# THE **BIG** BOOK OF
# PASTA

HILAIRE WALDEN

# THE **BIG** BOOK OF **PASTA**

## 365

### QUICK AND
### VERSATILE RECIPES

dbp

DUNCAN BAIRD PUBLISHERS

LONDON

**The Big Book of Pasta**
Hilaire Walden

Distributed in the USA and Canada by
Sterling Publishing Co., Inc.
387 Park Avenue South
New York, NY 10016-8810

This edition first published in the UK and USA in 2007 by
Duncan Baird Publishers Ltd
Sixth Floor, Castle House
75–76 Wells Street
London W1T 3QH

MANAGING EDITOR: Grace Cheetham
EDITOR: Gillian Haslam
MANAGING DESIGNER: Manisha Patel
DESIGNER: Sailesh Patel
STUDIO PHOTOGRAPHY: William Lingwood
FOOD STYLIST: Marie-Ange La-Pierre
PROP STYLIST: Helen Trent

Library of Congress Cataloging-in-Publication Data Available

ISBN-13: 978-1-84483-393-1
ISBN-10: 1-84483-393-3

10 9 8 7 6 5 4 3 2 1

Typeset in Gill Sans Condensed
Colour reproduction by Scanhouse, Malaysia
Printed in China by Imago

For information about custom editions, special sales, premium
and corporate purchases, please contact Sterling Special Sales
Department at 800-805-5489 or specialsales@sterlingpub.com.

PUBLISHER'S NOTE: While every care has been taken in compiling
the recipes in this book, Duncan Baird Publishers, or any other
persons who have been involved in working on this publication,
cannot accept responsibility for any errors or omissions,
inadvertent or not, that may be found in the recipes
or text, nor for any problems that may arise as
a result of preparing one of these recipes.

UNLESS OTHERWISE STATED:
• Use medium eggs
• Use fresh herbs

# Contents

INTRODUCTION                                    7

## FIRST COURSES & SNACKS
### CHAPTER 1                                   21

## FISH & SHELLFISH
### CHAPTER 2                                   61

## MEAT & POULTRY
### CHAPTER 3                                   105

## VEGETABLE & VEGETARIAN DISHES
### CHAPTER 4                                   153

INDEX                                          214

# Introduction

Although internationally popular and wonderfully versatile,
pasta remains quintessentially Italian, and it is arguably most
enjoyable when it is accompanied by other Mediterranean ingredients.

Pasta is a healthy food, and its nutrition can be enhanced by
the ingredients used with it in the traditional, restrained Italian
style, rather than large amounts of fattening cream, butter, and
cheese. Tossed with judicious amounts of freshly cooked vegetables,
herbs, and perhaps a little cheese, pasta makes a nutritious dish.

Pasta can be dressed up or down. Despite its inherent simplicity,
it can still be the ideal dish for a special occasion, provided the
ingredients are first class and fresh. What's more, many dishes
can be prepared and cooked in a matter of minutes.

The range of pasta that is available continues to increase, but it
is important to buy good-quality brands, which are usually Italian.
Simply look for the words "durum wheat," and "pure egg" if it is egg
pasta, on the packaging. If other ingredients are present, even water,
put the package back on the shelf. Good fresh pasta can also be found
in quality Italian delicatessens. With such a wide choice of commercially
produced pasta, few people make their own. It does take a little while
to get the knack of making it, especially if the stretching is done
by hand, but once the skill has been acquired, the superiority
of the results makes the effort of learning worthwhile.

## PASTA QUANTITIES

The amount of pasta you cook per person depends on appetite, the role the pasta dish is to play in the meal, and the character of the sauce: less pasta will be needed if a rich creamy sauce is to accompany it rather than a light vegetable one.

As a general guide, allow 2½ ounces dried pasta for a first course portion, 3 to 4 ounces for a main course serving. Slightly more fresh pasta is usually needed.

## DRIED PASTA

Semolina flour, made from durum wheat, is traditionally used in dried pasta. The flour is much tougher than other wheat flours and it is this quality that gives dried pasta its durability, preventing it from breaking easily when dried. It is a very "hard" flour and the dough needs industrial machinery to work it properly, and atmosphere- and temperature-controlled conditions for the drying that is required for long storage. Dried flour-and-water pasta made from durum wheat includes spaghetti, as well as many other shapes.

Dried egg pasta also includes some soft flour with the durum wheat flour. It has a silkier, smoother texture when cooked, a richer flavor, and is more expensive.

It is sometimes considered that fresh egg pasta is always better than dried, but this is not the case. Good-quality dried pasta (pasta made from durum wheat by a reputable, and usually Italian, company) is far better than poor-quality bought fresh egg pasta (some don't even contain much egg). The growing popularity of pasta in general, and fresh pasta in particular, however, has meant an increase in sales of low-quality fresh pasta. The best fresh egg pasta is usually found in Italian delicatessens that make their own.

## QUICK GUIDE TO PASTA SHAPES

There are hundreds of pasta shapes. Names can be confusing as sometimes one name can refer to different shapes, while different names can be used in various parts of Italy. The name ending provides a clue: -ini and -ette imply small, while -oni implies large. See page 12 for more information on shapes and sizes of homemade pasta.

**LONG ROUND PASTA** includes spaghetti; spaghettini (thin spaghetti); vermicelli (fine spaghetti); capelli d'angelo, "angel hair" (threadlike pasta); tonnarelli (homemade square spaghetti); bucatini or perciatelli (chunky spaghetti with hollow middles); bigoli (the only traditional pasta made with wholewheat flour).
**LONG FLAT RIBBONS** include tagliatelle; taglierini, taglioni, and bavette (thinner tagliatelle); fettuccine (narrower than tagliatelle); frappe (delicate ribbons with wavy edges); trenette (a cross between tagliatelle and linguine); linguine (resembling flattened spaghetti); paglia e fieno, "straw and hay" (nests of green and plain fettuccine); tagliolini (homemade version of linguine); pappardelle (wide ribbons); lasagnette (wide with fluted edges).
**TUBULAR PASTA** includes macaroni; ziti (similar to macaroni); penne (short tubes cut on the diagonal, penne lesce is smooth and penne rigate is ridged); pennette (shorter, thinner penne); rigatoni (ridged, hollow chunky tubes); marille (double rigatoni); sedani (short, ridged tubes with straight ends); elicoidali (narrower rigatoni with spiral ridges and straight ends), denti d'elefante, "elephants' teeth," (fairly long, ridged tubes with straight ridges and flat ends); garganelli (homemade ridged scroll-shapes); cavatappi (corkscrew shapes); chifferi (small curved tubes).
**SHAPED PASTA** includes fusilli (spirals); orecchiette (ear shapes); rotelle (wheels); farfalle (butterfly shapes); conchiglie (shells); smooth or ribbed conchigliette/conchiglioni (small/large conchiglie); riccioli (short with wide ridges); radiatori (shaped like old-fashioned radiators); gnocchi (dumplings); cavatieddi (small, mussel shaped); lumache (shells formed out of hollow pasta), eliche (short, thin spirals); trofie (rolls of pasta with pointed ends, sometimes open along one side); strozzapreti (twists), gemelli and caserecce (similar to strozzapreti); ballerine (bell shaped, with frilly edges); campanelle (similar to ballerine).
**FILLED PASTA (RIPIENA)** includes cannelloni (tubes); cappelletti (small squares folded into hat shapes); ravioli (squares); ravioloni (large ravioli); agnolotti or raviolini (half-moons); tortelli (squares, larger than raviolini —the smaller version, tortellini, are rounder in shape, although tortelloni can also be large, square shapes).
**SOUP PASTA** are small shapes (pastina) that are used in soups, with names often ending in -ini, -etti, or -ette. For example, tubettini, anellini, quadretti, conchigliette, stelline, and ditali.

# HOMEMADE PASTA

The best pasta is undoubtedly homemade pasta, particularly homemade egg pasta. In fact, very few people make anything but egg pasta. You need only two ingredients, flour and eggs. Both influence the flavor. A wide range of different flours can be used—see below. Good-quality, free-range, and preferably organic eggs will give the best flavor; the richer the color of the yolk, the better the color of the pasta. Any size can be used; simply adjust the amount of flour accordingly. See page 10 for the different flavor variations you can experiment with.

## Flours

The type of flour used governs the texture of the pasta:

**DURUM WHEAT:** This is not used for homemade pastas. Fresh egg pasta is usually undried so it is not necessary to use durum wheat, although some people like to use plain semolina in the dough to give it some durability.

**GOOD-QUALITY, UNBLEACHED ALL-PURPOSE FLOUR:** This makes a dough that is malleable and easy to roll, and pasta that is soft and not particularly resilient (springy and slightly elastic).

**HARD BREAD FLOUR:** This produces a firmer dough that requires more effort to roll, but the pasta will have a more conventional, firmer, more chewy texture with a decent amount of resilience.

**GROUND SEMOLINA/SEMOLINA FLOUR:** These add to the texture, color, and firmness of pasta, making it chewy and quite coarse, but not very resilient. Dough that contains only semolina and no other flour is much harder to roll, tears more easily, and is the hardest to stretch thinly. It is, however, easier to cut and is less likely to stick. Dough made with semolina requires more flour per egg than other flours, and it can be tricky getting the proportions right. A good compromise, therefore, is to use one quarter to one half semolina to bread flour.

**TIPO/DOPIO 00:** This is a very soft, highly refined Italian flour. The dough is more grainy than other pasta doughs at first, but it becomes smoother and more silky after kneading for a few minutes. The dough is the easiest to work with and produces pasta that is lighter, softer, and not particularly firm, but it has greater resilience. It also takes slightly less time to cook than pasta made with other flours.

The consistency of the dough also influences the texture of the pasta. A stiff dough will produce firmer pasta, whereas a soft dough makes pasta that is soft and silky. However, a soft dough is also more difficult to handle, tends to stick when cut, and takes longer to dry. It is easiest to add more flour to a dough that is too soft.

## PASTA-MAKING EQUIPMENT

If you wish to make your own pasta, there are just a few essential pieces of kitchen equipment that you will require:

• Spacious, firm working area, at least 24 inches deep, 36 inches wide.
• Smooth, warm surface—traditionally, pasta is made on a large, smooth wooden board. In modern kitchens, laminated worktops are good alternatives. Marble, slate, or granite are too cold.
• Long rolling pin—a 24-inch long rolling pin, up to 2 inches in diameter, is ideal for rolling a 3-egg quantity of pasta.
• Dish towels—several clean dish towels are needed for absorbing moisture from the pasta dough when it is left to dry.
• Plastic wrap—for covering the ball of dough lightly when it is left to rest.
• Pasta machine—this makes stretching the pasta dough much easier in terms of effort and skill. Made of stainless steel, the machine has rollers for pressing out the dough as thinly as possible. The distance between the rollers can be adjusted, so the dough can be rolled progressively thinner and thinner until the required thickness is achieved. Cutters for producing various widths of noodles are available for attaching to the machine. A hand-operated pasta machine is usually considered to give better results than one operated by a motor.
• Large, sharp knife for cutting noodles and shapes.
• Pastry wheel for cutting stuffed pasta shapes, and for giving wavy edges to wide noodles, such as pappardelle and lasagnette.
• Cookie cutters for cutting out circles for stuffed pasta shapes.

## FRESH PASTA DOUGH

**PREPARATION TIME**: it's difficult to be precise as so much depends on whether you work by hand or use a machine, your skill and experience, and the shape required. With a little experience, doing everything by hand and cutting simple noodles will take about 35 to 40 minutes, plus drying, making about 12 ounces pasta.

1¼ CUPS **FLOUR (SEE PREVIOUS PAGE)**

2 **EXTRA-LARGE FREE-RANGE EGGS, PREFERABLY ORGANIC, AT ROOM TEMPERATURE**

### Flavor variations

Try adding the following ingredients for different flavors. A little extra flour will probably be needed for most variations during the kneading, cutting, and rolling stages.

**HERB:** stir 3 tablespoons finely chopped mixed herbs, such as basil, rosemary, parsley, or oregano, into the eggs.

**BLACK PEPPER:** stir 1½ tablespoons coarsely ground black peppercorns into the eggs.

**LEMON:** add 2 tablespoons lemon juice and the finely grated zest of 2 lemons to the eggs; about 2 tablespoons or more extra flour will probably be needed.

**SPINACH:** cook 5 ounces spinach in a covered pan, shaking the pan occasionally, until it wilts and is tender. Drain well, chop finely, and squeeze out surplus moisture; spread on paper towels to dry. Add to the eggs. As much as an extra ½ cup flour will be needed.

**SAFFRON:** crush a pinch of saffron threads, soak for 30 minutes in 1 tablespoon boiling water, then add to the eggs. About 2 tablespoons extra flour will probably be needed.

**CHILI:** stir 1–2 teaspoons crushed chili flakes into the eggs.

**BLACK OLIVE:** beat 2 tablespoons black olive paste into the eggs.

**SQUID:** add a 0.15 ounce package of squid ink to the eggs.

**SUN-DRIED TOMATO PASTE:** beat 2 tablespoons sun-dried tomato paste into the eggs.

**PESTO OR RED PESTO:** beat 2 tablespoons pesto into the eggs.

For a 3-egg quantity, use 2¼ cups flour and 3 extra-large eggs. This produces about 18 ounces of pasta.

You can either mix the dough by hand (see below) or use a food processor or food mixer (see below and facing page for instructions).

### Hand mixing

This is generally considered better than using a food processor, because it is easier to judge the moistness of the dough and thus add the right amount of flour. Flours vary in the amount of liquid they absorb depending on their storage conditions and the humidity and temperature of the kitchen. Eggs can also vary slightly in size. It is far easier to add more flour to a soft dough than it is to add more egg to a dry dough.

1   Tip the flour into a bowl and make a well in the middle. Add the eggs. Using a fork, break up the eggs slightly while bringing in some of the flour from the sides. Continue working with your hands, mixing in as much flour as needed to make a rough, semisoft dough. You might not need all the flour, but if the dough is too sticky, sprinkle on a little more. If you add too much flour, correct it by adding a little more egg or good-quality olive oil.

2   Form the dough into a ball and transfer to a work surface lightly dusted with flour. Knead the dough about 10 minutes, pushing a portion of the dough away from you with the heel of your hand, then fold the dough back on itself, so it faces toward you.

3   Continue with this action, turning the dough a few degrees occasionally so all the dough is worked, until it is elastic, smooth, and soft. If the dough is to be passed through a machine, it does not have to be kneaded for quite as long as hand-rolled dough. Avoid using too much flour during the kneading, otherwise the dough will become too dry and will be tough. Just add enough flour to stop the dough sticking is all that is needed.

### Using a food processor

Put all the ingredients in the bowl and work until they come together into a ball that leaves the sides of the bowl clean. Transfer the dough to a floured work surface and knead by hand about 2 minutes.

## Using a food mixer

With the dough hook attached, put the flour and eggs into the bowl and mix on medium speed until they come together to form a tight dough. Transfer the dough to a floured work surface and work by hand about 1 minute.

## Resting the dough

Place the kneaded dough under a bowl or wrap in plastic wrap and leave to relax at room temperature for 30 minutes. If the kitchen is hot, refrigerate the dough, but leave it to warm up again to room temperature before rolling.

## Rolling by hand

Hand rolling produces pasta that has a more interesting texture, is more porous, and absorbs a sauce better than machine-rolled pasta. It does require a certain amount of energy, practice, and time until you get used to the technique.

1   Divide the unwrapped dough into four balls; re-cover three balls. Working on a lightly floured surface, knead the unwrapped ball for a minute or so, then, with the flat of your hand, flatten it slightly into a disk before rolling out from the middle, and stopping at the edge.

2   Using a fair amount of pressure and always rolling away from you, stretch the dough rather than flatten it. Without using any pressure, roll the pin back to the middle and repeat four times. Give the dough a slight turn and repeat. Continue in this way until the dough is about ¼ inch thick all over. Dust the work surface and the pin frequently with flour.

3   Next, roll the top (far) edge of the dough, about one third of the way down, onto the rolling pin. Grip it with one hand, curling your fingers around the dough and pin. Grab the bottom edge of the dough with your other hand and, pulling gently in both directions, stretch the dough slightly. Be careful: too much pressure and you'll tear the dough, too little pressure and it won't stretch. Unroll the pin, give the dough a quarter turn and repeat, working your way around the dough, until it is about ½₂ to ⅛ inch thick.

4   Place the rolling pin on the dough. Gently stretch and roll the dough tightly onto the pin from the top toward you, with both your hands cupped over the middle of the pin (keep a firm hold of the edge of the dough nearest you). Stop when you have rolled up about one quarter of the dough on to the pin.

5   Place the balls of your hands on the dough on the pin, right on top. Begin rolling the pin toward you, while at the same time sliding the palms of your hands away from each other toward the ends of the pin, dragging them against the surface of the dough. Roll up some more of the dough, quickly roll backwards and forwards while repeating the same stretching action with the palms of your hands until the sheet is completely rolled up. Aim for a total of about 12 to 14 stretching actions.

6   Unroll the pasta, turn it slightly, and dust lightly with flour if sticky. Working as quickly as possible, repeat the rolling and stretching action until the pasta is wafer-thin, less than ½₂ inch thick, depending on the type of pasta you are making. If a hole appears, simply patch it with a piece of dough from the edge. If you take more than 8 to 10 minutes to achieve this, the pasta will dry out and lose its elasticity, making it impossible to roll farther.

7   If you are making stuffed pastas, omit steps 4, 5, and 6. Roll up the pasta sheet onto the rolling pin, then roll it out again onto a large clean dry towel spread on a table, letting about one third of the sheet hang over the edge of the table. Leave for 10 minutes before turning it so another third hangs down. Repeat with the last third. When the surface begins to look leathery and the dough is still pliable, it is ready for cutting. If the kitchen is very hot, the drying time will probably need to be reduced; if the dough dries out too much, it will become brittle and crack.

8   Roll the dough onto the rolling pin and unroll it again on the work surface. Cut into the required sizes using a large sharp knife or a pastry wheel. Push the noodles slightly apart so the air can circulate. Alternatively, the dough can be folded over and over into a flat roll, about 2½ inches wide, then cut across the roll to make the width of noodles you require. With floured fingertips, tweeze the noodles apart. This is a quicker method, but you will have to unravel the folded strips and they might have fold marks in them.

## Using a pasta machine

Divide the dough into four balls; re-cover three of them so they do not dry out. Using the base of your palm, flatten the fourth ball slightly, then pass it through a lightly floured pasta machine on the thickest setting. Fold the two ends of the sheet in toward the middle and repeat four more times. Move the notch or handle of the machine down one setting and repeat.

Continue passing the sheet through the machine in this way until you have gone through all the settings, or all but the last one (this is often considered too thin), until the pasta is about ¹⁄₁₆ inch thick (or the required thickness for the noodles you are making—see below for traditional thicknesses). Repeat with the remaining balls of dough. See page 13 for storage instructions.

Cut sheets about 8 to 9 inches long. Pass them through the appropriate cutters on the machine or cut noodles by hand. Leave for 5 minutes to firm up before cooking.

## Pasta size

These are the traditional widths for the different types of flat pasta:
Tagliatelle (rolled to just under ¹⁄₁₆ inch thick): ⅓ inch
Tagliarini (rolled to just under ¹⁄₁₆ inch thick): ¹⁄₁₂ inch
Tagliolini (rolled to just under ¹⁄₁₆ inch thick): ¹⁄₁₂ inch
Tonnarelli (rolled to ¹⁄₁₆ inch thick): ¹⁄₁₆ inch
Fettuccine/trenette (rolled to just under ¹⁄₁₆ inch thick): ⅓ inch
Pappardelle (rolled slightly thicker, about ¹⁄₁₆ inch): ¾ inch
Lasagnette (rolled slightly thicker, about ¹⁄₁₆ inch): 1 to 1¼ inch
Lasagne (rolled slightly thicker, about ¹⁄₁₆ inch): 5 to 6 x 3 to 4 inches, or whatever your preference

## Making pasta shapes

When making shapes, be sure to keep the dough you are not working on covered, and work as quickly as possible, otherwise the dough will become too dry. Listed below are the easiest shapes to create with homemade pasta—see page 8 for details of the many dried pasta shapes now available in supermarkets and Italian delicatessens.

**BRANDELLI:** this is the simplest of all pasta shapes: simply tear pieces of the rolled-out pasta sheet into pieces.

**FARFALLE:** using a fluted pasta or pastry wheel, cut the pasta sheets into rectangles measuring 1¼ x 1 inch. Pinch the long sides of each rectangle between your index finger and thumb, squeezing hard enough to make a bow-tie shape. If the pasta fails to hold its shape, moisten your fingers with water and squeeze again. Lay the bow ties out on dish towels, sprinkle with a little flour, and leave to dry for about 15 minutes before cooking.

**GARGANELLI:** cut the pasta sheets into 2-inch squares. Lay an old-fashioned butter pat (paddle), ridged side uppermost, on the work surface. Lay a pasta sheet across the pat so a pointed end of the sheet is in the middle of the top side of the pat. Put a lightly floured clean pencil or round chopstick diagonally across the corner of the sheet that is nearest you, and, pressing down on the uncovered sides of the pencil, roll it away from you across the pat, enclosing the pasta, which should be marked with the pat ridges. Stand the pencil on its end, give a light tap on the surface so the roll slips off. Spread the garganelli on a dish towel to dry for 10 to 15 minutes.

**GNOCCHI:** roll a small amount of pasta into a small link sausage, about 1 inch long. Press the piece onto a ridged butter pat, and press and push firmly to form a hollow sausage.

**MALTAGLIATI:** as the name means "badly cut," these can be made from pieces of leftover dough, as well as being especially cut. They can be random shapes, or cut into neater triangles. Traditionally, maltagliati are used in soups, but they can also be used in other dishes.

**ORECCHIETTE:** roll lengths of pasta into link sausages about 12 inches long and ½ inch thick. Cut into ½-inch pieces and roll each piece into an even ball. Press on each ball in turn, at the same time pushing it away from you slightly so the pasta curls into an ear or shell shape.

**QUADRUCCI:** these are similar to maltagliati, but cut into squares.

## Stuffed pastas

The sizes given here are the most usual ones, but they can vary according to preference. Any dough that is leftover can be cut into shapes such as brandelli and maltagliati (see page 12). Surplus filling can be used as sandwich or omelet filling, for filling mushroom caps, or formed into balls and fried, depending on type.

**AGNOLOTTI (ALSO KNOWN AS RAVIOLINI):** using a 2-inch fluted or plain pastry cutter, cut out circles of pasta dough. Place or pipe about ½ teaspoon of filling on one half of each circle. Dampen the edges of the circles using a pastry brush and fold the uncovered halves of the circles over the filling. Press the edges together to seal.

**CAPPELLETTI/CAPPELLACCI:** these are made in the same way as tortellini (see below) except that the dough is cut into squares. When formed, they should resemble bishops' miters.

**RAVIOLI (CALLED TORTELLONI IN ROMAGNA):** if necessary, using a floured large, sharp knife, cut the rolled sheet into 18- to 20-inch pieces. Fold in half lengthwise to mark a central long fold. Keep the sheets you are not working on covered. Using a teaspoon or piping bag fitted with a large plain tip, place or pipe small mounds of filling about 1½ to 2 inches apart along each side of the fold of one of the lengths, spacing them evenly. With a pastry brush, carefully brush a little water around each mound. Lay a second sheet of dough over the first one. Press gently with your fingertips, between the mounds, pushing out all trapped air. Sprinkle lightly with flour. Cut along each long side of the strip with a pastry or pasta wheel, then in between the mounds to make squares; repeat with the remaining sheets and filling. The ravioli can now be cooked, or dried farther by being laid on a dish towel, spaced apart, until dried.

**RAVIOLONI:** the same as ravioli, but larger.

**TORTELLINI:** using a fluted or plain pastry cutter, cut out 2-inch circles of pasta dough. Place or pipe about ½ teaspoon of filling on one half of each circle. Dampen the edges of the circles with water using a pastry brush and fold the uncovered halves of the circles over the filling. Press the edges together to seal. Bend the two corners toward each other, wrapping them around the end of your index finger. Pinch the tips together to seal.

**TORTELLINI (FROM BOLOGNA):** these are made like cappelletti with the dough being cut into 3-inch squares.

Once the pasta dough has been cut and shaped as required, make sure the strands or shapes do not touch because they will stick to each other. Leave for 5 minutes to dry slightly and become firmer, if you are going to cook them straightaway.

## STORING FRESH PASTA

If you are not using the pasta straightaway, or if you have made a large quantity, sprinkle noodles lightly with flour or semolina and then form into loose "nests" for longer storage. Alternatively, spread on clean dish towels laid on baskets or trays, or drape the pasta over a clean broom handle suspended between two chairs. Leave to dry for 24 hours and wrap carefully.

The pasta should then keep for three to four days stored in a rigid container in a cool place. Lacking durum wheat, homemade pasta can become brittle and crack if it is kept for longer. Lasagne sheets and shapes should be left to dry, spread out.

**PASTA DOUGH:** This freezes well for up to one month, rolled into a ball and covered.

**FILLED PASTAS:** These can be kept for up to three days in the refrigerator. Leave them spread out to dry, then store on sheets of waxed paper in an airtight container in the refrigerator. Filled pastas with moist fillings do not freeze successfully, but meat-filled pastas freeze well. Spread out the shapes on a tray and open-freeze for 2 to 3 hours, then carefully transfer them to a rigid freezerproof container. Freeze up to three months. Cook from frozen, allowing them an extra 5 minutes cooking.

**PASTA DISHES:** Uncooked pasta dishes for baking, such as lasagne or cannelloni, can be covered and refrigerated up to a day. Return the dish to room temperature 1 to 2 hours before cooking, or bake for an additional 5 to 10 minutes (uncovered) in the oven, depending on the size of the dish. Pasta dishes can also be frozen: cover and chill before freezing for up to two months. Thaw overnight in the refrigerator before baking as instructed in the recipe.

## SAUCES

Italians are very adept at matching a pasta shape to a sauce and only use certain combinations, but there are no rules set in stone. Some combinations, however, are more successful than others. The shape and thickness of pasta are significant. They are an integral part of its texture, which affects the way it combines with a sauce. As a general guideline match the thickness of the pasta to the weight of the sauce.

- Long, thin pasta, such as linguine, spaghettini, and spaghetti, is thought to be best with simple sauces based on olive oil, and with sauces containing finely chopped ingredients. Spaghetti is sturdy enough to also go with a wide variety of sauces.
- Long, thick pasta, such as bucatini, and flat ribbons like tagliatelle go well with cream sauces, and with sauces containing small amounts of vegetables, fish, and meat.
- Pappardelle and other wide noodles, pasta tubes such as penne, and pasta shapes like orecchiette are usually partnered with robust vegetable or meat sauces, or used in baked dishes.
- Tubular pasta, twists, shells, and similar shapes go well with chunky meat and vegetable sauces.
- Fresh pasta is traditionally considered to suit delicate cream sauces better than dried pasta.

The "ideal" amount of sauce to an Italian is enough to coat the pasta lightly without leaving a covering or pool on the plate when the pasta is eaten. Again, this is a matter of taste, and if you prefer more sauce, use it.


## EQUIPMENT FOR COOKING AND SERVING PASTA

These are the basics you will need:
- Large, deep saucepan: the most useful and safest pans if you cook pasta frequently are those with an inner perforated draining basket that can simply be lifted from the pan when the pasta is cooked.
- Wide, deep skillet: for cooking lasagne.
- Long-handled fork: for stirring pasta during cooking to keep the strands separate, and for tossing the pasta with the sauce.
- Wooden pasta rake: resembles a flat wooden spoon with prongs attached to one side, at right angles. It is effective because pasta does not slip off when it is lifted.
- Tongs: these are very effective for lifting strands of spaghetti and other tubular pastas.
- Long-handled slotted spoon or straining/skimming spoon: for lifting shapes and stuffed pastas from the water.
- Parmesan grater: a special, very sharp grater that is specifically designed for grating hard cheeses, such as Parmesan or pecorino.
- Parmesan knife: a short-bladed knife for cutting Parmesan and pecorino and for creating shavings.


## COOKING PASTA

To be at its best, pasta should be served as soon as it is cooked (unless being used for a salad), so it is important to time the cooking of the sauce to be ready at the same time. This might occasionally mean taking the sauce off the heat when it is cooked, then reheating it just before the pasta is done. Because of the time taken for the pasta water to boil, it often makes sense to bring it to a boil before preparing the sauce. This is especially true for fresh pastas.

While it is important to have enough water, there is no need, and indeed is wasteful, to have vast amounts. Provided the pasta is covered by about 3 inches of water, it will cook perfectly well if it is stirred immediately after being added to the water and two or three times during cooking, and the water is kept at a gentle, rolling boil.

Bring a covered pan of water to a boil, add salt if you like (this is purely a matter of taste and not essential), then add all the pasta at once (oil is unnecessary), without breaking it; coil spaghetti into the water as it softens. Stir, cover the pan, and return the water quickly to a boil. Remove the lid and boil the pasta until shortly before you think it will be done, and start testing. The pasta should be just firm to the bite: it will continue to cook in its own heat after draining.

Fresh pasta can be cooked in as little as 1 minute or as much as 5 minutes, depending on the type of flour and the length of drying. The normal range is 2 to 4 minutes. Commercial dried pastas should be cooked according to the directions on the package, but begin testing a couple of minutes before the stated time. Stuffed pastas take 4 to 7 minutes.

Drain pasta as soon as it is ready, either by tipping it into a large, preferably warm, colander in the sink, or by lifting out the saucepan's integral straining basket. Give the colander or basket two or three sharp shakes, but do not drain the pasta too thoroughly. Long pasta should remain slippery and slightly dripping with water. Shapes and short tubes should be drained slightly more thoroughly to dislodge any trapped water, but they should still be slippery. Fresh egg pasta needs the least thorough draining, and should remain very slippery because it will tend to absorb more of the sauce than dried pasta.

It is a good idea to get into the habit of reserving a little of the cooking water (some recipes specify this), to moisten the dressed pasta if it is too dry. This water is better than hot tap water because the starch it contains will add body as well as moisture to the sauce.

## Combining pasta and sauce

Pasta should be tossed with its sauce as soon as it is cooked, or with a little olive oil or cooking water to prevent it sticking together. If it does happen to stick, tip it into a colander and pour boiling water through it. For tossing, the pasta can returned to the hot pan in which it was cooked, the sauce ingredients added, and everything tossed together; or the pasta can be added to the pan of sauce; or it can be tipped into a hot, roomy serving bowl, the sauce added and the two tossed together. Some recipes specify gently heating the pasta and sauce together, and care must be taken not to use too high a temperature or heat for too long. To toss pasta and sauce, use two large, long-handled spoons or forks, or a spoon and a fork and lift the pasta, reaching right down into the bottom of the bowl, and toss gently. If, after tossing, the sauce seems too thick, add a little reserved cooking water.

## Cooking stuffed pastas

Stuffed pastas, such as ravioli, are more fragile than ordinary types so they require more gentle handling and cooking to prevent them being damaged and the filling escaping. Don't boil them too hard, and, for preference, use a large slotted spoon or a draining/skimming spoon to remove them from the pan when cooked.

## Pasta for baked dishes

Because of the cooking in the oven, pasta for a baked dish should be boiled for slightly less time than normal: usually 1 to 2 minutes, depending on the length of time in the oven.

Lasagne sheets and cannelloni tubes should be cooked in batches, in a shallow, wide pan, rather than a deep, narrower one. As they are difficult to stir to separate, and don't move about as much as other pastas, it is worth adding 1 to 2 tablespoons olive oil to the water. Cook according to the package directions, then drain well and rinse under running cold water to remove surplus starch and prevent sticking. Drain again, and then spread on a dish towel to dry. Cannelloni tubes should be handled more gently than lasagne sheets.

The texture of no-precook types will benefit from similar cooking until they are just pliable, which will probably be about 1 minute. If a recipe specifies precooking and you do not give it, it is a good idea to use a little more sauce than the recipe specifies, or make the sauce thinner.

## Cooking in a microwave

Short pasta shapes and soup pasta, and quantities under 8 ounces are the only types that are worth cooking in a microwave, although the results won't be quite as good as conventionally cooked pasta.
It doesn't really make sense to cook larger amounts because the large volume of water required means they have to be cooked in batches, so time is not saved.

Microwave ovens can be useful, though, for thawing frozen dishes, and for reheating precooked pasta dishes, such as lasagne and cannelloni, especially individual portions. Microwaves can also be used for thawing and reheating pasta sauces.

To cook less than 8 ounces pasta shapes in a microwave, put the pasta in a suitable large bowl, pour boiling water over to cover by 1 inch, stir, and put the bowl in the microwave. Cook on 100% (HIGH) power for 3 to 4 minutes for fresh pasta, 8 to 10 minutes for dried. Leave to stand for 5 minutes before draining.

## SERVING PASTA

Pasta bowls or deep soup plates make the best serving dishes. Because pasta loses its heat so quickly, be sure to warm the dishes well. Pasta salads are best served warm or cold, not chilled.

# 001
# ragù

PREPARATION TIME 10 minutes COOKING TIME 1¾ to 2¼ hours SERVES 4

I ONION, FINELY CHOPPED
I SMALL CARROT, FINELY CHOPPED
I SMALL CELERY STALK, FINELY CHOPPED
OLIVE OIL
2 GARLIC CLOVES, FINELY CHOPPED
12 ounces LEAN GROUND BEEF
I cup MILK

¾ cup MEDIUM-BODIED DRY WHITE WINE
1½ cups CHOPPED RIPE WELL-FLAVORED TOMATOES
I tablespoon SUN-DRIED TOMATO PASTE
I BOUQUET GARNI
SALT AND FRESHLY GROUND BLACK PEPPER

1   Fry the onion, carrot, and celery in a little olive oil in a heavy pan until soft and light brown.
    Add the garlic and fry 1 to 2 minutes longer. Stir in the beef to break it up, and cook, stirring,
    until it loses its pink color.
2   Once the meat has changed color, pour in the milk in 3 stages; let the liquid simmer and evaporate
    between each addition. Repeat with the wine. Do not let the sauce boil otherwise the meat will
    become tough.
3   Stir in the tomatoes, tomato paste, bouquet garni, seasoning, and 1 cup water. Continue to simmer,
    uncovered, very slowly for 1½ to 2 hours, stirring occasionally, until the sauce is thick; discard the
    bouquet garni.
4   Use immediately, or leave to cool, cover, and refrigerate for 2 to 3 days. Alternatively, freeze for up to
    1 month. Thaw in the fridge overnight before using; the sauce will probably thicken so it might be
    necessary to stir in a little additional liquid.

# 002
# quick ragù

PREPARATION TIME 10 minutes COOKING TIME 50 minutes SERVES 4

I LARGE ONION, FINELY CHOPPED
I CARROT, FINELY CHOPPED
I CELERY STALK, FINELY CHOPPED
OLIVE OIL
2 GARLIC CLOVES, FINELY CHOPPED
I pound GROUND BEEF
1¼ cups RED WINE

1¼ cups BEEF STOCK
I CAN (15-oz.) CRUSHED TOMATOES
I tablespoon SUN-DRIED TOMATO PASTE
2 teaspoons DRIED OREGANO
SALT AND FRESHLY GROUND BLACK PEPPER
2 tablespoons CHOPPED FLAT-LEAF PARSLEY

1   Fry the onion, carrot, and celery in a little oil until soft and flecked with brown. Add the garlic and fry
    1 minute, then stir in the beef and cook, stirring, until light brown. Stir in the wine, stock, tomatoes,
    tomato paste, and oregano.
2   Heat until just simmering, half cover, and then simmer, stirring occasionally, about 40 minutes until the
    beef is very tender and the sauce reduced. If the sauce becomes too dry, add a little water, or remove
    the lid if the sauce has not reduced enough. Season and stir in the parsley.

## 003
# béchamel sauce

PREPARATION TIME 5 minutes, plus 30 minutes infusing COOKING TIME 10 minutes SERVES 4

2½ cups MILK
1 BAY LEAF
1 ONION SLICE
1 CLOVE

2 PARSLEY SPRIGS
3½ tablespoons UNSALTED BUTTER
4 tablespoons ALL-PURPOSE FLOUR
SALT AND FRESHLY GROUND BLACK PEPPER

1   Gently heat the milk with the bay leaf, onion, clove, and parsley until bubbles appear around the edge. Cover, remove from the heat, and leave 30 minutes.
2   Melt the butter in a heavy pan until sizzling but not brown, then stir in the flour and cook 1 to 2 minutes. Off the heat, slowly strain in the milk, whisking or stirring. Return the pan to the heat and bring to a boil, stirring or whisking. Lower the heat and simmer 5 minutes, stirring occasionally; season.
3   If not using the sauce straightaway, cover the surface closely with plastic wrap, leave to cool, then store in the refrigerator for up to 3 days. When reheating the sauce, it might be necessary to stir in a little more milk to restore the correct consistency.

Note:
   The thickness of a béchamel sauce (and therefore the proportions of butter, flour, and milk) can vary from recipe to recipe. The flavorings—the bay leaf, onion, clove, and parsley—remain the same.

## 004
# simple white sauce

PREPARATION TIME 5 minutes COOKING TIME 10 minutes SERVES 4

2½ cups MILK
3 tablespoons ALL-PURPOSE FLOUR
2½ tablespoons UNSALTED BUTTER

1 BAY LEAF
SALT AND FRESHLY GROUND BLACK PEPPER

1   Put all the ingredients into a small saucepan and bring to a boil over medium heat, whisking constantly, and simmer until the sauce thickens, still whisking.
2   Reduce the heat and let the sauce simmer 2 to 3 minutes, stirring occasionally. Discard the bay leaf and season.

Variation:
   Cheese sauce: stir ½ cup grated Parmesan cheese into the sauce after discarding the bay leaf. Do not boil once the cheese has been added.

## 005
# fresh tomato sauce

PREPARATION TIME 5 minutes COOKING TIME 25 to 30 minutes SERVES 4

I SMALL ONION, FINELY CHOPPED
VIRGIN OLIVE OIL
2 GARLIC CLOVES, LEFT WHOLE
I BAY LEAF
3 THYME SPRIGS

3 PARSLEY SPRIGS
ABOUT 3½ cups VERY FINELY CHOPPED
 WELL-FLAVORED TOMATOES (2½ pounds)
SALT AND FRESHLY GROUND BLACK PEPPER
SUGAR OR SUN-DRIED TOMATO PASTE (OPTIONAL)

1   Fry the onion in a little oil in a large skillet 2 minutes. Stir in the garlic and herbs and cook over
    medium heat 8 to 10 minutes until the onion is soft but not colored.
2   Add the tomatoes, raise the heat, and cook until the sauce is no longer watery. Season and add a
    pinch or two of sugar, or a little sun-dried tomato paste, if necessary, to enhance the flavor;
    discard the garlic and herbs.
3   The sauce should have some texture; if you prefer a smooth sauce, puree it and pass through a
    nonmetallic strainer. Use immediately, or leave to cool, cover, and refrigerate 2 to 3 days.
    Alternatively, freeze up to 1 month; thaw in the refrigerator overnight before using.

**Variation:**
    Broiled tomato sauce: broil 3½ cups tomatoes on the lowest rung under the broiler, turning as required,
    until evenly blistered and lightly charred. Remove any blackened skin, then puree coarsely so there is still
    some texture. Fry two chopped shallots in a little oil until soft, then stir in the puree and simmer until
    thick. Season and add a pinch of sugar, if necessary, to bring out the flavor. Store as above.

## 006
# pesto

PREPARATION TIME 5 minutes COOKING TIME 5 minutes SERVES 4

2 ounces BASIL LEAVES
2 GARLIC CLOVES, CRUSHED
2 tablespoons PINE NUTS
½ cup EXTRA-VIRGIN OLIVE OIL

½ cup FRESHLY GRATED PARMESAN
SALT AND FRESHLY GROUND BLACK PEPPER
SQUEEZE OF LEMON JUICE (OPTIONAL)

1   Put the basil, garlic, pine nuts, and a little of the oil into a blender and pulse to a fairly smooth paste.
    Mix in the remaining oil.
2   Transfer to a bowl and stir in the Parmesan. Season and add a squeeze of lemon juice, if liked.
    Pesto will keep in a covered container in the refrigerator for up to 1 week.

# 007
# red pesto

PREPARATION TIME 5 minutes COOKING TIME 5 minutes SERVES 4

2 OUNCES SUN-DRIED TOMATOES IN OIL, DRAINED
2 GARLIC CLOVES, CRUSHED
1½ OUNCES BASIL LEAVES
3 TABLESPOONS PINE NUTS, LIGHTLY TOASTED
6 TABLESPOONS MIXED EXTRA-VIRGIN OLIVE OIL AND
    OIL FROM THE TOMATOES

4 TABLESPOONS FRESHLY GRATED PARMESAN CHEESE
SALT AND FRESHLY GROUND BLACK PEPPER
½–2 TEASPOONS BALSAMIC VINEGAR

1   Put the tomatoes, garlic, basil, pine nuts, and a little of the oils into a blender and pulse to a fairly
    smooth paste. Mix in the remaining oils.
2   Transfer to a bowl and stir in the Parmesan. Season, taking care with the salt but adding plenty
    of black pepper. Add balsamic vinegar, to taste. Red pesto will keep in a covered container in the
    refrigerator for up to 1 week.

# 008
# winter tomato sauce

PREPARATION TIME 20 minutes COOKING TIME 30 to 35 minutes SERVES 4

1 ONION, CHOPPED
1 CARROT, CHOPPED
1 CELERY STALK, CHOPPED
OLIVE OIL OR OIL FROM
    THE SUN-DRIED TOMATOES
2 GARLIC CLOVES, CHOPPED
2 CANS (15-oz.) CRUSHED TOMATOES

2 TABLESPOONS SUN-DRIED TOMATO PASTE
⅔ CUP RED OR MEDIUM-BODIED DRY WHITE WINE
⅔ CUP VEGETABLE STOCK
4 TABLESPOONS DRAINED AND
    SLICED SUN-DRIED TOMATOES IN OIL
SALT AND FRESHLY GROUND BLACK PEPPER

1   Fry the onion, carrot, and celery in a little oil until soft and beginning to color. Add the garlic and
    cook 1 minute, then stir in the canned tomatoes, tomato paste, wine, and stock. Simmer, uncovered,
    about 30 minutes until thick, stirring occasionally.
2   Puree the sauce, then add the sun-dried tomatoes and seasoning.

# first courses & snacks

First-course pasta dishes are lighter than those served for main courses, containing less pasta and with fewer ingredients. If you would like to serve one of the recipes in this chapter as a main course, simply serve larger portions to fewer people. First-course pasta dishes are generally quick and easy to prepare, and often made from simple pantry or refrigerator ingredients. An exception to the "quick" rule is gnocchi, the dumplings made from mashed potatoes, spinach, and ricotta, or semolina, but these can be made in advance. Some simple classics appear in this chapter, such as Spaghetti alla Carbonara and Herb Fettuccine all'Alfredo, plus some variations on traditional recipes, like Trenette with Red Pesto and Ricotta and Spaghetti with Summer Puttanesca Sauce. This chapter also features soup recipes containing pasta.

**CHAPTER**

**1**

# vegetable, borlotti, & pasta soup

PREPARATION TIME 10 minutes COOKING TIME 50 minutes SERVES 6

1 ONION, CHOPPED
1 SMALL LEEK, THINLY SLICED
2 CELERY STALKS, CHOPPED
3 GARLIC CLOVES, CHOPPED
3–4 THYME SPRIGS
OLIVE OIL
1¼ QUARTS VEGETABLE STOCK
1 CAN (15-oz.) BORLOTTI BEANS, DRAINED
   AND RINSED
1 ZUCCHINI, DICED

5 TOMATOES, CHOPPED
5 OUNCES HALVED THIN GREEN BEANS
5 OUNCES BABY FAVA BEANS
⅓ CUP FRESH MALTAGLIATI,
   OR SMALL PASTA SHAPES FOR SOUP
LEAVES FROM A SMALL BUNCH OF
   FLAT-LEAF PARSLEY, CHOPPED
SALT AND FRESHLY GROUND BLACK PEPPER
PESTO (SEE PAGE 18) AND SHAVED PECORINO,
   TO SERVE

1 Fry the onion, leek, celery, garlic, and thyme in oil in a large saucepan until soft but not colored. Add the stock, cover, and simmer 30 minutes.
2 Add the borlotti beans, zucchini, tomatoes, and green and fava beans, simmer 10 minutes longer, then add the pasta and parsley, stir, and cook about 5 minutes until the pasta is tender.
3 Season, discard the thyme, and serve with pesto swirled in and scattered with pecorino shavings.

010

# chunky vegetable & pasta soup

PREPARATION TIME 5 minutes COOKING TIME 25 minutes SERVES 6 to 8

2½ QUARTS VEGETABLE STOCK
2–3 GARLIC CLOVES, CHOPPED
4 CUPS DICED POTATOES
2 LEEKS, THINLY SLICED
3 CARROTS, DICED
2½ CUPS DICED ZUCCHINI
1¼ CUPS HALVED THIN GREEN BEANS

1 CAN (15-oz.) CANNELLINI BEANS, DRAINED
   AND RINSED
1 CAN (15-oz.) CRUSHED PLUM TOMATOES
⅔ CUP FARFALLINE OR OTHER SMALL PASTA FOR SOUP
1½ CUPS SLICED CREMINI MUSHROOMS
OLIVE OIL FOR FRYING
PESTO (SEE PAGE 18) AND FRESHLY GRATED
   PECORINO, TO SERVE

1 Bring the stock and garlic to a boil in a large saucepan. Add the potatoes, leeks, and carrots, cover, and simmer slowly 20 minutes until the vegetables are very tender.
2 Add the zucchini, green beans, cannellini beans, and tomatoes and bring to a boil. Stir in the pasta and simmer about 10 minutes until the pasta is al dente.
3 Meanwhile, fry the mushrooms in a little oil until soft. Add to the soup for the final 5 minutes of its cooking. Serve in warm large soup bowls accompanied by pesto and pecorino.

## 011
# chicken soup with tortellini

PREPARATION TIME 5 minutes COOKING TIME 10 minutes SERVES 4

I QUART **GOOD CHICKEN STOCK**
I QUANTITY **SPICED CHICKEN TORTELLINI**
   **(SEE PAGE 120), OR BOUGHT FRESH**
   **CHICKEN TORTELLINI OR RAVIOLI**

2 **WELL-FLAVORED PLUM TOMATOES,**
   **SEEDED AND FINELY CHOPPED**
**FINELY CHOPPED FLAT-LEAF PARSLEY AND**
   **FRESHLY GRATED PARMESAN, TO SERVE**

1  Bring the stock to a boil in a saucepan, add the tortellini, and cook 4 to 5 minutes.
2  Lower the heat so the stock is just simmering, add the tomatoes and warm through
   for a couple of minutes. Serve sprinkled with Parmesan and parsley.

## 012
# golden squash & conchigliette soup

PREPARATION TIME 15 minutes COOKING TIME 30 minutes SERVES 4

1 ONION, FINELY CHOPPED

VIRGIN OLIVE OIL

2 GARLIC CLOVES, FINELY CHOPPED

3½ CUPS BUTTERNUT OR ONION SQUASH,
   ½-INCH PIECES

1 LARGE BAY LEAF, TORN ACROSS

1¼ QUARTS VEGETABLE STOCK

½ CUP DRY WHITE VERMOUTH

⅔ CUP CONCHIGLIETTE, OR OTHER SMALL
   PASTA SHAPES FOR SOUP

FRESHLY GRATED PARMESAN, TO SERVE

1   Fry the onion in a little oil until soft. Stir in the garlic, squash, and bay leaf and cook slowly 2 minutes. Pour in the stock and wine and simmer 10 to 15 minutes until the squash is tender.

2   Remove 1 to 2 cups of the soup, puree the liquid, and then return to the pan. Bring to a boil, add the conchigliette, stir, and cook 6 to 8 minutes until the pasta is just tender. Serve with grated Parmesan.

**Note:**

This soup is particularly good served with Parmesan croûtons: cut 3 thick slices of bread, remove the crusts, and spread with garlic butter made by pounding a small knob of unsalted butter with a crushed garlic clove. Sprinkle 2 tablespoons freshly grated Parmesan over. Place on a greased baking sheet and cut into cubes, spacing them well apart. Bake in a heated oven at 400°F 8 to 10 minutes until golden.

# 013
# crab & shrimp soup

PREPARATION TIME 10 minutes COOKING TIME 30 minutes SERVES 4

1 ONION, FINELY CHOPPED
1 SMALL FENNEL BULB, FINELY CHOPPED,
   FEATHERY TOPS RESERVED
OLIVE OIL
2 GARLIC CLOVES, FINELY CHOPPED
2 THYME SPRIGS
PINCH OF CHILI FLAKES
1 QUART SHELLFISH OR FISH STOCK
1½ CUPS PASSATA (BOTTLED STRAINED PUREED
   TOMATOES)

HEAPED ½ CUP FUNGHETTI OR
   OTHER SMALL PASTA SHAPES
6 OUNCES CRAB MEAT
4 OUNCES SHELLED COOKED SHRIMP
1 LARGE BOTTLED BROILED RED PEPPER IN OIL,
   DRAINED AND CHOPPED
SALT AND FRESHLY GROUND BLACK PEPPER
PINCH OF SUGAR (OPTIONAL)
LEAVES FROM A SMALL BUNCH OF
   FLAT-LEAF PARSLEY, CHOPPED

1   Fry the onion and fennel in a little oil until soft and translucent, adding the garlic, thyme, and chili
    flakes toward the end of cooking. Pour in the stock and passata, bring to a boil and then simmer
    about 15 minutes.
2   Return the soup to a boil, stir in the pasta, and cook according to the package directions.
    Lower the heat, add the crab, shrimps, and red pepper and heat through slowly; do not boil.
    Season, adding a pinch of sugar, if necessary. Sprinkle the reserved fennel tops and parsley over.

## 014
# chicken & pasta soup

PREPARATION TIME 10 minutes COOKING TIME 25 minutes SERVES 4

4–6 CHICKEN THIGHS, PREFERABLY UNBONED
I ROSEMARY SPRIG
2 BAY LEAVES
5 GARLIC CLOVES
¾ cup MEDIUM-BODIED DRY WHITE WINE
2⅔ cups CHICKEN STOCK
I ONION, FINELY CHOPPED
I CARROT, DICED

OLIVE OIL
⅓ cup SMALL FARFALLINE, OR OTHER
   SMALL PASTA SHAPE FOR SOUP
I SMALL ROMAINE LETTUCE, SHREDDED
2 TABLESPOONS CHOPPED FLAT-LEAF PARSLEY
SALT AND FRESHLY GROUND BLACK PEPPER
FRESHLY GRATED PARMESAN, TO SERVE

1  Put the chicken, rosemary, bay, 4 garlic cloves, wine, and stock into a saucepan. Slowly bring just to a boil, then simmer 10 to 15 minutes, depending on size and whether the chicken has bone, until the chicken is just cooked through. Transfer the chicken to a plate using a slotted spoon; reserve the stock.
2  Chop the reserved garlic clove. Fry the onion, carrot, and chopped garlic in a little oil in a saucepan until soft. Strain in the stock and bring to a boil, then add the pasta. Stir and cook about 5 minutes until the pasta is tender.
3  Meanwhile, chop the chicken very finely. Add to the soup with the lettuce and parsley when the pasta is cooked. Heat gently until the lettuce wilts. Season. Serve sprinkled with Parmesan.

## 015
# zucchini, fava bean, & tagliatelle soup

PREPARATION TIME 5 minutes COOKING TIME 25 minutes SERVES 4

I ONION, FINELY CHOPPED
2 GARLIC CLOVES, CRUSHED
4 TABLESPOONS OLIVE OIL
1½ cups FAVA BEANS
2¼ cups GRATED ZUCCHINI
1¼ QUARTS VEGETABLE STOCK, BOILING

5 ounces TAGLIATELLE, BROKEN INTO
   SHORT PIECES
2 TABLESPOONS FINELY CHOPPED
   FLAT-LEAF PARSLEY
SALT AND FRESHLY GROUND BLACK PEPPER
FRESHLY GRATED PARMESAN, TO SERVE

1  Fry the onion and the garlic in the oil in a saucepan until soft and very lightly colored. Stir in the beans and zucchini and stir 1 to 2 minutes, then add the stock. Bring to a boil, stir, and then simmer, uncovered, 10 to 15 minutes.
2  Remove half the vegetables, puree them, and then return to the soup.
3  Meanwhile, cook and drain the pasta according to the package directions. Add to the soup with the parsley, season, and reheat. Serve sprinkled with freshly grated Parmesan.

# spring minestrone

PREPARATION TIME 10 minutes COOKING TIME 15 minutes SERVES 4 to 6

1 cup MINCED CARROTS
4 MINIATURE FENNEL BULBS, MINCED, OR 1 SMALL
  FENNEL BULB
OLIVE OIL
3 BABY LEEKS, THINLY SLICED
HEAPED 1 cup MINCED ZUCCHINI
1.3 quarts GOOD-QUALITY VEGETABLE STOCK
3 ounces VERMICELLI OR
  SMALL PASTA SHAPES FOR SOUP
1¼ cups SHELLED PEAS

1¼ cups SHELLED FAVA BEANS,
  OR FROZEN BABY FAVA BEANS
3 WELL-FLAVORED TOMATOES,
  SEEDED AND SLICED
4 ounces BABY SPINACH LEAVES
SALT AND FRESHLY GROUND BLACK PEPPER
PESTO (SEE PAGE 18), TO SERVE

1   Fry the carrots and fennel in a little oil until beginning to soften. Add the leeks and
    zucchini, fry 2 to 3 minutes, then add the stock. Bring to a boil, add the pasta,
    and cook until just tender, adding the peas, beans, and tomatoes 4 to 5 minutes
    before the end of the cooking.
2   Stir in the spinach. Season as soon as it wilts and serve with pesto.

# anelli siciliani, garbanzo beans, & sage soup

PREPARATION TIME 10 minutes COOKING TIME 25 minutes SERVES 4

1 CELERY STALK, CHOPPED,
1 LEEK, CHOPPED
1 CARROT, FINELY CHOPPED
VIRGIN OLIVE OIL
3 GARLIC CLOVES, FINELY CHOPPED
8 SMALL SAGE LEAVES, FINELY CHOPPED
1 CAN (15-oz.) GARBANZO BEANS, DRAINED AND
  RINSED
1 CAN (15-oz.) CRUSHED PLUM TOMATOES
ABOUT 3½ cups VEGETABLE STOCK
⅔ cup ANELLI SICILIANI, OR OTHER
  SMALL PASTA SHAPES FOR SOUP
SALT AND FRESHLY GROUND BLACK PEPPER
FRESHLY GRATED PARMESAN, TO SERVE

1   Fry the celery, leek, and carrot in a little oil in a saucepan until light brown. Add the garlic and sage, fry 1 minute, then add the garbanzo beans, tomatoes, and stock. Simmer 15 to 20 minutes. Pour most of the soup into a food processor and reduce to a thick, nubbly puree. Return to the pan.
2   Meanwhile, cook and drain the pasta. Add to the soup and heat through, adjusting the thickness, if necessary, by boiling so any excess water evaporates, or adding more stock if too thick; season. Serve with freshly grated Parmesan.

## 018
# linguine with herbs, lemon, & garlic crumbs

PREPARATION TIME 10 minutes COOKING TIME 10 minutes SERVES 4

10 OUNCES LINGUINE*
EXTRA-VIRGIN OLIVE OIL
1 PLUMP GARLIC CLOVE, CRUSHED
1 CUP FRESH BREAD CRUMBS
1 SHALLOT, FINELY CHOPPED

LEAVES FROM A BUNCH OF MIXED HERBS, SUCH
    AS PARSLEY, OREGANO, BASIL, AND FENNEL,
    PLUS A FEW CHIVES, ALL FINELY CHOPPED
JUICE OF 1 LEMON
1 TEASPOON LEMON ZEST
SALT AND FRESHLY GROUND BLACK PEPPER

1   Cook and drain the pasta according to the package directions.
2   Meanwhile, heat about 3 tablespoons oil in a skillet. Add the garlic and bread crumbs and cook over low heat, stirring frequently, until golden. Stir in the shallot toward the end.
3   At the same time, gently warm 2 tablespoons oil with the herbs, lemon juice and zest, and seasoning in a pan.
4   Toss the pasta with the herb mixture, scatter the bread crumbs over, and serve.

*   Spaghetti or bucatini can also be used.

## 019
# tagliarini with artichokes & gremolata

PREPARATION TIME 10 minutes, plus 30 minutes standing COOKING TIME 10 minutes SERVES 4

8 ROASTED ARTICHOKES IN OIL, RINSED AND
    QUARTERED
2 TABLESPOONS SMALL CAPERS
6 SCALLIONS, FINELY CHOPPED
2–3 TABLESPOONS LEMON JUICE, TO TASTE
EXTRA-VIRGIN OLIVE OIL

SALT AND FRESHLY GROUND BLACK PEPPER
GRATED ZEST OF 1 LEMON
3 GARLIC CLOVES, FINELY SLICED
HANDFUL OF FLAT-LEAF PARSLEY, CHOPPED
9 OUNCES TAGLIARINI
FRESHLY GRATED PARMESAN, TO SERVE

1   Put the artichokes, capers, scallions, and lemon juice into a small bowl and pour enough oil to cover over. Season using plenty of black pepper; leave 30 minutes.
2   To make the gremolata, combine the lemon zest, garlic, and parsley in a small bowl.
3   Cook and drain the tagliarini according to the package directions. Toss with the artichoke mixture and serve with the lemon and garlic gremolata scattered over, accompanied by freshly grated Parmesan.

## 020

# spaghetti with lemon, basil, & parmesan

PREPARATION TIME 5 minutes COOKING TIME 10 minutes SERVES 4 to 6

6 TABLESPOONS VIRGIN OLIVE OIL
2 GARLIC CLOVES, FINELY CHOPPED
JUICE AND GRATED ZEST OF 1 LEMON
14 OUNCES SPAGHETTI

½ CUP PARMESAN, FRESHLY GRATED
HANDFUL OF BASIL LEAVES, SHREDDED
SALT AND FRESHLY GROUND BLACK PEPPER

1   Warm the oil, garlic, and lemon juice in a small saucepan over very low heat.
2   Meanwhile, cook and drain the spaghetti according to the package directions. Toss with the warmed oil, the Parmesan, basil, and seasoning. Serve with the lemon zest sprinkled over.

## 021

# pasta, basil, & goat cheese frittata

PREPARATION TIME 10 minutes COOKING TIME 15 to 20 minutes SERVES 3 to 4

4 OUNCES COOKED ANGELS' HAIR PASTA
   (2 OUNCES UNCOOKED WEIGHT)
4 EGGS, LIGHTLY BEATEN
2 GARLIC CLOVES, FINELY CHOPPED
2 TABLESPOONS CHOPPED FLAT-LEAF PARSLEY
SALT AND FRESHLY GROUND BLACK PEPPER
OLIVE OIL

3 OUNCES GOAT CHEESE, FINELY CHOPPED
   OR CRUMBLED
2 WELL-FLAVORED TOMATOES, CHOPPED
2 TEASPOONS BALSAMIC VINEGAR
1 TABLESPOON SHREDDED BASIL LEAVES
1½ TABLESPOONS FRESHLY GRATED PARMESAN

1   Stir the pasta into the eggs with the garlic, parsley, and seasoning.
2   Heat a thin layer of oil in an ovenproof skillet. Pour in the egg mixture and spread it out evenly. Cook over low-medium heat until most of the mixture is set, but the top is still creamy.
3   Scatter the goat cheese over and put under a heated broiler until the cheese is bubbling.
4   Meanwhile, combine the tomatoes with the balsamic vinegar and basil.
5   Sprinkle the Parmesan over the frittata and serve in wedges, accompanied by the tomatoes.

## 022

# spaghetti with garlic, anchovies, & parsley

PREPARATION TIME 5 minutes COOKING TIME 10 minutes SERVES 6

15 OUNCES SPAGHETTI
3 GARLIC CLOVES, FINELY CHOPPED
VIRGIN OLIVE OIL
1 CAN (2-OZ.) ANCHOVIES IN OIL, DRAINED
2 TEASPOONS DRIED OREGANO

LEAVES FROM A SMALL BUNCH OF FLAT-LEAF
   PARSLEY, COARSELY CHOPPED
SALT AND FRESHLY GROUND BLACK PEPPER
FRESHLY GRATED PECORINO OR PARMESAN, TO SERVE

1   Cook and drain the spaghetti according to the package directions.
2   Meanwhile, fry the garlic in a little oil with the anchovies, oregano, and parsley, stirring frequently, until the anchovies have dissolved and the garlic is soft and lightly colored. Season, using plenty of black pepper.
3   Toss with the spaghetti and serve with pecorino or Parmesan.

## 023
# cavatappi with arugula, tomatoes, & olives

PREPARATION TIME 10 minutes COOKING TIME 10 minutes SERVES 4

9 OUNCES **CAVATAPPI**
3 PLUMP GARLIC CLOVES, FINELY SLICED
4 TABLESPOONS **EXTRA-VIRGIN OLIVE OIL**
1¼ POUNDS **RIPE WELL-FLAVORED TOMATOES, SEEDED AND CHOPPED**

2 OUNCES **ARUGULA**
12 OIL-CURED BLACK OLIVES, PITTED
1 TABLESPOON **PINE NUTS, LIGHTLY TOASTED**
SALT AND FRESHLY GROUND BLACK PEPPER
FRESHLY GRATED PECORINO OR PARMESAN, TO SERVE

1  Cook and drain the cavatappi according to the package directions.
2  Meanwhile, fry the garlic in the oil in a small pan until just beginning to color. Scoop the garlic from the pan and reserve. Add the tomatoes to the oil and warm over low heat; do not let them soften.
3  Toss the pasta with the oil and tomatoes, garlic, arugula, olives, pine nuts, and seasoning. Serve with pecorino or Parmesan.

## 024
# herb fettuccine all'alfredo

PREPARATION TIME 5 minutes COOKING TIME 10 minutes SERVES 6

3 TABLESPOONS **UNSALTED BUTTER**
1 CUP **HEAVY CREAM**
SMALL PINCH OF FRESHLY GRATED NUTMEG (OPTIONAL)

SALT AND FRESHLY GROUND BLACK PEPPER
1 POUND **FRESH HERB FETTUCCINE (SEE PAGE 10)***
½ CUP **FRESHLY GRATED PARMESAN, PLUS EXTRA TO SERVE (OPTIONAL)**

1  Bring a pan of water for the pasta to a boil.
2  Meanwhile, boil the butter with the cream in a large skillet until reduced by almost a half, stirring frequently. Add the nutmeg, if using, salt and plenty of black pepper.
3  Cook and drain the pasta. Toss with the cream sauce and the cheese. Serve with extra Parmesan, if liked.

*  Plain fettuccine can also be used.

## 025
# linguine with anchovies, chili, & olives

PREPARATION TIME 5 minutes COOKING TIME 10 minutes SERVES 6

14 OUNCES **LINGUINE**
2 WIDE STRIPS OF PARED LEMON PEEL
4 TABLESPOONS **EXTRA-VIRGIN OLIVE OIL**
1 CAN (2-oz.) ANCHOVIES, DRAINED AND CHOPPED
2 GARLIC CLOVES, FINELY CHOPPED
PINCH OF DRIED CHILI FLAKES

¾ CUP **MIXED PITTED GREEN AND BLACK OLIVES, FINELY CHOPPED**
2 TABLESPOONS **CHOPPED FRESH FLAT-LEAF PARSLEY**
FRESHLY GROUND BLACK PEPPER
FRESHLY GRATED PARMESAN, TO SERVE

1  Cook and drain the pasta according to the package directions, reserving ½ cup of the cooking water.
2  Meanwhile, heat the lemon peel in the oil in a large skillet over low heat about 2 minutes, until sizzling. Stir in the anchovies until they dissolve, then add the garlic, chili flakes, and olives and cook over fairly high heat 2 to 3 minutes. Discard the lemon peel. Add the parsley and season with black pepper. Toss with the pasta and add enough cooking water to moisten. Serve with Parmesan.

## 026
# spaghetti with mixed herb sauce

PREPARATION TIME 10 minutes COOKING TIME 10 minutes SERVES 4 to 6

6 TABLESPOONS EXTRA-VIRGIN OLIVE OIL

1 GARLIC CLOVE, FINELY CHOPPED

2 TABLESPOONS CHOPPED FLAT-LEAF PARSLEY

LEAVES FROM A SMALL BUNCH OF SAGE, CHIVES,
PARSLEY, AND THYME, FINELY CHOPPED

SALT AND FRESHLY GROUND BLACK PEPPER

2 TEASPOONS LEMON JUICE

13 OUNCES SPAGHETTI

1   Slowly heat the oil, garlic, and herbs in a saucepan 1 to 2 minutes, stirring. Season and then add
    the lemon juice.
2   Meanwhile, cook and drain the spaghetti according to the package directions, reserving ½ cup of the
    cooking water. Toss with the herb mixture, adding enough reserved water, if necessary, to moisten.

## 027
# linguine with gorgonzola & watercress

PREPARATION TIME 5 minutes COOKING TIME 10 minutes SERVES 4

7 OUNCES LINGUINE

1 BUNCH OF WATERCRESS, THICK STEMS REMOVED

3 TABLESPOONS VIRGIN OLIVE OIL

2 TEASPOONS LEMON JUICE, TO TASTE

SALT AND FRESHLY GROUND BLACK PEPPER

½ CUP CRUMBLED GORGONZOLA

1   Cook and drain the pasta according to the package directions.
2   Meanwhile, put the watercress, oil, and lemon juice into a blender. Pulse until the watercress is finely
    chopped. Season and adjust the lemon juice, if necessary. Toss with the pasta and Gorgonzola.

## 028
# fusilli with artichokes, tomatoes, & olives

PREPARATION TIME 5 minutes COOKING TIME 10 minutes SERVES 4 to 6

10 OUNCES FUSILLI*

1 RED ONION, FINELY CHOPPED

6 PIECES SUN-BLUSH TOMATOES IN OIL, OR PLUMP
   SUN-DRIED TOMATOES IN OIL, DRAINED (OIL
   RESERVED) AND SLICED

10 ROAST ARTICHOKES IN OIL, DRAINED

⅓ CUP PITTED BLACK OLIVES

4 OUNCES ARUGULA

½ CUP PECORINO, FRESHLY GRATED

1   Cook and drain the fusilli according to the package directions.
2   Meanwhile, fry the onion in 1 tablespoon of the reserved tomato oil until soft and turning golden.
3   Coarsely chop the artichokes with the olives and add to the pan with the tomatoes. Heat through. Add
    the arugula and toss with the pasta and half the cheese. Serve with the remaining cheese scattered over.

*   Eliche can also be used.

## 029
# fidelini with walnut sauce

PREPARATION TIME 5 minutes COOKING TIME 10 minutes SERVES 4

11 ounces FIDELINI
⅔ cup WALNUT HALVES, LIGHTLY TOASTED
1 GARLIC CLOVE, CRUSHED
1 tablespoon VIRGIN OLIVE OIL

⅔ cup RICOTTA
SALT AND FRESHLY GROUND BLACK PEPPER
FINELY CHOPPED FLAT-LEAF PARSLEY AND FRESHLY
    GRATED PECORINO, TO SERVE

1   Cook and drain the pasta according to the package directions, reserving ½ cup of the cooking water.
2   Meanwhile, put the walnuts and garlic into a small blender and pulse to chop finely. Add the oil and
    mix briefly to a coarse paste. Transfer to a bowl and work in the ricotta and seasoning. Toss with
    the pasta, adding enough of the reserved cooking water to moisten, if necessary. Serve scattered
    with the parsley and pecorino.

## 030
# tagliatelle with ricotta pesto

PREPARATION TIME 5 minutes COOKING TIME 20 minutes SERVES 4

2 GARLIC CLOVES
HEAPED 1 cup RICOTTA
2 tablespoons VIRGIN OLIVE OIL
LEAVES FROM A LARGE BUNCH OF BASIL,
    A FEW RESERVED FOR GARNISH

SALT AND FRESHLY GROUND BLACK PEPPER
8 ounces TAGLIATELLE
FRESHLY GRATED PARMESAN, TO SERVE

1   Simmer the garlic cloves in a little water 10 minutes. Drain well and put into a blender with the ricotta,
    oil, and basil and mix until smooth; season.
2   Cook and drain the tagliatelle according to the package directions, reserving ½ cup of the cooking water.
    Toss immediately with the ricotta pesto, adding some of the reserved cooking water, if necessary,
    to moisten. Serve garnished with basil leaves and accompanied by Parmesan.

## 031
# spaghetti with sun-dried tomato tapenade

PREPARATION TIME 5 minutes COOKING TIME 10 minutes SERVES 4 to 6

14 ounces SPAGHETTI
3 GARLIC CLOVES, CRUSHED
PINCH OF CHILI FLAKES
¼ cup VIRGIN OLIVE OIL
SCANT ½ cup PITTED OIL-CURED BLACK OLIVES

2 ounces SUN-DRIED TOMATOES IN OIL
3 tablespoons CAPERS
LEAVES FROM A SMALL BUNCH OF FLAT-LEAF
    PARSLEY, CHOPPED

1   Cook and drain the pasta according to the package directions.
2   Meanwhile, put the garlic, chili flakes, and oil into a blender and add three-quarters of the olives,
    sun-dried tomatoes, and capers. Mix together to a smooth sauce. Thinly slice the remaining sun-dried
    tomatoes and quarter the remaining olives.
3   Toss the spaghetti with the sauce, parsley, and remaining sun-dried tomatoes, olives, and capers.

# warm pasta salad with spinach, tomatoes, & olives

PREPARATION TIME 10 minutes COOKING TIME 10 minutes SERVES 4

8 OUNCES **LINGUINE***

3 TABLESPOONS **VIRGIN OLIVE OIL**

2 TEASPOONS **WHITE WINE VINEGAR**

1 TEASPOON **BALSAMIC VINEGAR**

2 TEASPOONS **OREGANO**

1 SMALL **GARLIC CLOVE, CRUSHED**

**SALT AND FRESHLY GROUND BLACK PEPPER**

2 OUNCES **BABY LEAF SPINACH**

⅓ CUP **HALVED PITTED KALAMATA OLIVES**

4 OUNCES **CHERRY TOMATOES, HALVED**

HEAPED ¾ CUP **CRUMBLED FETA**

½ SMALL **RED ONION, FINELY CHOPPED**

1   Cook and drain the pasta according to the package directions.

2   Meanwhile, whisk the oil with the vinegars, oregano, garlic, and seasoning until emulsified.

3   Toss the pasta with the oregano dressing and the remaining ingredients. Serve warm.

*   Cavatappi, cavatelli, eliche, fusilli, or orecchiette can also be used.

## 033

# fusilli, arugula, & tomato frittata

PREPARATION TIME 5 minutes COOKING TIME 25 minutes SERVES 4 to 6

4 OUNCES **FUSILLI**
5 OUNCES **WELL-FLAVORED CHERRY TOMATOES, HALVED**
4 OUNCES **ARUGULA**
7 **EGGS**
2 OUNCES **SOFT GOAT CHEESE, CHOPPED**

I TABLESPOON **THYME**
**SALT AND FRESHLY GROUND BLACK PEPPER**
**VIRGIN OLIVE OIL**
4 OUNCES **TALEGGIO, FINELY CHOPPED**

1   Cook and drain the pasta according to the package directions. While it is still warm, stir in the tomatoes and arugula.
2   Meanwhile, beat the eggs into the goat cheese and add the thyme, pasta mixture, and seasoning.
3   Heat a little oil in a large ovenproof skillet. Pour in the egg mixture and cook slowly until the frittata is almost set; it should remain creamy on top. Scatter the Taleggio over and place under a heated broiler until it melts. Serve cut into wedges.

## 034

# trenette with tuscan herb sauce

PREPARATION TIME 10 minutes COOKING TIME 10 minutes SERVES 4 to 6

I POUND **FRESH TRENETTE (SEE PAGE 10)**
2 **GARLIC CLOVES, FINELY CHOPPED**
4 TABLESPOONS **VIRGIN OLIVE OIL**
6 **CANNED ANCHOVY FILLETS, DRAINED**
2 TABLESPOONS **PASSATA (BOTTLED STRAINED PUREED TOMATOES)**
**PINCH OF CHILI FLAKES**

**LEAVES FROM A SMALL BUNCH OF FLAT-LEAF PARSLEY, FINELY CHOPPED**
I TABLESPOON **THYME**
I TABLESPOON **CHOPPED MARJORAM**
I½ TEASPOONS **FINELY CHOPPED ROSEMARY**
**SALT AND FRESHLY GROUND BLACK PEPPER**
**FRESHLY GRATED PARMESAN, TO SERVE**

1   Cook and drain the pasta.
2   Meanwhile, gently fry the garlic in the oil 2 minutes, then stir in the anchovies until they dissolve. Stir in the passata. After 1 minute add the chili flakes and herbs. Heat slowly for a couple of minutes; season.
3   Toss with the trenette and serve with Parmesan.

## 035

# trenette with wilted tomatoes

PREPARATION TIME 5 minutes COOKING TIME 10 minutes SERVES 4

10 OUNCES **TRENETTE**
14 OUNCES **WELL-FLAVORED CHERRY PLUM TOMATOES OR WELL-FLAVORED ORDINARY CHERRY TOMATOES, HALVED OR QUARTERED**
**VIRGIN OLIVE OIL**
ABOUT 2 TABLESPOONS **BALSAMIC VINEGAR, TO TASTE**

**PINCH OF SUGAR, TO TASTE (OPTIONAL)**
**SALT AND FRESHLY GROUND BLACK PEPPER**
**LEAVES FROM A SMALL HANDFUL OF BASIL, SHREDDED**
**SHAVINGS OF PECORINO OR PARMESAN, TO SERVE**

1   Cook and drain the trenette according to the package directions.
2   Meanwhile, cook the tomatoes briskly in a large skillet in a little oil 1 to 2 minutes until just beginning to soften. Remove from the heat and immediately stir in balsamic vinegar to taste. Add a pinch of sugar, to taste, if liked. Season and toss with the pasta. Serve with the basil and pecorino or Parmesan shavings scattered over.

## 036
# fusilli with spinach, sun-dried tomatoes, & olives

PREPARATION TIME 5 minutes COOKING TIME 10 minutes SERVES 4

8 OUNCES FUSILLI*
GOOD HANDFUL OF BABY SPINACH LEAVES
12 SUN-DRIED TOMATOES IN OIL, DRAINED (OIL
    RESERVED) AND SLICED
2–3 GARLIC CLOVES, FINELY CHOPPED
12 PITTED KALAMATA OLIVES, SLICED

1–2 TEASPOONS BALSAMIC VINEGAR
PINCH OF CHILI FLAKES (OPTIONAL)
5 TABLESPOONS MIXED EXTRA-VIRGIN OLIVE OIL AND
    OIL FROM THE SUN-DRIED TOMATOES
SALT AND FRESHLY GROUND BLACK PEPPER

1    Cook and drain the pasta according to the package directions.
2    Toss with the spinach, and then with the remaining ingredients. Season and serve warm.

*    Eliche or farfalle can also be used.


## 037
# tagliatelle with lemon & parsley sauce

PREPARATION TIME 5 minutes COOKING TIME 5 minutes SERVES 4 to 6

½ CUP RICOTTA
3 TABLESPOONS LEMON JUICE
2 TABLESPOONS GRATED LEMON ZEST
2 TABLESPOONS CHOPPED FLAT-LEAF PARSLEY

SALT AND FRESHLY GROUND BLACK PEPPER
14 OUNCES FRESH TAGLIATELLE (SEE PAGE 10)
4 TABLESPOONS FRESHLY GRATED PARMESAN

1    Mash the ricotta with the lemon juice and zest until smooth. Mix in the parsley and seasoning.
2    Cook and drain the pasta. Toss with the ricotta mixture and serve sprinkled with the Parmesan.


## 038
# spaghetti with sun-dried tomatoes, garlic, & chilies

PREPARATION TIME 5 minutes COOKING TIME 10 minutes SERVES 6

14 OUNCES SPAGHETTI*
12–14 SUN-DRIED TOMATOES IN OIL,
    DRAINED AND SLICED
3 GARLIC CLOVES, FINELY CHOPPED

1 TABLESPOON CHOPPED FLAT-LEAF PARSLEY
PINCH OF DRIED CHILI FLAKES
¼ CUP EXTRA-VIRGIN OLIVE OIL

1    Cook and drain the spaghetti according to the package directions.
2    Meanwhile, combine the sauce ingredients and warm slowly in a small saucepan.
3    Toss the spaghetti with the sauce and serve.

*    Bucatini or fusilli can also be used.

# 039
# pancetta-stuffed tomatoes

PREPARATION TIME 15 minutes COOKING TIME 35 minutes SERVES 4

4 RIPE LARGE TOMATOES

⅓ CUP MACARONI

3 OUNCES PANCETTA, CHOPPED

VIRGIN OLIVE OIL

1 SMALL ONION, FINELY CHOPPED

1 GARLIC CLOVE, FINELY CHOPPED

1 CUP FINELY CHOPPED MOZZARELLA

8 PITTED KALAMATA OLIVES, CHOPPED

2 TABLESPOONS CHOPPED FLAT-LEAF PARSLEY

2 TABLESPOONS SNIPPED CHIVES

SALT AND FRESHLY GROUND BLACK PEPPER

MAYONNAISE OR AÏOLI, TO SERVE (OPTIONAL)

1   Heat the oven to 375°F.

2   Slice the tops from the tomatoes and reserve. Scoop the seeds and central flesh from the tomatoes into a strainer, leaving the walls intact. Press the flesh and seeds through the strainer into a bowl and reserve the juice. Leave the tomato shells upside down on paper towels to drain.

3   Cook the macaroni 1 minute less than specified; drain.

4   Meanwhile, fry the pancetta in a little oil until lightly golden and the fat runs; remove from the pan. Fry the onion and garlic in the pancetta fat until soft but not colored. Add the reserved tomato flesh and juice and boil until thick. Toss with the pasta, pancetta, mozzarella, olives, herbs, and seasoning.

5   Stand the tomato shells upright in a shallow baking dish and fill with the pasta mixture. Replace the lids and bake in the heated oven 20 to 25 minutes until the tomatoes are soft and beginning to color. Serve with mayonnaise or aïoli, if liked.

## 040

# tagliatelle with sicilian tomato pesto

PREPARATION TIME 5 minutes, COOKING TIME 10 minutes, SERVES 4 to 6

2 OUNCES BASIL LEAVES
2 GARLIC CLOVES, CHOPPED
⅓ CUP BLANCHED ALMONDS
1¼ CUPS SEEDED AND CHOPPED WELL-FLAVORED
   TOMATOES
3 TABLESPOONS PECORINO, FRESHLY GRATED,
   PLUS EXTRA TO SERVE

ABOUT ⅔ CUP VIRGIN OLIVE OIL
SALT AND FRESHLY GROUND BLACK PEPPER
ABOUT 1 TABLESPOON SUN-DRIED TOMATO PASTE
   (OPTIONAL)
12 OUNCES TAGLIATELLE

1   Put the basil, garlic, and almonds into a blender and mix to a nubbly paste. Add the tomatoes and
    cheese and, with the motor running, pour in the oil in a slow, steady stream. Season and add sun-dried
    tomato paste if necessary, to boost the tomato flavor.
2   Cook and drain the pasta according to the package directions. Toss with half the pesto. Serve with the
    remaining pesto, if liked.

**Note:**
It is not practical to make a smaller quantity of the pesto, but any remaining can be kept in a jar,
covered by a layer of oil, in the refrigerator for up to 1 week.

38

## 041

# fusilli with sun-blush tomatoes, anchovies, & olives

PREPARATION TIME 10 minutes COOKING TIME 10 minutes SERVES 4

2 SHALLOTS, FINELY CHOPPED
2 GARLIC CLOVES, FINELY CHOPPED
OLIVE OIL
8 CANNED ANCHOVY FILLETS, DRAINED
4 OUNCES SUN-BLUSH TOMATOES, OR PLUMP SUN-
   DRIED TOMATOES IN OIL, DRAINED AND COARSELY
   CHOPPED

8 PITTED BLACK OLIVES, FINELY CHOPPED
12 OUNCES FUSILLI
1 TABLESPOON SMALL CAPERS
LEAVES FROM A SMALL BUNCH OF
   FLAT-LEAF PARSLEY, CHOPPED
FRESHLY GROUND BLACK PEPPER

1   Fry the shallots and garlic in a little oil 1 to 2 minutes. Stir in the anchovies, tomatoes,
    and olives and heat slowly.
2   Meanwhile, cook and drain the pasta according to the package directions.
3   Toss the fusilli with the tomato mixture, capers, and parsley. Season with plenty of black pepper;
    salt probably won't be necessary because of the salty flavor of the capers.

## 042

# spaghetti with anchovies, lemon, chilies & thyme pangritata

PREPARATION TIME 5 minutes COOKING TIME 15 minutes SERVES 4

2 THICK SLICES OF CRUSTLESS BREAD,
   MADE INTO CRUMBS
2½ TEASPOONS THYME LEAVES
2 PLUMP GARLIC CLOVES,
   FINELY CHOPPED
VIRGIN OLIVE OIL

12 OUNCES SPAGHETTI
PINCH OF CHILI FLAKES
12 CANNED ANCHOVY FILLETS, DRAINED
ZEST AND JUICE OF 1 SMALL LEMON,
   PLUS EXTRA TO TASTE, IF NECESSARY
SALT AND FRESHLY GROUND BLACK PEPPER

1  To make the pangritata, fry the bread crumbs, thyme, and 1 garlic clove in ½ cup oil, stirring frequently, until very crisp and golden. Season and scoop onto paper towels to drain.
2  Cook and drain the spaghetti according to the package directions.
3  Meanwhile, fry the remaining garlic and the chili in a little oil 30 seconds. Stir in the anchovies until they dissolve. Remove from the heat and add the lemon juice and zest and season. Taste and add more lemon juice, if necessary. Toss with the spaghetti and serve with the crumbs sprinkled over.

## 043

# cavatelli with fresh tomatoes, herbs, & mozzarella

PREPARATION TIME 10 minutes COOKING TIME 10 minutes SERVES 4 to 6

8 OUNCES BUFFALO MOZZARELLA,
   CUT INTO ¼-INCH CUBES
2¼ CUPS DICED WELL-FLAVORED PLUM TOMATOES
1 TABLESPOON SHREDDED BASIL
2 TEASPOONS OREGANO
2 TEASPOONS THYME

5 TABLESPOONS EXTRA-VIRGIN OLIVE OIL
2 TEASPOONS LEMON JUICE
SALT AND FRESHLY GROUND BLACK PEPPER
14 OUNCES CAVATELLI*

1  Combine the cheese, tomatoes, herbs, oil, lemon juice, and seasoning in a large bowl.
2  Cook and drain the pasta according to the package directions. Toss immediately with the tomato mixture. If the cheese does not begin to melt, cover 2 minutes. Serve straightaway.

*  Cavatappi or eliche can also be used.

## 044
# herb carbonara

PREPARATION TIME 5 minutes COOKING TIME 10 minutes SERVES 4 to 6

12 ounces LINGUINE*
3 tablespoons SHREDDED BASIL
2 tablespoons FINELY CHOPPED FLAT-LEAF PARSLEY
HEAPED ¾ cup FRESHLY GRATED PARMESAN

4 tablespoons UNSALTED BUTTER, MELTED
SALT AND FRESHLY GROUND BLACK PEPPER
4 EGG YOLKS

1 Cook and drain the linguine according to the package directions.
2 Meanwhile, stir the herbs, Parmesan, butter, and seasoning into the egg yolks. Toss with the linguine to make a creamy sauce and serve.

* Tagliarini or spaghetti can also be used.

## 045
# spaghetti with summer puttanesca sauce

PREPARATION TIME 10 minutes COOKING TIME 10 minutes SERVES 4

10 ounces SPAGHETTI
1 GARLIC CLOVE, FINELY CHOPPED
EXTRA-VIRGIN OLIVE OIL
3 CANNED ANCHOVY FILLETS, CHOPPED
1¼ cups SEEDED AND CHOPPED WELL-FLAVORED
   TOMATOES

1 tablespoon CAPERS
10 PITTED BLACK OLIVES, SLICED
1 tablespoon CHOPPED FLAT-LEAF PARSLEY
FRESHLY GROUND BLACK PEPPER

1 Cook and drain the pasta according to the package directions.
2 Meanwhile, cook the garlic in a little oil until it just begins to change color. Stir in the anchovies until they dissolve, then add the tomatoes, capers, and olives. Stir around for a few minutes to warm the tomatoes. Remove from the heat and add the parsley and black pepper. Toss with the pasta.

## 046
# spaghetti alla carbonara

PREPARATION TIME 5 minutes COOKING TIME 10 minutes SERVES 4

9 ounces SPAGHETTI
3 ounces PANCETTA, CUT ACROSS INTO STRIPS
SMALL KNOB OF UNSALTED BUTTER
4 tablespoons MEDIUM-BODIED DRY WHITE WINE
2 EGGS

1½ tablespoons CHOPPED FLAT-LEAF PARSLEY
2 tablespoons FRESHLY GRATED PECORINO
2 tablespoons FRESHLY GRATED PARMESAN
SALT AND FRESHLY GROUND BLACK PEPPER

1 Cook the pasta according to the package directions.
2 Meanwhile, fry the pancetta in the butter until crisp but not colored. Add the wine and boil until reduced by half.
3 While the pancetta is cooking, in a bowl that is large enough to hold the cooked pasta, beat the eggs with the parsley, half of each of the cheeses, a pinch of salt, and plenty of black pepper.
4 Drain the pasta and immediately add it to the bowl of eggs. Quickly toss together, adding the pancetta, until the eggs are creamy. Toss lightly with the remaining cheese and serve.

## 047
# pasta, shrimp, & pesto

PREPARATION TIME 5 minutes COOKING TIME 10 minutes SERVES 4 to 6

12 OUNCES FUSILLI*
4 TABLESPOONS VIRGIN OLIVE OIL
4 TABLESPOONS PESTO (SEE PAGE 18)
8 OUNCES SHELLED COOKED SHRIMP

5 PLUM TOMATOES, CHOPPED
SALT AND FRESHLY GROUND BLACK PEPPER
SHREDDED BASIL LEAVES, TO SERVE

1    Cook and drain the pasta according to the package directions.
2    Meanwhile, stir the oil into the pesto.
3    Toss the pesto mixture, shrimp, and tomatoes with the pasta. Season and serve sprinkled with basil leaves.

*    Cavatappi, conchiglie, or eliche can also be used.

## 048
# spaghetti with simple red bell pepper sauce

PREPARATION TIME 10 minutes COOKING TIME 10 minutes SERVES 6

2 LARGE, FLESHY RED BELL PEPPERS, BROILED,
    PEELED, AND CHOPPED (SEE PAGE 67)
2 GARLIC CLOVES, CHOPPED
PINCH OF CHILI FLAKES (OPTIONAL)
5 TABLESPOONS PINE NUTS, LIGHTLY TOASTED

5 TABLESPOONS EXTRA VIRGIN OLIVE OIL
½ TEASPOON BALSAMIC VINEGAR, TO TASTE
SALT AND FRESHLY GROUND BLACK PEPPER
14 OUNCES SPAGHETTI
FRESHLY GRATED PARMESAN, TO SERVE

1    Put the bell peppers, garlic, chili (if using), pine nuts, and oil into a food processor and pulse until just
     smooth. Add the balsamic vinegar and seasoning, to taste.
2    Cook and drain the pasta according to the package directions, reserving ½ cup of the cooking water.
     Toss with the red pepper sauce, adding a little of the reserved cooking water, if necessary.
     Serve with the freshly grated Parmesan.

## 049
# spaghetti with capers, olives, & anchovies

PREPARATION TIME 5 minutes COOKING TIME 10 minutes SERVES 6

14 OUNCES SPAGHETTI
1 GARLIC CLOVE, FINELY CHOPPED
2 TABLESPOONS DRIED BREAD CRUMBS
½ CUP EXTRA-VIRGIN OLIVE OIL
6 ANCHOVY FILLETS, CHOPPED

2 TABLESPOONS CAPERS
10 PITTED BLACK OLIVES, SLICED
1 TABLESPOON CHOPPED FLAT-LEAF PARSLEY
FRESHLY GROUND BLACK PEPPER

1    Cook and drain the pasta according to the package directions, reserving ½ cup of the cooking water.
2    Meanwhile, cook the garlic and bread crumbs in the oil until the garlic just begins to change color, but
     do not let the bread crumbs brown. Stir in the anchovies until they dissolve, then add the capers and
     olives. Stir around a minute or so, remove from the heat, and add the parsley and black pepper.
     Toss with the pasta and add enough cooking water to moisten.

## 050
# fidelini-stuffed bell peppers

PREPARATION TIME 10 minutes COOKING TIME 20 to 25 minutes SERVES 4

1½ OUNCES FIDELINI

2 LARGE RED BELL PEPPERS

2 TABLESPOONS MILK

2 TABLESPOONS SOFT CHEESE WITH GARLIC AND HERBS

2 LARGE EGGS, BEATEN

2 TABLESPOONS CHOPPED FLAT-LEAF PARSLEY

1 WELL-FLAVORED TOMATO, SEEDED AND CHOPPED

6 TABLESPOONS FRESHLY GRATED PARMESAN

1   Heat the oven to 350°F.
2   Cook and drain the fidelini according to the package directions, but for 1½ minutes less than specified. Snip the strands into shorter pieces.
3   Meanwhile, cut the bell peppers in half lengthwise, carefully removing the stem ends and seeds. Blanch in boiling water 3 minutes; leave upside down to drain.
4   Stir the milk into the soft cheese until smooth, then mix in the eggs and parsley.
5   Stand the pepper halves in a shallow baking dish or pan, propping them upright with foil, if necessary. Divide the fidelini between the halves. Carefully spoon in the cheese mixture, easing it with the point of a knife to flow between the pasta strands. Sprinkle the Parmesan over and bake in the heated oven 20 to 25 minutes until the filling is just set.

## 051
# tonnarelli with tomato & red pesto sauce

PREPARATION TIME 10 minutes COOKING TIME 10 minutes SERVES 6

4 RIPE PLUM TOMATOES, CHOPPED

4 PIECES OF SUN-DRIED TOMATOES, DRAINED AND CHOPPED

2 TABLESPOONS PINE NUTS, LIGHTLY TOASTED

3 TABLESPOONS EACH OIL FROM THE TOMATOES AND EXTRA-VIRGIN OLIVE OIL

SMALL HANDFUL OF BASIL LEAVES, SHREDDED, PLUS EXTRA TO GARNISH

SALT AND FRESHLY GROUND BLACK PEPPER

4 TABLESPOONS HOME-DRIED BREAD CRUMBS

2 GARLIC CLOVES, FINELY CHOPPED

12 OUNCES FRESH TONNARELLI*

1   Put all the tomatoes and the pine nuts in a food processor. With the motor running, slowly pour in 4 tablespoons oil to make a chunky mixture. Remove from the processor and add the basil and seasoning.
2   Fry the bread crumbs and garlic in the remaining oil over low heat, stirring, until the crumbs are golden; take care the garlic does not burn.
3   Cook and drain the pasta, reserving ½ cup of the cooking water. Toss the pasta with the pesto; if it seems too dry, add 2 tablespoons of the reserved water. Serve with the bread crumbs and extra basil sprinkled over.

*   Spaghetti can also be used.

## 052
# mediterranean vegetable & pasta salad

PREPARATION TIME 10 minutes COOKING TIME 10 minutes SERVES 4

8 OUNCES RADIATORI*
6 SUN-DRIED TOMATOES IN OIL, DRAINED
  (OIL RESERVED) AND SLICED
5 TABLESPOONS VIRGIN OLIVE OIL
1 TABLESPOON RED WINE VINEGAR
1 GARLIC CLOVE, FINELY CHOPPED
SALT AND FRESHLY GROUND BLACK PEPPER
6 PITTED KALAMATA OLIVES, QUARTERED
5 OUNCES CHERRY PLUM TOMATOES, HALVED

¼ CUP SLICED BABY ZUCCHINI, SLICED
6 ROAST ARTICHOKE HEARTS IN OIL,
  DRAINED AND SLICED
1 LARGE (OR 2 HALVES) BOTTLED ROASTED
  RED BELL PEPPER IN OIL, CUT INTO STRIPS
LEAVES FROM A SMALL BUNCH OF BASIL, SHREDDED
2–3 HANDFULS OF SMALL CRISP SALAD LEAVES,
  INCLUDING SOME ARUGULA

1   Cook and drain the pasta according to the package directions. Rinse in cold water and toss immediately
    with 1 tablespoon oil from the tomatoes; leave to cool.
2   Meanwhile, make the dressing by whisking the oil, vinegar, garlic, and seasoning together. Toss with
    the pasta, olives, tomatoes, zucchini, artichokes, peppers, and basil. Serve on a bed of salad leaves.

*   Fusilli and cavatelli can also be used.

## 053
# potato gnocchi with bell pepper & red pesto sauce

PREPARATION TIME 25 minutes COOKING TIME 30 to 35 minutes SERVES 4

1 LARGE RED BELL PEPPER, BROILED, PEELED, AND
  CHOPPED (SEE PAGE 67)
1 QUANTITY RED PESTO (SEE PAGE 19)
2 POUNDS FLOURY POTATOES, UNPEELED
4 TABLESPOONS UNSALTED BUTTER, DICED

1 EGG, BEATEN
SALT AND FRESHLY GROUND BLACK PEPPER
SCANT 2 CUPS ALL-PURPOSE FLOUR
BASIL LEAVES AND OIL-CURED PITTED BLACK OLIVES,
  TO SERVE

1   Put the red bell pepper and red pesto into a blender and puree together; set aside.
2   Boil the potatoes until very tender; the time will depend on their size. Drain well and press through a
    potato ricer, or peel and press through a strainer. While still warm, beat in the butter, egg, and seasoning.
    Then, using a fork, lightly mix in half the flour. Turn on to a floured surface and lightly knead in enough
    flour to give a soft, smooth, slightly sticky dough.
3   Roll the dough into rope shapes about 1 inch thick. Cut into ¾-inch pieces. Using a lightly floured thumb,
    roll each piece over the back of the tines of a fork, so there are ridges on one side and a slight
    depression on the other. Place the gnocchi on a floured dish towel as they are done.
4   Cook the gnocchi in batches in a large saucepan of slowly boiling water 2 to 3 minutes per batch
    until they float. Give them a few seconds more before removing with a slotted spoon on to a dish
    towel to drain. Keep warm while cooking the remaining batches. Combine lightly with the sauce
    and serve scattered with basil and black olives.

## 054
# fusilli, chicken, & fennel salad

PREPARATION TIME 10 minutes, plus cooling time COOKING TIME 10 minutes SERVES 4 to 6

5 ounces FUSILLI
3 tablespoons RED PESTO (SEE PAGE 19)
1½ tablespoons LEMON JUICE
3 tablespoons VIRGIN OLIVE OIL
9 ounces COLD SKINLESS ROAST OR
POACHED CHICKEN, SLICED ACROSS THE GRAIN
1 SMALL FENNEL BULB,
FINELY SLICED ACROSS THE BULB

1 PLUMP GARLIC CLOVE, FINELY CHOPPED
5 SCALLIONS, INCLUDING SOME GREEN PARTS, FINELY
CHOPPED
7 ounces CHERRY TOMATOES, QUARTERED
2 tablespoons MIXED FINELY CHOPPED PARSLEY,
OREGANO, AND THYME
PINE NUTS, LIGHTLY TOASTED, AND
FRESHLY GRATED PARMESAN, TO SERVE

1   Cook and drain the pasta according to the
    package directions.
2   Meanwhile, whisk together the pesto, lemon
    juice, and oil. Toss with the hot, drained
    pasta and leave to cool.
3   Combine the chicken, fennel, garlic, scallions,
    tomatoes, and herbs. Toss with the cooled
    pasta and sprinkle some pine nuts and
    Parmesan over.

## 055
# cavatappi with crab & basil

PREPARATION TIME 5 minutes COOKING TIME 10 minutes SERVES 4

8 ounces CAVATAPPI
½ SMALL RED CHILI, SEEDED
  AND FINELY CHOPPED
SMALL BUNCH OF SCALLIONS,
  THINLY SLICED ON THE DIAGONAL
SMALL KNOB OF UNSALTED BUTTER

4 TABLESPOONS MEDIUM-BODIED DRY WHITE WINE
7 ounces FRESH OR FROZEN CRABMEAT, THAWED
¼ cup CRÈME FRAÎCHE
SALT AND FRESHLY GROUND BLACK PEPPER
1 TABLESPOON SHREDDED BASIL, PLUS A LITTLE EXTRA
  FOR GARNISH

1  Cook and drain the pasta according to the package directions, reserving ½ cup of the cooking water.
2  Meanwhile, fry the chili and scallions in the butter 1 minute. Pour in the wine, bring to a boil, lower the heat, and stir in the crabmeat. Warm through slowly, then toss with the pasta, crème fraîche, and basil. Add a little of the reserved water, if necessary, to moisten. Season and serve lightly garnished with basil.

## 056
# linguine with watercress & capers

PREPARATION TIME 5 minutes COOKING TIME 10 minutes SERVES 4

10 ounces LINGUINE*
1 TABLESPOON CAPERS
6 CANNED ANCHOVY FILLETS, DRAINED
1 GARLIC CLOVE

2 ounces WATERCRESS LEAVES AND FINE STEMS
6 TABLESPOONS VIRGIN OLIVE OIL
SALT AND FRESHLY GROUND BLACK PEPPER
FRESHLY GRATED PARMESAN, TO SERVE

1  Cook and drain the pasta according to the package directions, reserving ¼ cup of the cooking water.
2  Meanwhile, put the capers, anchovies, and garlic into a small blender; mix until well blended. Add the watercress and chop finely, then, with the motor running, slowly pour in the olive oil to make a smooth paste. Season and add the reserved cooking water. Toss with the pasta and serve with freshly grated Parmesan.

\*  Spaghetti can also be used.

## 057
# fettuccine with fresh tomatoes & basil

PREPARATION TIME 5 to 10 minutes COOKING TIME 5 minutes SERVES 4

4 LARGE, WELL-FLAVORED TOMATOES, ABOUT 1¼
  POUNDS TOTAL WEIGHT, SEEDED AND CHOPPED
LEAVES FROM A BUNCH OF BASIL, SHREDDED
1 GARLIC CLOVE, FINELY CHOPPED
5 TABLESPOONS EXTRA-VIRGIN OLIVE OIL

SALT AND FRESHLY GROUND BLACK PEPPER
2-EGG QUANTITY FRESH FETTUCCINE (SEE PAGE 10),
  OR 12 ounces DRIED FETTUCCINE
FRESHLY GRATED PARMESAN, TO SERVE

1  Combine the tomatoes, basil, and garlic in a bowl. Pour in the oil in a thin, steady stream, stirring. Season and set aside.
2  Cook (see page 14) and drain the pasta or according to the package directions. Toss with the tomato mixture and serve with plenty of freshly grated Parmesan.

## 058
# spaghetti with garlic, parsley, & chili

PREPARATION TIME 5 minutes COOKING TIME 10 minutes SERVES 4 to 6

14 OUNCES **SPAGHETTI**
4 **GARLIC CLOVES, FINELY CHOPPED**
3 TABLESPOONS **CHOPPED FLAT-LEAF PARSLEY**

**PINCH OF CRUSHED CHILI FLAKES**
6 TABLESPOONS **EXTRA-VIRGIN OLIVE OIL**

1   Cook and drain the pasta according to the package directions, reserving ½ cup of the cooking water.
2   Meanwhile, fry the garlic, parsley, and chilies in the oil until the garlic has turned golden.
    Toss with the pasta, adding enough of the reserved water, if necessary, to moisten.

## 059
# spaghetti with parsley & pine nuts

PREPARATION TIME 5 minutes, COOKING TIME 10 minutes, SERVES 4

10 OUNCES **SPAGHETTI**
**LEAVES FROM 1 BUNCH OF FLAT-LEAF PARSLEY,**
   **CHOPPED**
3 TABLESPOONS **PINE NUTS**

⅓ CUP **VIRGIN OLIVE OIL**
1 TABLESPOON **BALSAMIC VINEGAR**
**SALT AND FRESHLY GROUND BLACK PEPPER**
**FRESHLY GRATED PARMESAN, TO SERVE**

1   Cook and drain the pasta according to the package directions.
2   Meanwhile, put the parsley in a heatproof bowl. Fry the pine nuts in 1 tablespoon of the oil until turning
    golden; add to the bowl. Pour the remaining oil into the pan and heat until it is beginning to give
    off a heat haze. Pour over the parsley, which should sizzle slightly. Toss with the pasta, balsamic
    vinegar, and seasoning. Serve with freshly grated Parmesan.

## 060
# gnocchi, arugula,
# tomato, & black olive salad

PREPARATION TIME 10 minutes COOKING TIME 10 minutes SERVES 4

6 OUNCES **GNOCCHI***
**HANDFUL OF ARUGULA**
**HANDFUL OF BABY SPINACH LEAVES**
4 **SCALLIONS, SLICED ON THE DIAGONAL**
4 OUNCES **CHERRY PLUM TOMATOES, HALVED**
8 **SUN-DRIED TOMATOES IN OIL, DRAINED AND SLICED**
10 **PITTED KALAMATA OLIVES**

**DRESSING**
5 **SUN-DRIED TOMATOES IN OIL**
6 TABLESPOONS **OIL FROM THE TOMATOES**
2 TABLESPOONS **RED WINE VINEGAR**
1 **GARLIC CLOVE, CHOPPED**
**SALT AND FRESHLY GROUND BLACK PEPPER**

1   Cook the pasta according to the package directions.
2   Meanwhile, put all the dressing ingredients into a blender and process to make a thick dressing; season.
3   Drain the pasta and toss immediately with the arugula and dressing so the arugula wilts.
    Toss with the remaining ingredients and serve.

*   Other pasta shapes such as conchiglie can be used.

## 061
# farfalle with arugula, walnuts, & dolcelatte

PREPARATION TIME 5 minutes COOKING TIME 10 minutes SERVES 6

14 OUNCES **FARFALLE**
3 OUNCES **ARUGULA**
7–8 OUNCES **DOLCELATTE OR GORGONZOLA, CRUMBLED**

⅓ CUP **WALNUT HALVES, LIGHTLY TOASTED**
1 TABLESPOON **WALNUT OIL**
**SALT AND FRESHLY GROUND BLACK PEPPER**

1    Cook and drain the pasta according to the package directions, reserving ½ cup of the cooking water.
2    Toss with the arugula, cheese, walnuts, and oil. Season and add enough of the reserved cooking water to moisten, if necessary.

## 062
# tagliatelle with arugula pesto

PREPARATION TIME 5 minutes COOKING TIME 10 minutes SERVES 6

2 OUNCES **ARUGULA**
1 **GARLIC CLOVE, CHOPPED**
1 TABLESPOON **PINE NUTS, LIGHTLY TOASTED**
⅔ CUP **VIRGIN OLIVE OIL**

5 OUNCES **SOFT GOAT CHEESE**
**SALT AND FRESHLY GROUND BLACK PEPPER**
2 TABLESPOONS **FRESHLY GRATED PARMESAN**
1 POUND **TAGLIATELLE**

1    Put the arugula, garlic, and pine nuts into a blender and mix to a puree, slowly pouring in the oil. Add the cheeses and mix again until just forming a smooth sauce; do not overmix. Season.
2    Cook and drain the pasta according to the package directions, reserving ½ cup of the cooking water. Toss with the pesto, adding enough of the cooking water, if necessary, to moisten.

## 063
# orecchiette with tomatoes, arugula, & pine nuts

PREPARATION TIME 5 minutes COOKING TIME 10 minutes SERVES 6

13 OUNCES **ORECCHIETTE**
2 TABLESPOONS **PINE NUTS**
3 TABLESPOONS **VIRGIN OLIVE OIL**
18 OUNCES **RIPE WELL-FLAVORED CHERRY PLUM TOMATOES, HALVED**

**SALT AND FRESHLY GROUND BLACK PEPPER**
3 OUNCES **ARUGULA**
2 OUNCES **PARMESAN, SHAVED**

1    Cook and drain the pasta according to the package directions.
2    Meanwhile, fry the pine nuts in 2 tablespoons of the oil 1 to 2 minutes until they are just turning golden. Add the tomatoes, season, and warm through 1 to 2 minutes, shaking the pan frequently to avoid breaking up the tomatoes.
3    Toss the pasta with the remaining oil, the arugula, and tomato sauce, then most of the Parmesan shavings. Serve with the remaining Parmesan shavings on top.

## 064

# eliche with tomatoes, black olives, & basil

PREPARATION TIME 10 minutes, plus 30 minutes standing COOKING TIME 10 minutes SERVES 4 to 6

1 POUND **WELL-FLAVORED TOMATOES, SEEDED AND CUT INTO ¼-INCH CUBES**
1 **GARLIC CLOVE, FINELY CHOPPED**
12 **PITTED KALAMATA OLIVES, COARSELY CHOPPED**

4 TABLESPOONS **SHREDDED BASIL**
5 TABLESPOONS **EXTRA-VIRGIN OLIVE OIL**
**SALT AND FRESHLY GROUND BLACK PEPPER**
12 OUNCES **ELICHE**

1 Combine the tomatoes, garlic, olives, basil, oil, and seasoning, cover and set aside at least 30 minutes.
2 Cook and drain the pasta according to the package directions.
3 Meanwhile, warm the tomato mixture over low heat, shaking the pan from time to time. Toss with the pasta and serve.

## 065

# spaghetti with goat cheese, arugula, & walnuts

PREPARATION TIME 5 minutes COOKING TIME 10 minutes SERVES 4

9 OUNCES **SPAGHETTI**
⅓ CUP **WALNUT HALVES, VERY LIGHTLY TOASTED**
**VIRGIN OLIVE OIL**
3 OUNCES **FRESH, SOFT GOAT CHEESE, CRUMBLED**

**SMALL HANDFUL OF ARUGULA, TORN IN HALF**
**SALT AND FRESHLY GROUND BLACK PEPPER**
**PARMESAN SHAVINGS (OPTIONAL)**

1 Cook and drain the spaghetti according to the package directions.
2 Meanwhile, grind the walnuts coarsely in a blender using a pulse action; do not chop too finely.
3 Toss the spaghetti with a little olive oil, the nuts, cheese, arugula, and seasoning, using plenty of black pepper. Serve with Parmesan shavings, if liked.

## 066

# spaghetti with broiled bell peppers & garlic

PREPARATION TIME 10 minutes COOKING TIME 15 minutes SERVES 4 to 6

2 **LARGE, FLESHY RED BELL PEPPERS, HALVED LENGTHWISE**
3 **PLUMP GARLIC CLOVES, UNPEELED**
5 TABLESPOONS **EXTRA-VIRGIN OLIVE OIL**
5 TABLESPOONS **PINE NUTS, LIGHTLY TOASTED**

**SALT AND FRESHLY GROUND BLACK PEPPER**
**FEW DROPS OF BALSAMIC VINEGAR**
13 OUNCES **SPAGHETTI**
**FRESHLY GRATED PARMESAN, TO SERVE**

1 Broil the bell peppers and garlic until the peppers are charred and blistered and the garlic is soft.
2 When the peppers are cool enough to handle, peel and coarsely chop, then put into a blender. Squeeze the garlic flesh from the skins into the blender. Add the oil and pine nuts and pulse until just smooth. Season with salt, pepper, and balsamic vinegar.
3 Cook and drain the pasta according to the package directions, reserving ½ cup of the cooking water. Toss thoroughly with the sauce, adding enough reserved water to moisten, if necessary. Serve with Parmesan.

# green and white tagliatelle with pine nuts & parmesan

PREPARATION TIME 5 minutes COOKING TIME 10 minutes SERVES 4 to 6

LEAVES FROM A LARGE BUNCH OF HERBS, SUCH AS
   BASIL, PARSLEY, ROSEMARY, THYME, AND OREGANO
1 PLUMP GARLIC CLOVE, COARSELY CHOPPED
1 POUND FRESH GREEN AND WHITE TAGLIATELLE
   (PAGLIA E FIENO)*

5 TABLESPOONS EXTRA-VIRGIN OLIVE OIL
5 TABLESPOONS PINE NUTS, LIGHTLY TOASTED
¼ CUP FRESHLY GRATED PARMESAN
SALT AND FRESHLY GROUND BLACK PEPPER

1   Finely chop the herbs and garlic in a food processor. Set aside.
2   Cook and drain the pasta according to the package directions.
3   Toss the pasta with the garlic and herb mixture, the oil, pine nuts, Parmesan, and seasoning.

*   Plain fettuccine or tagliatelle can also be used.

49

## 068

# spaghetti with butter & parmesan

PREPARATION TIME 5 minutes COOKING TIME 10 minutes SERVES 4 to 6

12 OUNCES **SPAGHETTI**
6 TABLESPOONS **UNSALTED BUTTER, DICED**

¾ CUP **FRESHLY GRATED PARMESAN**
**SALT AND FRESHLY GROUND BLACK PEPPER**

1   Cook and drain the pasta according to the package directions.
2   Toss with the butter until it melts, then toss with most of the Parmesan. Season, using plenty of black pepper. Serve with the remaining Parmesan.

## 069

# pasta e piselli (pasta & peas)

PREPARATION TIME 5 minutes COOKING TIME 10 minutes SERVES 4

1 **ONION, HALVED AND THINLY SLICED**
**OLIVE OIL**
4 **SLICES OF PROSCIUTTO, CUT INTO STRIPS**
1 QUART **CHICKEN STOCK, HOT**
1 CUP **CONCHIGLIETTE OR OTHER SMALL**
  **DRIED PASTA SHAPES**

1½ CUPS **PEAS, FRESH OR FROZEN**
**HANDFUL BASIL LEAVES, SHREDDED**
**SALT AND FRESHLY GROUND BLACK PEPPER**
4 **SMALL KNOBS OF UNSALTED BUTTER**

1   Fry the onion in a little olive oil until soft but not colored. Stir in the prosciutto and cook 1 minute, then pour in the stock. Bring to a boil, add the pasta, and cook until al dente, adding fresh peas 4 minutes before the end of the cooking, frozen ones 2 minutes.
2   Add the basil and seasoning and serve with a knob of butter on each portion.

## 070

# warm pasta with mixed bell peppers & tomatoes

PREPARATION TIME 10 minutes COOKING TIME 10 minutes SERVES 4

5 TABLESPOONS **VIRGIN OLIVE OIL**
½ **RED BELL PEPPER, THINLY SLICED**
½ **YELLOW BELL PEPPER, THINLY SLICED**
6 OUNCES **YELLOW CHERRY PLUM TOMATOES, HALVED**
6 OUNCES **CHERRY TOMATOES, HALVED**
  **OR QUARTERED**
**LEAVES FROM A HANDFUL OF FRESH HERBS, SUCH**
  **AS THYME, PARSLEY, MARJORAM, AND OREGANO**
12 **PITTED BLACK OLIVES**

3 TABLESPOONS **CAPERS**
2 **NARROW STRIPS OF LEMON ZEST,**
  **CUT INTO FINE SHREDS**
**SALT AND FRESHLY GROUND BLACK PEPPER**
1½ CUPS **PASTA SHAPES, SUCH AS**
  **CONCHIGLIE OR FUSILLI**
**LEMON JUICE, TO TASTE**
4 TABLESPOONS **FRESHLY GRATED PARMESAN**

1   Combine the oil with the peppers, tomatoes, herbs, olives, capers, lemon zest, and seasoning; set aside.
2   Cook and drain the pasta according to the package directions. Toss with the salad and add lemon juice to taste. Scatter the Parmesan over and serve warm.

## 071
# trenette with red pesto & ricotta

PREPARATION TIME 5 minutes COOKING TIME 10 minutes SERVES 4 to 6

14 OUNCES **TRENETTE**                      3 TABLESPOONS **RICOTTA**
1 **QUANTITY RED PESTO (SEE PAGE 19)**

1   Cook and drain the pasta according to the package directions, reserving ½ cup of the cooking water.
2   Meanwhile, combine the red pesto with the ricotta. Toss thoroughly with the pasta, adding enough reserved
    water to moisten, if necessary.


## 072
# spaghetti with tomatoes, olives, & walnuts

PREPARATION TIME 10 minutes COOKING TIME 10 minutes SERVES 4

10 OUNCES **SPAGHETTI**                         16 **PITTED KALAMATA OLIVES, COARSELY CHOPPED**
¾ CUP **WALNUT HALVES**                         **SMALL HANDFUL OF BASIL LEAVES, SHREDDED**
3 **WELL-FLAVORED PLUM TOMATOES,**              3 TABLESPOONS **VIRGIN OLIVE OIL**
  **SEEDED AND CHOPPED**                        **SALT AND FRESHLY GROUND BLACK PEPPER**

1   Cook and drain the spaghetti according to the package directions.
2   Meanwhile, lightly toast the walnuts in a heavy, dry skillet, stirring constantly, until they are just fragrant.
    Break into large pieces.
3   Toss the spaghetti with the walnuts, tomatoes, olives, basil, olive oil, and seasoning.
    Serve warm or at room temperature.


## 073
# spinach & ricotta gnocchi

PREPARATION TIME 10 to 15 minutes, plus 30 minutes chilling COOKING TIME 15 minutes SERVES 4

14 OUNCES **SPINACH**                           SCANT 1 CUP **FRESHLY GRATED PARMESAN,**
½ CUP **ALL-PURPOSE FLOUR,**                      **PLUS EXTRA TO SERVE**
  **PLUS EXTRA FOR ROLLING**                    ⅔ CUP **RICOTTA, STRAINED**
1 **EGG YOLK**                                  **SALT AND FRESHLY GROUND BLACK PEPPER**
                                                5 TABLESPOONS **UNSALTED BUTTER, MELTED**

1   Cook the spinach in a large pan, stirring frequently until wilted and tender. Drain, chop finely, and squeeze
    out the surplus moisture. Combine the spinach, flour, egg yolk, and two-thirds of the Parmesan. When mixed,
    lightly but evenly mix in the ricotta and a little salt but plenty of black pepper; chill 30 minutes.
2   With floured hands, break off heaped teaspoons of the mixture and form into short pieces about
    ½—¾-inch in diameter.
3   Bring a large pan of water to a boil. Add the gnocchi in batches and simmer slowly about 3 minutes until
    they have been on the surface 30 to 60 seconds. Using a slotted spoon, transfer to paper towels to drain,
    then carefully transfer the gnocchi to a shallow baking dish.
4   When all the gnocchi are in the dish, pour over the melted butter and sprinkle with the remaining
    Parmesan. Place under a heated broiler until the cheese melts. Serve with extra Parmesan.

## 074
# riccioli with peas & saffron

PREPARATION TIME 5 minutes, plus 20 minutes soaking COOKING TIME 10 minutes SERVES 4

PINCH OF SAFFRON THREADS, CRUSHED
⅓ CUP HEAVY CREAM
8 OUNCES RICCIOLI OR GNOCCHI

1½ CUPS FRESH OR FROZEN PEAS
SMALL KNOB OF UNSALTED BUTTER
FRESHLY GRATED PARMESAN, TO SERVE

1　Soak the saffron in about 1 tablespoon of the cream about 20 minutes.
2　Cook the riccioli according to the package directions, adding the peas for the last 4 minutes if fresh, 2 minutes if frozen; drain.
3　Meanwhile, slowly heat the remaining cream with the butter and saffron cream until the butter melts, stirring occasionally. Warm through completely but do not let boil. Season and toss with the pasta and peas. Serve sprinkled with freshly grated Parmesan and accompanied by more Parmesan.

## 075
# trenette with pine nuts & herbs

PREPARATION TIME 5 minutes COOKING TIME 10 minutes SERVES 4

2 GARLIC CLOVES, THINLY SLICED
½ FRESH RED CHILI, SEEDED AND FINELY SLICED
5 TABLESPOONS EXTRA-VIRGIN OLIVE OIL
⅓ CUP PINE NUTS
HANDFUL OF FLAT-LEAF PARSLEY, FINELY CHOPPED

10–14 BASIL LEAVES, SHREDDED
SALT AND FRESHLY GROUND BLACK PEPPER
10 OUNCES FRESH TRENETTE
FRESHLY GRATED PARMESAN, TO SERVE

1　Bring a saucepan of water for the pasta to a boil.
2　Meanwhile, fry the garlic and chili in the oil for 1 minute. Add the pine nuts and parsley and fry a minute longer, stirring so the nuts do not burn. Remove from the heat and add the basil and seasoning.
3　Add the pasta to the boiling water, cook and drain, but not too thoroughly. Toss with the pine nuts and herb mixture. Serve with freshly grated Parmesan.

## 076
# cavatappi with tomatoes, avocado, & basil

PREPARATION TIME 10 minutes COOKING TIME 10 minutes SERVES 4

8 OUNCES CAVATAPPI
1 GARLIC CLOVE, FINELY CRUSHED
VIRGIN OLIVE OIL
3 WELL-FLAVORED TOMATOES,
　SEEDED AND CHOPPED

1 AVOCADO, PITTED AND VERY FINELY CHOPPED
4 SCALLIONS, THINLY SLICED ON THE DIAGONAL
LEAVES FROM A SMALL BUNCH OF BASIL, SHREDDED
SALT AND FRESHLY GROUND BLACK PEPPER
FRESHLY GRATED PARMESAN, TO SERVE

1　Cook and drain the pasta according to the package directions.
2　Meanwhile, fry the garlic in a little oil 1 to 2 minutes. Add the tomatoes and heat slowly, just to warm through. Toss with the pasta, avocado, scallions, basil, and seasoning. Serve warm or cold with freshly grated Parmesan.

# 077
# cavatappi with spinach, raisins, & pine nuts

PREPARATION TIME 5 minutes COOKING TIME 10 minutes SERVES 4

2 TABLESPOONS **RAISINS**
8 OUNCES **CAVATAPPI**
18 OUNCES **BABY SPINACH**
**KNOB OF UNSALTED BUTTER**

**SALT AND FRESHLY GROUND BLACK PEPPER**
3–4 TABLESPOONS **PINE NUTS, LIGHTLY TOASTED**
**FRESHLY GRATED PARMESAN, TO SERVE**

1   Soak the raisins in a little hot water 3 to 5 minutes to plump up, then drain.
2   Meanwhile, cook and drain the pasta according to the package directions.
3   While the pasta is cooking, cook the spinach in a covered pan, shaking the pan occasionally, until it wilts. Drain and press out surplus moisture. Gently reheat with the butter, stirring occasionally. Season and toss with the pasta, raisins, and pine nuts. Serve with freshly grated Parmesan.

53

## 078
# spaghetti with garlic & herb mayonnaise

PREPARATION TIME 5 minutes COOKING TIME 10 minutes SERVES 3 to 4

8 ounces SPAGHETTI
1 GARLIC CLOVE
SALT
4–5 tablespoons MAYONNAISE

LEAVES FROM A BUNCH OF MIXED HERBS,
    SUCH AS PARSLEY, THYME, CHIVES, BASIL
FRESHLY GRATED PARMESAN, TO SERVE

1   Cook and drain the pasta according to the pack instructions, reserving ½ cup of the cooking water.
2   Meanwhile, crush the garlic to a paste with a pinch of salt, and then mix into the mayonnaise with
    the herbs. Toss with the pasta and enough of the reserved water so it is moist, and serve with
    freshly grated Parmesan.

## 079
# pennette with tomato & almond sauce

PREPARATION TIME 10 minutes COOKING TIME 10 minutes SERVES 4 to 6

3 WELL-FLAVORED PLUM TOMATOES, SEEDED AND
    CHOPPED
2 tablespoons BLANCHED ALMONDS, LIGHTLY TOASTED
6 tablespoons EXTRA-VIRGIN OLIVE OIL
4 SUN-DRIED TOMATOES, DRAINED AND CHOPPED

12 BASIL LEAVES, SHREDDED
SALT AND FRESHLY GROUND BLACK PEPPER
12 ounces PENNETTE
2 GARLIC CLOVES
4 tablespoons DRIED BREAD CRUMBS

1   Put the tomatoes, almonds, three-quarters of the oil, and the sun-dried tomatoes into small blender;
    mix to a nubbly paste. Transfer to a heatproof bowl and stir in the basil and seasoning.
    Put to warm over a saucepan of gently simmering water.
2   Cook and drain the pasta according to the package directions, reserving ½ cup of the cooking water.
3   Meanwhile, fry the garlic and bread crumbs in the remaining oil in a small frying pan over
    a low heat until the crumbs are golden; take care the garlic does not burn.
4   Toss the pasta with the tomato mixture, adding enough of the reserved water to moisten if necessary.
    Serve with the garlic crumbs scattered over.

## 080
# pasta with roast garlic, thyme, & crumbled goat cheese

PREPARATION TIME 5 minutes COOKING TIME 20 to 25 minutes SERVES 4

1 LARGE HEAD OF PLUMP GARLIC, SEPARATED
    INTO CLOVES
¼ cup EXTRA-VIRGIN OLIVE OIL
LEAVES FROM 8 LARGE THYME SPRIGS

8 ounces SPAGHETTI
7 ounces CRUMBLY GOAT CHEESE
SALT AND FRESHLY GROUND BLACK PEPPER

1   Lightly crush the garlic cloves to loosen the skins, then remove the skins. Heat the cloves gently in the oil
    in a small pan 20 to 25 minutes until soft and golden; do not let them fry and burn because
    they will taste bitter. Add the thyme leaves after 15 minutes cooking.
2   Meanwhile, cook and drain the pasta according to the package directions.
    Toss with the garlic, oil, thyme, goat cheese, and seasoning.

## 081
# tagliatelle with arugula, pine nuts, & thyme

PREPARATION TIME 10 minutes COOKING TIME 10 minutes SERVES 6

2 PLUMP GARLIC CLOVES, CRUSHED
4 TABLESPOONS PINE NUTS
EXTRA-VIRGIN OLIVE OIL
15 CHERRY TOMATOES, HALVED
LEAVES FROM 6 THYME SPRIGS

SALT AND FRESHLY GROUND BLACK PEPPER
18 OUNCES FRESH TAGLIATELLE
LARGE BUNCH OF ARUGULA, TORN IN HALF
¾ CUP FRESHLY GRATED PARMESAN

1   Fry the garlic and pine nuts in a little oil 1½ minutes, stirring frequently, until beginning to color;
    do not let them burn. Add the tomatoes and half the thyme and cook, stirring slowly,
    so the tomatoes are warmed through but not broken up; season.
2   Cook and drain the pasta.
3   Toss the tagliatelle with the arugula, sauce, remaining thyme, 3 tablespoons oil,
    and half the cheese. Serve with the remaining cheese.

## 082
# pappardelle with provolone
# & black olive paste

PREPARATION TIME 5 minutes COOKING TIME 15 minutes SERVES 4

10 OUNCES PAPPARDELLE
VIRGIN OLIVE OIL
5 TABLESPOONS BLACK OLIVE PASTE

FRESHLY GROUND BLACK PEPPER
1½ TABLESPOONS PINE NUTS
4 OUNCES PROVOLONE, FINELY GRATED

1   Cook and drain the pappardelle according to the package directions.
2   Tip the cooked pasta into an ovenproof gratin dish. Mix with a little oil, the olive paste, and black pepper.
    Spread out evenly in the dish. Scatter the pine nuts and provolone over and season with black pepper.
    Place under a heated broiler, not too close to the heat, until the cheese is crisp and golden.

## 083
# fettuccine with pesto, ricotta,
# & sun-blush tomatoes

PREPARATION TIME 5 minutes COOKING TIME 5 minutes SERVES 4

10 SUN-BLUSH TOMATOES WITH THEIR OIL, OR
  PLUMP SUN-DRIED TOMATOES IN OIL,
  CUT INTO STRIPS
2 TABLESPOONS VIRGIN OLIVE OIL
2–3 TABLESPOONS PESTO (SEE PAGE 18)

4 TABLESPOONS RICOTTA
1½ TABLESPOONS FRESHLY GRATED PARMESAN
FRESHLY GROUND BLACK PEPPER
12 OUNCES FRESH FETTUCCINE (SEE PAGE 10),
  OR 10 OUNCES DRIED FETTUCCINE

1   Stir the oil from the tomatoes, the olive oil, and pesto into the ricotta until smooth,
    then add the Parmesan and season with black pepper.
2   Cook and drain the pasta (see page 14 or according to the package directions),
    and toss with the ricotta sauce and tomato strips.

## 084
# garlic-flavored crisp pasta with mozzarella

PREPARATION TIME 5 minutes COOKING TIME 10 minutes SERVES 4 to 6

10 OUNCES TAGLIATELLE
2 GARLIC CLOVES, SLICED
4 TABLESPOONS VIRGIN OLIVE OIL
6 OUNCES BUFFALO MOZZARELLA, GRATED

SMALL HANDFUL OF MIXED CHOPPED HERBS,
    TO SERVE (OPTIONAL)
COARSELY GROUND BLACK PEPPER

1   Cook and drain the pasta according to the package directions.
2   Meanwhile, cook the garlic in the oil in a large pan until it smells extremely aromatic; scoop out
    and discard the garlic.
3   Add the pasta to the oil, toss to coat evenly in oil, and fry over high heat a few minutes until
    the pasta begins to brown and become crisp. Toss with the mozzarella and herbs, if liked,
    so the cheese begins to melt. Season with plenty of coarsely ground black pepper.


## 085
# tonnarelli with sage & olive oil

PREPARATION TIME 5 minutes, COOKING TIME 5 minutes, SERVES 4

LEAVES FROM 1 SMALL BUNCH OF SAGE,
    FINELY SHREDDED
⅓ CUP VIRGIN OLIVE OIL

10 OUNCES FRESH TONNARELLI (SEE PAGE 10)*
SALT AND FRESHLY GROUND BLACK PEPPER
FRESHLY GRATED PARMESAN, TO SERVE

1   Put the sage leaves in a heatproof bowl. Heat the oil in a small pan until it begins to give off
    a heat haze. Pour over the sage, which should sizzle slightly.
2   Cook and drain the pasta. Toss with the sage, oil, and seasoning. Serve with freshly grated Parmesan.

*   Spaghetti can also be used.


## 086
# tagliatelle with lemon sauce

PREPARATION TIME 5 minutes, COOKING TIME 10 minutes, SERVES 4

12 OUNCES TAGLIATELLE
JUICE OF 1½–2 LARGE LEMONS*
¾ CUP HEAVY CREAM
3½ TABLESPOONS UNSALTED BUTTER, DICED

1 CUP FRESHLY GRATED PARMESAN
SALT AND FRESHLY GROUND BLACK PEPPER
SHREDDED BASIL, TO SERVE

1   Cook and drain the pasta according to the package directions.
2   Meanwhile, bring the lemon juice, cream, and butter to a boil and simmer about 5 minutes,
    stirring occasionally, until lightly thick.
3   Toss the pasta with the Parmesan and then with the lemon cream sauce and seasoning.
    Scatter the basil over and serve.

*   The juice from 2 lemons gives a very tangy flavor, so if you prefer a less sharp sauce,
    use the smaller quantity.

# 087
# conchiglie with gorgonzola & walnuts

PREPARATION TIME 10 minutes COOKING TIME 10 minutes SERVES 4

10 ounces CONCHIGLIE
1 teaspoon FINELY CHOPPED SAGE
SMALL KNOB OF UNSALTED BUTTER
3 tablespoons RICOTTA
5 tablespoons MILK

1 cup FINELY CHOPPED GORGONZOLA
SALT AND FRESHLY GROUND BLACK PEPPER
scant ½ cup WALNUT HALVES,
   LIGHTLY TOASTED AND FINELY CHOPPED
FRESHLY GRATED PARMESAN, TO SERVE

1   Cook and drain the pasta according to the package directions.
2   Meanwhile, gently heat the sage and butter in a small, heavy saucepan 1 to 2 minutes and then add the ricotta and milk, stirring until smooth, followed by the Gorgonzola. Continue stirring until smooth once more, but do not let it boil. Season with very little salt but plenty of black pepper.
3   Toss the sauce with the pasta and walnuts. Serve with freshly grated Parmesan.

# 088
# spaghetti with salmon eggs & chives

PREPARATION TIME 5 minutes COOKING TIME 10 minutes SERVES 4

10 ounces SPAGHETTI
2 tablespoons CRÈME FRAÎCHE
3 tablespoons UNSALTED BUTTER, DICED

2½ ounces SALMON EGGS (KETA)
1½ tablespoons FINELY SNIPPED CHIVES
SALT AND FRESHLY GROUND BLACK PEPPER

1   Cook and drain the pasta according to the package directions, reserving ½ cup of the cooking water.
2   Meanwhile, slowly heat the crème fraîche with the butter until warmed through, but do not boil. Toss with the pasta and then the salmon eggs, chives, and seasoning, taking care not to burst the eggs. Add enough of the pasta cooking water to moisten, if necessary.

# 089
# trenette with quick spinach
# & walnut sauce

PREPARATION TIME 10 minutes COOKING TIME 10 minutes SERVES 4 to 6

10 ounces TRENETTE*
1½ ounces BABY SPINACH LEAVES
3 GARLIC CLOVES, CRUSHED
heaped 3 tablespoons WALNUT HALVES,
  LIGHTLY TOASTED

5 tablespoons EXTRA-VIRGIN OLIVE OIL
½ cup PECORINO OR PARMESAN,
  FRESHLY GRATED
SALT AND FRESHLY GROUND BLACK PEPPER

1   Cook and drain the pasta according to the package directions, reserving ½ cup of the cooking water.
2   Meanwhile, put the spinach, garlic, nuts, and oil into a small blender or food processor and pulse until just smooth. Transfer to a bowl and stir in the cheese and seasoning. Toss with the pasta, adding reserved cooking water to moisten, if necessary.

\*   Linguine, tagliatelle, gnocchi rigate, or conchiglie rigate can also be used.

## 090
# gnocchi alla romana

PREPARATION TIME 5 minutes, plus 2 hours standing COOKING TIME 25 to 30 minutes SERVES 4

I CLOVE

I ONION

2 CUPS MILK

I BAY LEAF

½ CUP SEMOLINA

I EXTRA-LARGE EGG YOLK

4 TABLESPOONS FRESHLY GRATED PARMESAN

3½ TABLESPOONS UNSALTED BUTTER, MELTED

1½ TEASPOONS DIJON MUSTARD

SALT AND FRESHLY GROUND BLACK PEPPER

CRISP GREEN SALAD, TO SERVE

1    Stick the clove into the onion. Put into a saucepan with the milk and bay leaf. Bring to a boil slowly,
     cover, and leave to infuse 10 minutes. Strain the milk and return to the rinsed pan; bring to a boil.
     Over medium heat, gradually whisk in the semolina in a thin steady stream. Return to a boil and
     simmer 3 to 5 minutes until thick and smooth, stirring constantly.
2    Off the heat, gradually beat in the egg yolk, then add two-thirds of the cheese, half the butter, and the
     mustard. Season, using plenty of black pepper. Using a damp metal spatula or back of a spoon, spread
     in a layer approximately ½-inch thick on a moist baking sheet. Brush with the remaining butter.
     Cool and then chill about 2 hours until firm.
3    Heat the oven to 450°F.
4    Cut the gnocchi into 2-inch circles with a plain cookie cutter. Arrange in a buttered gratin dish
     or individual dishes and sprinkle with the remaining cheese. Bake in the heated oven for
     15 to 20 minutes until hot and brown. Serve accompanied by a crisp green salad.

## 091
# spinach & potato gnocchi with fontina

PREPARATION TIME 15 minutes COOKING TIME 20 to 25 minutes SERVES 4 to 6

1½ POUNDS **BAKING POTATOES, CHOPPED**
7 OUNCES **SPINACH**
⅓ CUP **ALL-PURPOSE FLOUR**
**SALT AND FRESHLY GROUND BLACK PEPPER**

6 OUNCES **FONTINA, THINLY SLICED**
2 TABLESPOONS **MELTED UNSALTED BUTTER**
**FINELY CHOPPED PARSLEY OR BASIL, TO SERVE**

1   Boil the potatoes about 15 minutes until very tender. Drain thoroughly, then put the pan over low heat to dry the potatoes farther. Mash with a potato masher, then press through a food mill or strainer.
2   Heat the oven to 425°F.
3   Meanwhile, cook the spinach in a dry pan, stirring frequently until tender and wilted; drain and then squeeze dry. Puree the spinach and work into the potatoes with enough flour to bind the mixture, and seasoning.
4   Transfer to a lightly floured surface and knead lightly and briefly; add a little more flour, if necessary, to bind the mixture. Divide the dough into 12 pieces and roll each one into a linked sausage shape about ½-inch thick. Cut across into ¾-inch pieces. Hold a lightly floured fork in one hand with the concave side toward you. Using the thumb of the other hand, roll each piece of dough along the inside curve of the fork to the tips of the tines, then let it drop on to a dish towel.
5   Cook the gnocchi in batches in simmering water 1 to 2 minutes until they float. Remove with a slotted spoon and drain on paper towels.
6   Lay half the gnocchi in a buttered large, shallow baking dish. Cover with half the fontina and pour half the butter over. Repeat the layering. Bake in the heated oven for about 10 minutes until the cheese melts. Scatter the parsley or basil over to serve.

## 092
# olive & triple tomato salad

PREPARATION TIME 10 minutes, plus 1 to 2 hours standing COOKING TIME about 10 minutes SERVES 4

1 CUP **PASTA SHAPES, SUCH AS CONCHIGLIE, RICCIOLI, OR GNOCCHETTI**
3 TABLESPOONS **OIL FROM THE SUN-DRIED TOMATOES**
6 **SUN-DRIED TOMATOES IN OIL, DRAINED AND SLICED**
ABOUT 10 **PITTED KALAMATA OLIVES, SLICED (OPTIONAL)**
8 OUNCES **WELL-FLAVORED CHERRY TOMATOES, HALVED**
**SMALL BUNCH OF SCALLIONS,**

**FINELY SLICED ON THE DIAGONAL**
1 **GARLIC CLOVE, COARSELY CHOPPED**
2 TEASPOONS **SUN-DRIED TOMATO PASTE**
1½–2 TABLESPOONS **RED WINE VINEGAR**
2 TABLESPOONS **EXTRA-VIRGIN OLIVE OIL**
**SALT AND FRESHLY GROUND BLACK PEPPER**
**SMALL HANDFUL OF BASIL LEAVES, SHREDDED**

1   Cook and drain the pasta according to the package directions. Toss with 1 tablespoon oil, 4 sun-dried tomatoes, the olives, cherry tomatoes, and scallions.
2   Meanwhile, put the remaining sun-dried tomato oil and tomatoes, the garlic, tomato paste, and vinegar into a blender. Mix together briefly, then, with the motor running, slowly pour in the olive oil and blend just until the fairly thick dressing has emulsified. Season and toss with the salad.
3   Cover the salad and leave in a cool place, preferably not the refrigerator, 1 to 2 hours. Toss with the shredded basil before serving.

# fish & shellfish

Mussels, clams, shrimp, crab, scallops, squid, tuna, sardines, and anchovies are the most-frequently used fish and seafood in Italian cooking. Many fish and seafood sauces are partnered with spaghetti, linguine, and other long pastas, but other types can work just as well. Fish and seafood can be combined in cream-based sauces, or a tomato sauce might be used for a different approach to what is essentially the same dish. For lighter, fresh-tasting dishes, the fish or shellfish will be cooked simply and quickly before being tossed with the pasta. Tagliatelle with Scallops, Red Peppers, and Basil is a good example. Salmon, both fresh and smoked, is also becoming popular in dishes, such as Green and White Tagliatelle with Smoked Salmon, Spinach, and Lemon.

**CHAPTER**
**2**

## 093
# fusilli with tuna, olives, & garlic

PREPARATION TIME 5 minutes COOKING TIME 20 minutes SERVES 4

3 GARLIC CLOVES, FINELY CHOPPED
VIRGIN OLIVE OIL
3 TABLESPOONS CHOPPED MIXED FLAT-LEAF PARSLEY
  AND OREGANO
1 CAN (15-oz.) CHERRY TOMATOES
13 OUNCES FUSILLI

10 OUNCES CANNED TUNA IN OIL,
  DRAINED AND FLAKED
16 OIL-CURED PITTED BLACK OLIVES, HALVED
SALT AND FRESHLY GROUND BLACK PEPPER
SMALL KNOB OF UNSALTED BUTTER
FINELY GRATED LEMON ZEST AND
  CHOPPED FLAT-LEAF PARSLEY, FOR GARNISH

1  Fry 2 of the garlic cloves in little oil for 1½ minutes. Add the herbs and cook 30 seconds longer before stirring in the tomatoes. Simmer slowly 15 to 20 minutes until thick.
2  Meanwhile, cook and drain the pasta according to the package directions.
3  Add the tuna, olives, and seasoning to the sauce, cover, and heat slowly about 5 minutes, or until the pasta is ready. Carefully stir the butter into the sauce, and then combine with the pasta. Serve sprinkled with the remaining garlic, lemon zest, and parsley.

## 094
# farfalle with bell peppers, anchovies, & capers

PREPARATION TIME 10 minutes COOKING TIME 10 minutes SERVES 4

12 OUNCES FARFALLE
2 GARLIC CLOVES, FINELY CHOPPED
PINCH OF CRUSHED CHILI FLAKES
VIRGIN OLIVE OIL
1 CAN (2-oz.) ANCHOVIES IN OIL,
  DRAINED AND CHOPPED
1 CAN (15-oz.) CHERRY TOMATOES

3 RED AND 2 YELLOW BELL PEPPERS, BROILED,
  PEELED, AND SLICED (SEE PAGE 67)
2 TABLESPOONS CAPERS
SALT AND FRESHLY GROUND BLACK PEPPER
LEMON JUICE, TO TASTE
CHOPPED FLAT-LEAF PARSLEY AND
  FRESHLY GRATED PARMESAN, TO SERVE

1  Cook and drain the pasta according to the package directions.
2  Meanwhile, fry the garlic and chili flakes in a little oil 1 minute. Stir in the anchovies, then stir in the tomatoes. Boil 5 minutes or so until lightly reduced, then add the peppers, capers, plus seasoning and lemon juice to taste. Heat through before tossing with the pasta. Sprinkle with parsley and Parmesan, and serve.

## 095
# salmon ravioli

PREPARATION TIME 45 minutes, plus 30 minutes resting COOKING TIME 8 to 12 minutes SERVES 4

2-EGG QUANTITY PASTA DOUGH (SEE PAGE 10)
8 ounces SALMON FILLET
4 ounces FLOUNDER FILLET
SQUEEZE OF LEMON JUICE
2 tablespoons HEAVY CREAM
2 EGG YOLKS
3 tablespoons FRESHLY GRATED PARMESAN
SALT AND FRESHLY GROUND BLACK PEPPER

TO SERVE
3½ tablespoons UNSALTED BUTTER
JUICE OF 1 SMALL LEMON
CHOPPED FLAT-LEAF PARSLEY,
   FOR SPRINKLING

1   While the pasta dough is resting for 30 minutes, lightly poach the salmon
    and flounder together in very slowly simmering water with the lemon juice
    2 to 3 minutes for the flounder, 3 to 4 minutes for the salmon, depending on
    thickness, until the flesh just flakes (do not overcook).
2   Remove the flounder with a slotted spoon when it is done, discard any skin and
    bones, and put into a blender. Repeat with the salmon. Add the cream and use
    the pulse button to mix to a nubbly puree. Transfer to a bowl and mix in the
    egg yolks, cheese, and seasoning, using a fork; chill until required.
3   Make the ravioli (see page 11) with the pasta dough and filling.
4   Cook the ravioli in gently boiling water, in batches, about 4 minutes per
    batch; drain well.
5   Meanwhile, melt the butter with the lemon juice in a small pan over low heat.
    Serve poured over with the ravioli and sprinkled with parsley and black pepper.

## 096
# linguine with white clam sauce

PREPARATION TIME 5 minutes COOKING TIME 10 minutes SERVES 4

10 OUNCES LINGUINE
2 GARLIC CLOVES, FINELY CHOPPED
PINCH OF CHILI FLAKES
VIRGIN OLIVE OIL

2 POUNDS CLAMS
½ CUP MEDIUM-BODIED DRY WHITE WINE
3 TABLESPOONS CHOPPED FLAT-LEAF PARSLEY

1   Cook the linguine until it is almost done (it will finish cooking in the sauce); drain.
2   Meanwhile, soften the garlic and chili in a little oil in a large saucepan. Add the clams, pour in the wine, cover the pan, and cook about 2 minutes until the clams open; discard any that remain closed.
3   Add the pasta and half the parsley, put on the lidm and toss the pan over the heat for a minute or so, shaking the pan frequently, until the pasta is tender and coated in the sauce. Serve with the remaining parsley sprinkled over.

## 097
# spaghetti alla puttanesca

PREPARATION TIME 5 minutes COOKING TIME 15 minutes SERVES 4

2 GARLIC CLOVES, CHOPPED
VIRGIN OLIVE OIL
6 ANCHOVY FILLETS, CHOPPED
2 CANS (14-oz.) CHOPPED PLUM TOMATOES
SALT AND FRESHLY GROUND BLACK PEPPER

1 POUND SPAGHETTI
1 TABLESPOON OREGANO
1 TABLESPOON CAPERS, RINSED
14 OIL-CURED PITTED BLACK OLIVES, SLICED

1   Fry the garlic in a little oil 1 minute, then stir in the anchovy fillets until they dissolve. Add the tomatoes, bring to a boil, and then simmer about 15 minutes, stirring occasionally, until the sauce has thickened. Season, using plenty of black pepper.
2   Meanwhile, cook and drain the spaghetti according to the package directions.
3   Add the oregano, capers, and olives to the sauce and toss with the pasta.

## 098
# farfalle with hot-smoked salmon & red bell peppers

PREPARATION TIME 5 minutes COOKING TIME 20 minutes SERVES 4

14 OUNCES FARFALLE
GENEROUS ½ CUP PINE NUTS
4 TABLESPOONS EXTRA-VIRGIN OLIVE OIL
3 LARGE, FLESHY RED BELL PEPPERS, BROILED, PEELED, AND SLICED (SEE PAGE 67)

8 OUNCES HOT-SMOKED SALMON, FLAKED
3 TABLESPOONS CHOPPED FRESH MIXED PARSLEY, THYME, BASIL, AND DILL
FRESHLY GROUND BLACK PEPPER

1   Cook and drain the pasta according to the package directions.
2   Meanwhile, heat the pine nuts in the oil in a large skillet until light brown. Add the pepper strips and their juices and heat 1 minute, then add the salmon. After a minute longer, remove from the heat and stir in the herbs and black pepper. Toss lightly with the pasta.

## 099

# quick linguine with seafood

PREPARATION TIME 5 minutes COOKING TIME 10 minutes SERVES 4

14 OUNCES LINGUINE
2 PLUMP GARLIC CLOVES, FINELY CHOPPED
EXTRA-VIRGIN OLIVE OIL
4 TABLESPOONS DRY MARSALA
1¼ POUNDS PREPARED SEAFOOD,
  PREFERABLY FRESH, THAWED IF FROZEN

LEAVES FROM A SMALL BUNCH
  OF FLAT-LEAF PARSLEY, CHOPPED
4 TABLESPOONS LOW-FAT CRÈME FRAÎCHE
JUICE OF 1 LEMON
SALT AND FRESHLY GROUND BLACK PEPPER

1   Cook and drain the pasta according to the package directions.
2   Meanwhile, fry the garlic in a little oil 30 seconds. Add the marsala, seafood, and half the parsley
    and cook, stirring, until the marsala reduces by half. Stir in the crème fraîche, and bubble briefly.
    Toss with the pasta, lemon juice, and seasoning. Serve sprinkled with the remaining parsley.

## 100

# spaghetti with cherry tomatoes, anchovies, & basil

PREPARATION TIME 10 minutes COOKING TIME 10 minutes SERVES 4

14 OUNCES SPAGHETTI
2 GARLIC CLOVES, FINELY CHOPPED
VIRGIN OLIVE OIL
8 ANCHOVY FILLETS, CHOPPED

1¼ POUNDS CHERRY TOMATOES, HALVED
JUICE FROM 1 LEMON
FRESHLY GROUND BLACK PEPPER
LEAVES FROM A BUNCH OF BASIL, SHREDDED

1   Cook and drain the spaghetti according to the package directions.
2   Meanwhile, fry the garlic in a little oil 1 minute. Stir in the anchovy fillets and 3 tablespoons water until
    the fillets begin to dissolve, then add the tomatoes, lemon juice, and black pepper. Warm through,
    shaking the pan frequently, then toss with the pasta and basil.

## 101

# strozzapreti with fresh tuna, chili, tomatoes, & olives

PREPARATION TIME 10 minutes COOKING TIME 10 minutes SERVES 4

14 OUNCES STROZZAPRETI
1 POUND FRESH TUNA, CUT INTO 1-INCH CUBES
1 GARLIC CLOVE, THINLY SLICED
1 FRESH RED CHILI, SEEDED AND FINELY CHOPPED
3 TABLESPOONS VIRGIN OLIVE OIL

12 CHERRY TOMATOES, QUARTERED OR HALVED
12–14 PITTED KALAMATA OLIVES, SLICED
LEAVES FROM A BUNCH OF FLAT-LEAF PARSLEY,
  FINELY CHOPPED
EXTRA-VIRGIN OLIVE OIL, TO SERVE

1   Cook and drain the pasta according to the package directions.
2   Meanwhile, slowly cook the tuna, garlic, and chili in a thick-bottomed pan in the virgin olive oil
    2 minutes; do not let the garlic brown. Add the tomatoes and olives, cover, and simmer 3 minutes.
3   Toss the tuna sauce with the pasta and most of the parsley. Serve with the remaining parsley sprinkled
    over and a trickle of extra-virgin olive oil.

# 102
# orecchiette with cauliflower, anchovies, & tomatoes

PREPARATION TIME 10 minutes, plus 20 minutes soaking COOKING TIME 25 minutes SERVES 4

I POUND CAULIFLOWER, DIVIDED INTO FLOWERETS

I ONION, THINLY SLICED

3 TABLESPOONS VIRGIN OLIVE OIL

2 CUPS CANNED PLUM TOMATOES, CHOPPED

14 OUNCES ORECCHIETTE

4 ANCHOVY FILLETS

PINCH OF CRUSHED DRIED CHILIES

12 PITTED BLACK OLIVES, SLICED

I TABLESPOON CHOPPED FLAT-LEAF PARSLEY

FRESHLY GROUND BLACK PEPPER

2 TABLESPOONS FRESHLY GRATED PECORINO

1   Cook the cauliflower 3 minutes in a saucepan of water that is large enough for the pasta; remove with a slotted spoon.
2   Meanwhile, fry the onion in 2 tablespoons oil until soft but not colored. Add the tomatoes and simmer about 3 minutes. Add the cauliflower, cover, and simmer slowly about 10 minutes until tender.
3   Meanwhile, cook and drain the pasta according to the package directions.
4   Fry the anchovies and chili in the remaining oil in a small pan about 2 minutes. Add to the tomato sauce with the olives and parsley. Toss with the pasta and black pepper, then serve with the pecorino sprinkled over.

# 103
# spaghetti with tuna, pancetta, & tomatoes

PREPARATION TIME 10 minutes, plus 20 minutes soaking COOKING TIME 25 minutes SERVES 4

½ OUNCE DRIED MUSHROOMS

2 GARLIC CLOVES, FINELY CHOPPED

2 OUNCES PANCETTA, CUT ACROSS INTO STRIPS

OLIVE OIL

2 CUPS SEEDED AND CHOPPED WELL-FLAVORED TOMATOES

I CAN (7-OZ.) TUNA, DRAINED

SALT AND FRESHLY GROUND BLACK PEPPER

14 OUNCES SPAGHETTI

FINELY CHOPPED FLAT-LEAF PARSLEY, TO SERVE

1   Place the dried mushrooms in a bowl and just cover with boiling water; soak 20 minutes. Drain, reserving the water. Chop the mushrooms finely.
2   Fry the garlic and pancetta in a little oil until the pancetta is flecked with brown, but do not let it burn. Add the dried mushrooms and the tomatoes and simmer about 15 minutes until thick. Add the reserved mushroom liquid and simmer 5 minutes longer. Gently stir in the tuna so it is not broken up too much, season, and heat through.
3   Meanwhile, cook and drain the pasta according to the package directions. Toss with the tuna sauce. Sprinkle the parsley over and serve.

## 104
# fusilli lunghi with fresh tuna
# & roast bell peppers

PREPARATION TIME 10 minutes COOKING TIME 20 minutes SERVES 4

2–3 FLESHY RED BELL PEPPERS, DEPENDING ON SIZE

10 OUNCES FUSILLI LUNGHI

1 RED ONION, THINLY SLICED

EXTRA-VIRGIN OLIVE OIL

1 PLUMP GARLIC CLOVE, FINELY CHOPPED

12 OUNCES FRESH TUNA,
   CUT INTO ½-INCH CHUNKS

6 TABLESPOONS FULL-BODIED DRY WHITE WINE

2 TABLESPOONS CAPERS

1½ TABLESPOONS CHOPPED FRESH
   FLAT-LEAF PARSLEY

SALT AND FRESHLY GROUND BLACK PEPPER

1   Broil the peppers until they are evenly charred and blistered. When cool enough to handle and working over a bowl to catch any juices, peel off the skins. Thinly slice the flesh.
2   Cook and drain the pasta according to the package directions, reserving ½ cup of the cooking water.
3   Meanwhile, fry the onion in a little oil in a large skillet until soft and golden. Add the garlic and fry 1 minute. Stir in the tuna and fry 1 minute until it changes color; do not overcook. Add the pepper strips and wine. Bubble until reduced by about half, then add the capers and parsley. Season. Toss with the pasta, adding a little of the reserved water, if necessary.

# bucatini with sardines, lemon, & fennel

PREPARATION TIME 10 minutes COOKING TIME 10 minutes SERVES 4

14 ounces **BUCATINI**

**1 FENNEL BULB, FINELY CHOPPED, FEATHERY**
**TOPS RESERVED**

**2 GARLIC CLOVES, FINELY CHOPPED**

**2** tablespoons **VIRGIN OLIVE OIL**

**8 FRESH SARDINE FILLETS**

**LEAVES FROM A SMALL BUNCH OF FLAT-LEAF**
**PARSLEY, CHOPPED**

**JUICE OF 1 JUICY LEMON**

**SALT AND FRESHLY GROUND BLACK PEPPER**

1   Cook and drain the pasta following the package directions, reserving about ½ cup of the cooking water.

2   Meanwhile, fry the fennel and garlic in the oil, stirring, about 1 minute. Add the sardine fillets, skin side down, and cook 1 minute. Turn them over and cook another minute until cooked through.

3   Add the parsley, reserved feathery fennel fronds, lemon juice, and seasoning, using plenty of black pepper. Toss with the pasta, adding enough of the reserved cooking water to moisten, if necessary.

# penne with tuna in tomato & olive sauce

PREPARATION TIME 5 minutes COOKING TIME 10 minutes SERVES 4

1 SMALL ONION, FINELY CHOPPED

4 TABLESPOONS VIRGIN OLIVE OIL

2 GARLIC CLOVES, FINELY CHOPPED

1 CAN (15-oz.) CRUSHED PLUM TOMATOES

1 CAN (7-oz.) TUNA, DRAINED AND FLAKED

12 PITTED BLACK OLIVES, QUARTERED

1 TABLESPOON SALTED CAPERS, RINSED AND DRAINED

SALT AND FRESHLY GROUND BLACK PEPPER

14 ounces PENNE

2 TABLESPOONS FINELY CHOPPED
   FLAT-LEAF PARSLEY

1 Fry the onion in the oil until soft, adding the garlic for the last minute. Pour in the tomatoes and boil until just thick. Add the tuna, olives, and capers and heat through gently; season.

2 Meanwhile, cook and drain the pasta according to the package directions. Toss with the tuna and tomato sauce and parsley.

# warm fusilli & seafood salad

PREPARATION TIME 10 minutes COOKING TIME 10 minutes SERVES 4

6 OUNCES FUSILLI

3 TABLESPOONS VIRGIN OLIVE OIL

1 TABLESPOON RICE WINE VINEGAR

GRATED ZEST AND JUICE OF 1 LEMON

1 GARLIC CLOVE, FINELY CHOPPED (OPTIONAL)

SALT AND FRESHLY GROUND BLACK PEPPER

12 OUNCES MIXED COOKED SEAFOOD, SUCH AS
   SHELLED SHRIMP, SHELLED JUMBO SHRIMP,
   SCALLOPS (QUARTERED, IF LARGE), AND MUSSELS

1 LARGE AVOCADO, SLICED

8 OUNCES MIXED RED AND YELLOW CHERRY
   TOMATOES, HALVED

BUNCH OF SCALLIONS, FINELY CHOPPED

SCANT ⅓ CUP SLICED PITTED GREEN OLIVES

LEAVES FROM A SMALL BUNCH OF MIXED
   HERBS, SUCH AS PARSLEY, BASIL, AND
   MARJORAM, CHOPPED

1 Cook and drain the fusilli according to the package directions.

2 Meanwhile, whisk the oil with the vinegar, lemon juice and zest, the garlic, and seasoning. Toss with the warm fusilli and the remaining ingredients. Serve warm.

# spaghetti with shrimp, tomatoes, & capers

PREPARATION TIME 10 minutes COOKING TIME 10 minutes SERVES 4

1 ONION, CHOPPED

VIRGIN OLIVE OIL

2 GARLIC CLOVES, CRUSHED

1¾ CUPS CHOPPED RIPE, WELL-FLAVORED
   PLUM TOMATOES

1 TEASPOON OREGANO

12 OUNCES MEDIUM RAW SHRIMP, SHELLED

1½ TABLESPOONS SALTED CAPERS,
   RINSED AND DRIED

SALT AND FRESHLY GROUND BLACK PEPPER

14 OUNCES SPAGHETTI

1 Fry the onion in a little oil in a large skillet until soft and beginning to color. Add the garlic and fry 1 to 2 minutes. Add the tomatoes and oregano and cook rapidly until the juice evaporates but the tomatoes should not disintegrate.

2 Add the shrimp to the sauce and cook over reduced heat about 2 minutes, just until they turn pink. Remove the pan from the heat and add the capers and seasoning.

3 Meanwhile, cook and drain the pasta according to the pack instructions. Toss with the sauce and serve.

## 109
# spaghetti with slivered sardines & tomatoes

PREPARATION TIME 10 minutes COOKING TIME 15 minutes SERVES 4 to 5

3 GARLIC CLOVES, FINELY CHOPPED
PINCH OF CRUSHED CHILI FLAKES
2–3 FRESH SAGE LEAVES, FINELY SHREDDED
2 TABLESPOONS VIRGIN OLIVE OIL
1¾ CUPS SEEDED AND CHOPPED WELL-FLAVORED TOMATOES
1 CAN (2-oz.) ANCHOVY FILLETS IN OIL, DRAINED

HEAPED ¾ CUP CHOPPED PITTED OIL-CURED BLACK OLIVES
2 TABLESPOONS CAPERS, RINSED
2–3 TEASPOONS CHOPPED OREGANO
SALT AND FRESHLY GROUND BLACK PEPPER
14 OUNCES SPAGHETTI
8–12 FRESH SARDINES, DEPENDING ON SIZE
3 TABLESPOONS CHOPPED FLAT-LEAF PARSLEY

1   Cook the garlic, chili, and sage in the oil 1½ minutes. Add the tomatoes, anchovies, olives, capers, and oregano and simmer 10 minutes longer; season.
2   Meanwhile, cook and drain the pasta according to the package directions.
3   While the pasta is cooking, season the sardines and broil about 2 minutes per side until just cooked through. Cool slightly, then remove the flesh from the bones in large pieces.
4   Toss the pasta with the sauce and parsley. Add the sardine flakes and toss gently.

## 110
# black olive pasta with broccoli, capers, & anchovies

PREPARATION TIME 5 minutes COOKING TIME 10 minutes SERVES 4

1 POUND BROCCOLI FLOWERETS
1 GARLIC CLOVE, CHOPPED
2 ANCHOVY FILLETS, CHOPPED
EXTRA-VIRGIN OLIVE OIL
2 TABLESPOONS SMALL CAPERS

FRESHLY GROUND BLACK PEPPER
18 OUNCES BLACK OLIVE TAGLIATELLE (SEE PAGE 10)
FRESHLY GRATED PARMESAN, TO SERVE

1   Bring enough water for cooking the pasta to a boil. Add the broccoli and cook 2 to 3 minutes; remove with a slotted spoon and drain. Cover the pan and keep warm.
2   Cook the garlic and anchovies in a little oil, stirring, 2 minutes. Add the broccoli and capers and cook over low heat, stirring occasionally, 4 to 5 minutes; season with black pepper.
3   Return the water to a boil and cook the pasta. Drain and toss with the broccoli sauce. Serve with freshly grated Parmesan.

# 111
# taglioni with mussels, wilted greens, & lardons

PREPARATION TIME 10 minutes COOKING TIME 10 minutes SERVES 4

7 OUNCES PANCETTA, CUT ACROSS INTO
 LARDONS (STRIPS)
2 GARLIC CLOVES, FINELY CHOPPED
OLIVE OIL
SCANT ½ CUP DRY WHITE WINE
LEAVES FROM A SMALL HANDFUL OF FLAT-LEAF
 PARSLEY, CHOPPED

3 SCALLIONS, CHOPPED
9 OUNCES COOKED MUSSELS OUT OF THE SHELL
5 OUNCES BABY SPINACH LEAVES
SALT AND FRESHLY GROUND BLACK PEPPER
1¼ POUNDS FRESH TAGLIONI

1  Bring a saucepan of water to a boil for cooking the taglioni.
2  Meanwhile, fry the lardons and garlic in a little oil in a saucepan until light brown; remove with
   a slotted spoon and drain on paper towels. Add the wine, parsley, and scallions to the pan and boil
   3 to 4 minutes. Add the pancetta, mussels, and spinach and heat until the spinach wilts. Season.
3  Immediately after adding the spinach to the pan, cook and drain the taglioni.
   Toss with the mussel mixture and serve.

# 112
# linguine with roast snapper & cherry tomatoes

PREPARATION TIME 5 minutes COOKING TIME 20 to 25 minutes SERVES 4

1 POUND CHERRY TOMATOES, HALVED
VIRGIN OLIVE OIL
SALT AND FRESHLY GROUND BLACK PEPPER
11 OUNCES LINGUINE

2 SNAPPERS, ABOUT 18 OUNCES EACH, FILLETED
1 TABLESPOON FRESH OREGANO
PINCH OF CRUSHED CHILI FLAKES
16 OIL-CURED PITTED BLACK OLIVES, HALVED

1  Heat the oven to 400°F.
2  Toss the tomatoes with a little oil and seasoning. Spread in a single layer on a baking sheet and roast
   in the heated oven 20 to 25 minutes.
3  Meanwhile, cook and drain the linguine according to the package directions.
4  At the same time, lay the snapper fillets in a single layer in another dish, sprinkle with the oregano,
   chili, and seasoning, and then trickle a little oil over. Put in the oven 5 minutes until the flesh flakes.
5  Toss the pasta with the tomatoes and any cooking juices, the olives and 1 tablespoon oil.
   Break the snapper into flakes over the top and toss gently.

## 113
# warm fresh tuna salad niçoise

PREPARATION TIME 10 minutes COOKING TIME 10 minutes SERVES 4

8 OUNCES FARFALLE

7 OUNCES THIN GREEN BEANS

VIRGIN OLIVE OIL

12 OUNCES FRESH TUNA STEAKS

SALT AND FRESHLY GROUND BLACK PEPPER

1 TABLESPOON BALSAMIC VINEGAR

1 TABLESPOON LEMON JUICE

1 GARLIC CLOVE, FINELY CHOPPED

2 TABLESPOONS CHOPPED MIXED HERBS, SUCH AS
    THYME, MARJORAM, PARSLEY, BASIL, AND FENNEL

2½ TABLESPOONS CAPERS

7 ANCHOVY FILLETS, CHOPPED

5 OUNCES CHERRY PLUM TOMATOES, HALVED

⅓ CUP PITTED BLACK OLIVES

1   Cook the pasta according to the package directions, adding the beans for the last 3 minutes.
    Drain, rinse in cold water, and drain thoroughly.
2   Meanwhile, brush the tuna with a little olive oil, season, and broil 3 to 4 minutes per side until
    still pink in the middle. Cut into bite-size pieces.
3   While the fish is cooking, whisk together the balsamic vinegar, 6 tablespoons oil, the lemon juice,
    garlic, herbs, capers, and black pepper until emulsified. Toss with the pasta and beans,
    the anchovies, tomatoes, olives, and tuna.

## 114
# spaghetti with cod & pangritata

PREPARATION TIME 10 minutes COOKING TIME 15 to 20 minutes SERVES 4

2 CUPS FRESH CIABATTA CRUMBS

1 CAN (2-oz.) ANCHOVY FILLETS, FINELY CHOPPED,
    OIL RESERVED

½ CUP VIRGIN OLIVE OIL

1 TEASPOON FENNEL SEEDS, CRUSHED

2 GARLIC CLOVES, FINELY CHOPPED

⅓ CUP PINE NUTS, CHOPPED

4 TABLESPOONS CHOPPED FLAT-LEAF PARSLEY

12 OUNCES SPAGHETTI

18 OUNCES COD FILLET

⅔ CUP MEDIUM-BODIED DRY WHITE WINE

1 BAY LEAF, TORN ACROSS

SALT AND FRESHLY GROUND BLACK PEPPER

LEMON WEDGES, TO SERVE

1   Heat the oven to 400°F.
2   Mix the bread crumbs with the anchovies and their oil, the olive oil, fennel seeds, garlic, and pine nuts
    in a roasting pan. Bake in the heated oven 15 to 20 minutes, stirring occasionally, until evenly brown and
    crisp; take care the mixture doesn't burn. Remove from the oven and add the parsley.
3   Meanwhile, cook and drain the pasta according to the package directions.
4   Also, poach the fish in the wine, ⅔ cup water, the bay leaf, and seasoning, about 5 minutes, depending
    on thickness, until the flesh just flakes; lift the fish from the liquid with a fish slice. Discard the bay leaf.
    Boil the liquid hard until reduced to about 4 tablespoons.
5   Meanwhile, discard the fish skin and break the fish into chunks. Toss with the pasta and reduced wine.
    Serve with the crumbs scattered over and accompanied by lemon wedges.

## 115
# green & white tagliatelle with smoked salmon, spinach, & lemon

PREPARATION TIME 5 minutes COOKING TIME 10 minutes SERVES 4

14 OUNCES **DRIED GREEN AND WHITE TAGLIATELLE**
14 OUNCES **BABY SPINACH LEAVES**
**SMALL KNOB OF UNSALTED BUTTER**
**GRATED ZEST AND JUICE OF 1 LEMON**
1¾ CUP **CRÈME FRAÎCHE OR SOUR CREAM**

**SALT AND FRESHLY GROUND BLACK PEPPER**
6 OUNCES **SMOKED SALMON TRIMMINGS,**
    **CUT INTO STRIPS**
**SNIPPED CHIVES, TO GARNISH**

1   Cook the pasta according to the package directions, pushing the spinach into the water 30 seconds before the end of the cooking time; drain.
2   Meanwhile, melt the butter in a small saucepan. Whisk in the lemon zest and juice, the crème fraîche, and seasoning and warm through. Toss with the pasta and smoked salmon. Serve garnished with snipped chives.

FISH & SHELLFISH

73

## 116
# pipe with tuna, lemon, & basil

PREPARATION TIME 5 minutes COOKING TIME 10 minutes SERVES 4

14 OUNCES PIPE*
9 OUNCES WELL-FLAVORED CHERRY TOMATOES
4 TABLESPOONS EXTRA-VIRGIN OLIVE OIL
2 TABLESPOONS LEMON JUICE
1 TABLESPOON CAPERS PACKED IN SALT,
  RINSED AND DRAINED

2 CANS (7-oz.) TUNA IN OIL, DRAINED
SALT AND FRESHLY GROUND BLACK PEPPER
½ TEASPOON LEMON ZEST
HANDFUL OF BASIL LEAVES, SHREDDED

1  Cook and drain the pasta according to the package directions.
2  Meanwhile, warm the tomatoes in the oil in a large skillet over a low heat. Just before the pasta is ready, gently stir in the lemon juice, capers, and tuna, making sure the tuna is not broken up too much; season and heat through.
3  Toss the pasta with the tomato and tuna mixture, the lemon zest, and basil.

*  Conchiglie, gnocchi, or chifferi can also be used.

## 117
# crab & dill cannelloni

PREPARATION TIME 15 minutes*, plus 1 to 8 hours standing COOKING TIME 35 minutes* SERVES 4

8 OUNCES MIXED WHITE AND BROWN CRABMEAT
1 CUP RICOTTA
ABOUT 1½ TABLESPOONS LEMON JUICE
ABOUT 1 TABLESPOON FINELY GRATED LEMON ZEST
1–2 TABLESPOONS CHOPPED DILL,
  ACCORDING TO THE FLAVOR OF THE DILL

2 LARGE SHALLOTS
SALT AND FRESHLY GROUND BLACK PEPPER
8 CANNELLONI TUBES, ABOUT 3 INCHES LONG
1 QUANTITY FRESH TOMATO SAUCE (SEE PAGE 18),
  WARM

1  Combine the crabmeat with the ricotta, lemon juice and zest, and dill to taste (the strength of flavor can vary quite considerably, especially in bought packages). Holding it over the crab mixture, squeeze the shallots through a garlic press to extract the juice. Stir in, then season. Cover and leave in a cool place 1 to 8 hours.
2  Heat the oven to 375°F.
3  Cook, drain, and rinse the cannelloni tubes, even if using the no-precook type (see page 15). Spread on a dish towel to dry.
4  Spoon or pipe the crab filling into the tubes, then place in an oiled shallow baking dish. Pour the sauce over and bake about 25 minutes until heated through.

*  Assumes the tomato sauce is already made.

## 118
# bucatini with melting onion & anchovy sauce

PREPARATION TIME 10 minutes COOKING TIME 25 to 35 minutes SERVES 4

1¼ POUNDS **LARGE ONIONS, VERY THINLY SLICED ON A MANDOLIN OR IN A FOOD PROCESSOR**
**VIRGIN OLIVE OIL**
**SALT AND FRESHLY GROUND BLACK PEPPER**
3 TABLESPOONS **DRY MARSALA**

7 OUNCES **BUCATINI**
2 TABLESPOONS **CAPERS**
6–8 **ANCHOVY FILLETS IN OIL**
2 TABLESPOONS **CHOPPED FLAT-LEAF PARSLEY, PLUS EXTRA TO SERVE**

1   Cook the onions in a little oil in a heavy-based pan about 5 minutes; season and add the marsala. Cover the onions closely with a disk of waxed paper. Put a lid on the pan and cook very slowly 20 to 30 minutes until the onions are almost melting; if they become too dry, add a few drops of water. Uncover and stir 1 to 2 minutes.
2   Meanwhile, cook and drain the pasta according to the package directions.
3   Add the capers to the sauce and stir in the anchovies until dissolved. Season and add the parsley. Toss with the pasta. Serve with extra parsley scattered over.

## 119
# salmon shells with pesto & tomato sauce

PREPARATION TIME 5 minutes, plus standing time COOKING TIME 30 minutes SERVES 4

1 CAN (7-OZ.) **SALMON, DRAINED**
½ CUP **RICOTTA**
2–3 TEASPOONS **LEMON ZEST**
**SALT AND FRESHLY GROUND BLACK PEPPER**
4 OUNCES **LARGE CONCHIGLIE, ABOUT 3 INCHES LONG**
2 TABLESPOONS **PESTO (SEE PAGE 18)**

2 **WELL-FLAVORED TOMATOES, SEEDED AND CHOPPED**

**WHITE SAUCE**
1¼ TABLESPOONS **UNSALTED BUTTER**
2 TABLESPOONS **ALL-PURPOSE FLOUR**
1¼ CUPS **MILK**

1   Combine the salmon with the ricotta, lemon zest, and seasoning. Cover and leave overnight if time allows, to let the flavor develop.
2   Heat the oven to 375°F.
3   Cook and drain the conchiglie according to the package directions and leave upside down to drain.
4   Divide the salmon mixture between the shells and place, open side up, in a shallow baking dish. Cover tightly and place in the heated oven 15 to 20 minutes to warm through.
5   While the shells are in the oven, make a simple white sauce (see page 17) with the butter, flour, and milk. Stir in the pesto and tomatoes. Pour over the shells and serve.

## 120
# seafood cannelloni

PREPARATION TIME 10 minutes COOKING TIME 35 minutes SERVES 4

8 ounces FRESH LASAGNE SHEETS (SEE PAGE 10)
2 SHALLOTS, FINELY CHOPPED
OLIVE OIL
2 GARLIC CLOVES, FINELY CHOPPED
1 TABLESPOON CHOPPED MIXED OREGANO, PARSLEY,
  AND TARRAGON
18 ounces MIXED MONKFISH AND SALMON, CUT INTO
  SMALL PIECES, AND LARGE SHRIMP, CHOPPED

2 WELL-FLAVORED TOMATOES, PEELED,
  SEEDED, AND VERY FINELY CHOPPED
4 TABLESPOONS FRESH BREAD CRUMBS
SALT AND FRESHLY GROUND BLACK PEPPER
1 POUND SPINACH
1 TABLESPOON UNSALTED BUTTER
1 QUANTITY FRESH TOMATO SAUCE (SEE PAGE 18)
  OR WINTER TOMATO SAUCE (SEE PAGE 19)
4 TABLESPOONS FRESHLY GRATED PARMESAN

1   Heat the oven to 375°F.
2   Cook and drain the lasagne sheets (see page 15) and spread on a dish towel to dry.
3   Meanwhile, fry the shallots in a little oil until soft. Add the garlic and fry 1 minute. Stir in the
    herbs, seafood, tomatoes, and three-quarters of the bread crumbs; season and remove from the heat.
4   Cook the spinach in a covered pan, stirring occasionally, until wilted and tender. Drain, chop coarsely,
    and squeeze out as much water as possible. Heat in a small pan with the butter and seasoning
    2 to 3 minutes, stirring frequently.
5   Divide the seafood mixture and the spinach between the lasagne sheets. Roll them up and place seam
    side down in a greased shallow baking dish that they just fit in. Pour the tomato sauce over, sprinkle
    over the remaining bread crumbs and the Parmesan.
6   Bake in the heated oven about 30 minutes until the top is golden.

## 121
# smoked fish raviolini

PREPARATION TIME 45 minutes, plus resting time COOKING TIME 20 minutes SERVES 4

2-EGG QUANTITY PASTA DOUGH (SEE PAGE 10)
1¼ POUNDS SMOKED COD OR HADDOCK FILLET
OLIVE OIL, FOR BRUSHING
2 SHALLOTS, FINELY CHOPPED
SMALL KNOB OF UNSALTED BUTTER
½ CUP RICOTTA, STRAINED
2 EGG YOLKS

2 TABLESPOONS FINELY CHOPPED
  FLAT-LEAF PARSLEY
FRESHLY GROUND BLACK PEPPER

TO SERVE
¼ CUP UNSALTED BUTTER
JUICE OF 1 SMALL LEMON

1   Wrap the dough in plastic wrap and leave to rest 30 minutes.
2   Meanwhile, brush the fish lightly with oil and broil, skin side up, 5 to 10 minutes until the flesh flakes
    when tested with a fork; the time will depend on the thickness of the fish. Discard the skin and any
    bones, and flake the fish into a bowl.
3   While the fish is cooking, fry the shallots in the butter until soft but not colored. Add to the fish with the
    ricotta, egg yolks, parsley, and black pepper. Using a fork, combine the ingredients.
4   Shape and stuff raviolini with the dough and filling (see page 11).
5   Cook the raviolini in batches in a large saucepan of gently boiling water about 3 minutes per batch;
    remove with a slotted spoon and drain thoroughly.
6   Meanwhile, melt the butter with the lemon juice. Pour over the raviolini to serve.

# smoked fish pie

PREPARATION TIME 15 mins, plus Tomato Sauce preparation COOKING TIME 45 mins SERVES 6

1 POUND **SPINACH**
**SMALL KNOB OF UNSALTED BUTTER**
1½ POUNDS **SMOKED HADDOCK FILLET,**
  **SKINNED AND CUBED**
1 **QUANTITY BROILED TOMATO SAUCE**
  **(SEE PAGE 18)**
2 TABLESPOONS **CHOPPED MIXED HERBS, SUCH**
  **AS BASIL, OREGANO, THYME, AND FENNEL**
12 OUNCES **CHIFFERI RIGATE OR**
  **CURVED MACARONI RIGATE**

2 TABLESPOONS **FRESHLY GRATED PARMESAN**
1 TABLESPOON **FRESH BREAD CRUMBS**

## CHEESE SAUCE
2 TABLESPOONS **BUTTER**
3 TABLESPOONS **ALL-PURPOSE FLOUR**
1½ CUPS **MILK**
3 TABLESPOONS **FRESHLY GRATED PARMESAN**

1  Cook the spinach in a covered pan without adding any water until wilted; drain and squeeze out the surplus moisture. Heat through with the butter, then spread in the bottom of a 2½-quart baking dish. Scatter the haddock evenly over the top. Mix the tomato sauce with the herbs and spoon over the haddock.

2  Meanwhile, cook and drain the pasta according to the package directions.

3  While the pasta is cooking, make the cheese sauce (see page 17) and mix with the pasta. Pile evenly over the tomato sauce. Sprinkle with the Parmesan and bread crumbs. Bake 25 to 30 minutes in an oven heated to 375°F, until golden.

FISH & SHELLFISH

77

# cod, shrimp, & leek lasagne

PREPARATION TIME 15 minutes COOKING TIME 45 minutes SERVES 6

1 POUND **COD FILLET, SKINNED**
1 **BAY LEAF, TORN ACROSS**
1 **SLICE EACH OF CARROT, FENNEL, AND ONION**
SCANT 1¼ CUPS **MEDIUM-BODIED DRY WHITE WINE**
ABOUT 2¾ CUPS **FISH STOCK**
7 OUNCES **SPINACH LASAGNE**
3 CUPS **SLICED SLIM LEEKS**
1 **GARLIC CLOVE, CHOPPED**
½ CUP **UNSALTED BUTTER**

⅔ CUP **ALL-PURPOSE FLOUR**
½ CUP **RICOTTA**
⅔ CUP **LOW-FAT CRÈME FRAÎCHE**
1 TABLESPOON **CHOPPED DILL**
**SALT AND FRESHLY GROUND BLACK PEPPER**
½ POUND **SHELLED COOKED SHRIMP**
4 TABLESPOONS **FRESHLY GRATED PARMESAN**
**LEMON WEDGES, TO SERVE**

1   Put the cod, bay leaf, vegetable slices, and half the wine in a saucepan. Cover with water and poach about 5 minutes until tender; lift out the fish and flake, discarding any skin and bones. Strain the cooking liquid and make up to 1 quart with fish stock.
2   Heat the oven to 400°F.
3   Meanwhile, cook, drain, and rinse the lasagne, even if using the no-precook type (see page 15). Spread on a dish towel to dry.
4   Cook the leeks and garlic in ¼ cup of the butter in a covered pan until tender; remove with a slotted spoon. Add the remaining butter to the pan, then continue to make a white sauce with the flour, reserved cooking liquid, and wine (see page 17). Off the heat, stir in the ricotta, crème fraîche, dill, and seasoning.
5   Spoon a little sauce into a large shallow baking dish. Cover with a layer of lasagne sheets followed by some of the fish, shrimp, and leeks then some more sauce; continue the layering, ending with sauce. Scatter the Parmesan over.
6   Bake in the heated oven about 30 minutes. Leave to stand 5 minutes before serving with lemon wedges.

## 124
# scallop & shrimp lasagne

PREPARATION TIME 10 minutes COOKING TIME 30 minutes SERVES 4

3 SHALLOTS, FINELY CHOPPED
PINCH OF CHILI FLAKES
OLIVE OIL
I TABLESPOONS CHOPPED FLAT-LEAF PARSLEY
8 OUNCES SHELLED MEDIUM SHRIMP, HALVED OR
   QUARTERED ACROSS
4 OUNCES SKINNED SEA BASS, COD, OR
   HADDOCK FILLET
8 OUNCES SCALLOPS, SHUCKED, QUARTERED, OR
   COARSELY CHOPPED, DEPENDING ON SIZE
2-EGG QUANTITY OF PASTA DOUGH (SEE PAGE 10),
   CUT INTO LASAGNE SHEETS

2 TABLESPOONS FRESHLY GRATED PARMESAN
   (OPTIONAL)
LEMON WEDGES, TO SERVE

### BÉCHAMEL SAUCE
I CUP MEDIUM-BODIED DRY WHITE WINE
1½ CUPS MILK
I BAY LEAF AND 2 PARSLEY SPRIGS
I ONION SLICE AND I CLOVE
3½ TABLESPOONS UNSALTED BUTTER
4 TABLESPOONS ALL-PURPOSE FLOUR
SALT AND FRESHLY GROUND BLACK PEPPER

1   Heat the oven to 400°F. Make the béchamel sauce (see page 17).
2   Fry the shallots and chili in a little oil until the shallots are soft and lightly colored. Add the parsley,
   shrimp, and sea bass, cod, or haddock, and cook fairly briskly about I minute. Add the scallops
   and cook I minute longer.
3   Cook, drain, and rinse the lasagne, even if using the no-precook type (see page 15). Spread on a dish
   towel to dry.
4   Spread a little of the béchamel sauce over the bottom of a shallow baking dish and cover with a layer
   of pasta. Stir the fish mixture into the remainder and use to coat the pasta in a fairly thin layer.
   Repeat the layering, ending with a layer of sauce. Sprinkle the Parmesan over, if using.
5   Bake in the heated oven 15 to 20 minutes until golden on top. Remove from the
   oven and leave to stand 5 minutes before serving with lemon wedges.

## 125
# smoked fish & mushroom cannelloni

PREPARATION TIME 10 minutes COOKING TIME 45 minutes SERVES 6

1½ POUNDS SMOKED HADDOCK FILLET
I BOUQUET GARNI OF 2 TARRAGON SPRIGS, I BAY
   LEAF, AND 2 THYME SPRIGS
3 GARLIC CLOVES
ABOUT 3 CUPS MILK
8 OUNCES DRIED LASAGNE SHEETS
5 TABLESPOONS UNSALTED BUTTER

⅓ CUP ALL-PURPOSE FLOUR
2 TABLESPOONS CHOPPED FLAT-LEAF PARSLEY
GRATED ZEST AND JUICE OF I LEMON
1⅓ CUPS FINELY SLICED MUSHROOMS
3 TABLESPOONS FRESHLY GRATED PARMESAN
LEMON WEDGES, TO SERVE

1   Put the haddock, bouquet garni, garlic, and 2½ cups of the milk into a saucepan. Cover and poach the
   fish about 10 minutes until it just flakes when tested with the tip of a knife. Remove the fish and flake
   it, discarding any skin and bones. Strain the milk and add more milk to make it up to 2½ cups.
2   Heat the oven to 375°F.
3   Meanwhile, cook, drain, and rinse the lasagne, even if using the no-precook type (see page 15).
   Spread on a dish towel to dry.
4   While the lasagne sheets are cooking, make a white sauce (see page 17) with the butter, flour,
   and milk. Off the heat, add the parsley and lemon zest and juice.
5   Mix one-quarter of the sauce with the fish and mushrooms. Divide between the lasagne sheets then
   carefully roll up each one from a short end. Place seam side down in a greased shallow baking dish.
   Spoon the remaining sauce evenly over the cannelloni and sprinkle with the Parmesan.
6   Bake in the heated oven about 30 minutes. Serve with lemon wedges.

## 126
# riccioli with shrimp & asparagus

PREPARATION TIME 10 minutes COOKING TIME 15 minutes SERVES 4

12 ounces SLIM ASPARAGUS
1 GARLIC CLOVE, CRUSHED
VIRGIN OLIVE OIL
1 pound MEDIUM RAW SHRIMP, SHELLED

SALT AND FRESHLY GROUND BLACK PEPPER
14 ounces RICCIOLI*
SMALL KNOB OF UNSALTED BUTTER
FRESHLY GRATED PARMESAN (OPTIONAL)

1   Blanch the asparagus in salted boiling water 3 to 4 minutes until just tender; drain (reserve the water), rinse in cold water, and drain again. Cut the asparagus into 1½-inch pieces.
2   Stir-fry the garlic and asparagus in a little oil in a large nonstick skillet 2 to 3 minutes. Add scant ½ cup reserved asparagus cooking water and boil until reduced by half. Add the shrimp and cook slowly 2 to 3 minutes, stirring, until they turn pink and the sauce is still slightly runny. If necessary, add a little more asparagus water; season.
3   Meanwhile, cook and drain the pasta according to the package directions. Toss with the butter, asparagus, and shrimp. Serve with freshly grated Parmesan, if liked.

*   Radiatori, fusilli, or eliche can also be used.

## 127
# smoked mussel & pimento pasta salad

PREPARATION TIME 10 minutes COOKING TIME 10 minutes SERVES 4

10 ounces CONCHIGLIE
4 ounces THIN GREEN BEANS, HALVED ACROSS
6 tablespoons VIRGIN OLIVE OIL, PLUS EXTRA FOR
   BRUSHING
ABOUT 1 tablespoon BALSAMIC VINEGAR, TO TASTE
1 GARLIC CLOVE, FINELY CHOPPED
½–1 RED CHILI, SEEDED AND FINELY CHOPPED
SALT AND FRESHLY GROUND BLACK PEPPER
1 AVOCADO, CHOPPED

5 SCALLIONS, FINELY CHOPPED
2 CANS (3½-oz.) SMOKED MUSSELS, DRAINED
1½ tablespoons CAPERS
1½ BOTTLED ROASTED PIMENTOS (RED PEPPERS)
   IN OIL, DRAINED AND THINLY SLICED
LEAVES FROM A SMALL HANDFUL OF FLAT-LEAF
   PARSLEY, CHOPPED
LEMON WEDGES, TO SERVE

1   Cook and drain the pasta according to the package directions, adding the beans 3 to 4 minutes before the end; rinse under running cold water.
2   Meanwhile, whisk the oil with the vinegar, garlic, and chili. Season to taste.
3   Toss the pasta and beans with the dressing and remaining ingredients. Serve cold but not chilled, with lemon wedges.

# linguine with mussels & zucchini

PREPARATION TIME 10 minutes COOKING TIME 10 minutes SERVES 4

14 OUNCES LINGUINE
2 SHALLOTS, FINELY CHOPPED
1 GARLIC CLOVE, FINELY CHOPPED
PINCH OF CRUSHED CHILI FLAKES
VIRGIN OLIVE OIL

1 POUND SMALL ZUCCHINI,
    CUT INTO ½-INCH PIECES
5 TABLESPOONS DRY WHITE VERMOUTH
1¾ POUNDS MUSSELS
LEAVES FROM A SMALL BUNCH OF BASIL, SHREDDED
SALT AND FRESHLY GROUND BLACK PEPPER

1   Cook the pasta 1 minute less than specified on the package, and then drain, reserving ½ cup of the cooking water.
2   Meanwhile, fry the shallots, garlic, and chili in a little oil about 1 minute in a pan that is large enough to hold all the mussels and cooked pasta. Add the zucchini and fry until softened and flecked with gold.
3   Pour in the vermouth and bring to a boil, then add the mussels. Cover and cook 3 to 4 minutes until they open; discard any that remain closed. Add the linguine, toss to mix, scatter the basil over and add a little of the reserved water, if necessary, to moisten. Season, cover, and heat together for 1 minute.

FISH & SHELLFISH

81

# cavatappi with shrimp, mushrooms, & tomatoes

PREPARATION TIME 10 minutes COOKING TIME 10 minutes SERVES 4

14 OUNCES CAVATAPPI
1 ONION, THINLY SLICED
VIRGIN OLIVE OIL
2 GARLIC CLOVES, CRUSHED
12 OUNCES MIXED OYSTER AND SHIITAKE MUSHROOMS,
    HALVED OR QUARTERED IF LARGE

¾ CUP MEDIUM-BODIED DRY WHITE WINE
4 RIPE WELL-FLAVORED PLUM TOMATOES, CHOPPED
18 OUNCES LARGE RAW SHRIMP, SHELLED
2 TABLESPOONS CHOPPED FLAT-LEAF PARSLEY
SALT AND FRESHLY GROUND BLACK PEPPER

1   Cook and drain the pasta according to the package directions.
2   Meanwhile, fry the onion in a little oil in a large skillet until soft but not colored. Add the garlic and fry 1 minute. Add the mushrooms and cook until tender and there is not any spare liquid. Add the wine and bubble the liquid until it reduces by half.
3   Add the tomatoes and shrimp and simmer very slowly 2 to 3 minutes until the shrimp just turn pink. Add the parsley and seasoning and toss with the pasta.

## 130
# taglioni with shrimp & spinach

PREPARATION TIME 5 minutes COOKING TIME 10 minutes SERVES 4

13 OUNCES TAGLIONI
VIRGIN OLIVE OIL
2 GARLIC CLOVES, FINELY CHOPPED
9 OUNCES LARGE RAW SHRIMP, SHELLED

8 OUNCES BABY SPINACH LEAVES
3 TABLESPOONS SHREDDED BASIL
SALT AND FRESHLY GROUND BLACK PEPPER

1   Cook and drain the taglioni according to the package directions.
2   Meanwhile, heat about 4 tablespoons oil with the garlic, then add the shrimp and stir-fry 2 to 3 minutes
    until they change color; take care not to overcook. Toss with the taglioni, spinach, basil, seasoning,
    and an additional 4 tablespoons oil. Serve.

## 131
# tagliatelle with mussels & pesto

PREPARATION TIME 10 minutes COOKING TIME 10 minutes SERVES 4

1 SHALLOT, FINELY CHOPPED
2 GARLIC CLOVES, THINLY SLICED
2 SPRIGS OF FLAT-LEAF PARSLEY
4 TABLESPOONS DRY WHITE VERMOUTH

2¼ POUNDS MUSSELS
14 OUNCES TAGLIATELLE
1–1½ QUANTITIES PESTO (SEE PAGE 18)

1   Put the shallot, garlic, parsley, vermouth, and mussels into a large pan over fairly high heat, cover.
    Bring to a boil, then cook 3 to 4 minutes, shaking the pan occasionally, until the shells open; discard
    any that remain closed. Remove the shells from half of the mussels. Strain off and reserve the liquid.
2   Meanwhile, cook and drain the pasta according to the package directions, reserving ½ cup
    of the cooking water.
3   At the same time, warm the pesto over very low heat. Add all the mussels and heat gently.
    Toss with the pasta, adding the reserved liquid, as necessary, to moisten.

## 132
# fidelini with lobster,
# basil, & wilted tomatoes

PREPARATION TIME 15 minutes COOKING TIME 10 minutes SERVES 4

13 OUNCES FIDELINI
1 GARLIC CLOVE, FINELY CHOPPED
4 TABLESPOONS VIRGIN OLIVE OIL
1 POUND WELL-FLAVORED CHERRY TOMATOES,
   QUARTERED

1½–2 POUNDS FRESH LOBSTER,
   SHELLED AND CUT INTO SMALL PIECES
2 TABLESPOONS DRY WHITE VERMOUTH
2 TABLESPOONS SHREDDED BASIL
SALT AND FRESHLY GROUND BLACK PEPPER

1   Cook and drain the fidelini according to the package directions, reserving ½ cup of the cooking water.
2   Meanwhile, fry the garlic in the oil for about 2 minutes. Add the tomatoes and lobster and cook,
    stirring occasionally, for 2 to 3 minutes until the tomatoes are just beginning to collapse.
3   Pour in the vermouth, add the basil and bubble for 1 to 2 minutes. Season and toss
    with the pasta, adding enough of the reserved cooking water to moisten, if necessary.

# 133
# black spaghettini with scallops, white wine, & parsley

PREPARATION TIME 5 minutes COOKING TIME 10 minutes SERVES 4

1 GARLIC CLOVE, FINELY CHOPPED

OLIVE OIL

1 TABLESPOON UNSALTED BUTTER

8 LARGE SCALLOPS, SHUCKED AND HALVED
  HORIZONTALLY

½ CUP MEDIUM-BODIED DRY WHITE WINE

2 TABLESPOONS CHOPPED FLAT-LEAF PARSLEY

SALT AND FRESHLY GROUND BLACK PEPPER

1 POUND FRESH BLACK SPAGHETTINI

1  Put the water for the pasta on to boil. Fry the garlic in little oil and the butter
   in a wide skillet about 2 minutes until soft. Over high heat, add the scallops and fry
   quickly on both sides until they just turn opaque and remain tender; remove from the pan.
2  Add the wine, parsley, and seasoning to the pan and boil until slightly reduced. Lower the heat
   and return the scallops to the pan; do not allow them to boil otherwise they will toughen.
3  About 2 minutes before the scallops are ready, cook and drain the pasta according to the
   package directions. Toss with the scallops and sauce.

## 134
# haddock, spinach, & pasta al forno

PREPARATION TIME 15 minutes* COOKING TIME 45 minutes SERVES 6

1 POUND 6 OUNCES SPINACH

SMALL KNOB OF UNSALTED BUTTER

1½ POUNDS SMOKED HADDOCK FILLET,
SKINNED AND CUBED

1 QUANTITY BROILED TOMATO SAUCE (SEE PAGE 18)

2 TABLESPOONS CHOPPED MIXED HERBS
SUCH AS BASIL, OREGANO, THYME, AND FENNEL

12 OUNCES CHIFFERI RIGATE OR
CURVED MACARONI RIGATE

2 TABLESPOONS FRESHLY GRATED PARMESAN

1 TABLESPOON FRESH BREAD CRUMBS

### CHEESE SAUCE

2 TABLESPOONS BUTTER

3 TABLESPOONS ALL-PURPOSE FLOUR

1¼ CUPS MILK

3 TABLESPOONS FRESHLY GRATED PARMESAN

1   Heat the oven to 375°F.
2   Cook the spinach in a covered pan, shaking the pan occasionally, until wilted; drain and squeeze out surplus moisture. Heat through with the butter, then spread in the bottom of a baking dish. Scatter the haddock evenly over the top. Mix the tomato sauce with the herbs and spoon over the haddock.
3   Cook and drain the pasta according to the package directions.
4   While the pasta is cooking, make the cheese sauce (see page 17) and mix with the pasta. Spoon evenly over the tomato sauce, then sprinkle with the Parmesan and bread crumbs.
5   Bake in the heated oven 25 to 30 minutes until golden.

*   Assumes the tomato sauce is already made.

## 135
# mediterranean seafood & pasta salad

PREPARATION TIME 15 minutes, plus cooling time COOKING TIME 15 minutes SERVES 4

1 CUP MEDIUM-BODIED DRY WHITE WINE

1 GARLIC CLOVE

1 SHALLOT, QUARTERED

1 BAY LEAF

1 LEMON, SLICED

4 TABLESPOONS EXTRA-VIRGIN OLIVE OIL

1½ TABLESPOONS LEMON JUICE

SALT AND FRESHLY GROUND BLACK PEPPER

8 OUNCES RAW JUMBO SHRIMP, SHELLED

4 OUNCES SHUCKED SCALLOPS, HALVED OR
QUARTERED ACCORDING TO SIZE

½ CUP COOKED SHELLED MUSSELS

7 OUNCES BLACK LINGUINE

2 RED BELL PEPPERS, BROILED, PEELED,
AND CHOPPED (SEE PAGE 67)

1 TABLESPOON CAPERS

LEAVES FROM A SMALL BUNCH OF
FLAT-LEAF PARSLEY, CHOPPED

2 HANDFULS OF CRISP SALAD LEAVES

1 LEMON, CUT INTO WEDGES

1   Put the wine, garlic, shallot, bay leaf, and lemon slices into a saucepan, cover, and bring to a boil. Remove the pan from the heat and leave to infuse 10 minutes.
2   Meanwhile, make the dressing by whisking the oil with the lemon juice and seasoning.
3   Return the liquid to a slow simmer, add the shrimp, and poach about 2 minutes until they turn pink. Using a slotted spoon, transfer them to the bowl of dressing. Poach the scallops 1 to 1½ minutes until they change color; add to the shrimp. Dunk the mussels into the poaching liquid to warm them, then add to the other seafood; set aside.
4   Strain the poaching liquid, return to the pan, and add enough water for cooking the pasta. Bring to a boil, then cook and drain the pasta according to the package directions. Toss the pasta with the seafood mixture and leave to cool.
5   Toss the cooled pasta and seafood with the red pepper, capers, and parsley and pile on to a bed of salad leaves. Serve with lemon wedges.

# 136
# pizza macaroni pie

PREPARATION TIME 20 minutes COOKING TIME 35 minutes SERVES 4 to 6

I CUP **MACARONI**

I **SMALL ONION, FINELY CHOPPED**

3 **GARLIC CLOVES, SLICED**

SCANT 2½ CUPS **MILK**

2½ TABLESPOONS **UNSALTED BUTTER**

5 TABLESPOONS **ALL-PURPOSE FLOUR**

**SALT AND FRESHLY GROUND BLACK PEPPER**

ABOUT 1½ TABLESPOONS **SUN-DRIED TOMATO PASTE**

6 TABLESPOONS **FRESHLY GRATED PARMESAN**

5 OUNCES **BUFFALO MOZZARELLA,**
  **THINLY SLICED**

3–4 **RIPE TOMATOES, THINLY SLICED**

ABOUT 12 **PITTED BLACK OLIVES, SLICED**

I CAN (2-oz.) **ANCHOVIES,**
  **DRAINED AND HALVED LENGTHWISE**

**HERBES DE PROVENCE, FOR SPRINKLING**

⅔ CUP **FRESH BREAD CRUMBS**

**OLIVE OIL**

1   Heat the oven to 350°F.

2   Cook the macaroni 2 minutes less than specified on the package, and then drain.

3   Meanwhile, simmer the onion and garlic with enough milk to just cover, until tender, then puree, unless you prefer to have pieces of onion.

4   Make a white sauce (see page 17) with the butter, flour, and the remaining milk. Season and add the tomato paste, Parmesan, and macaroni.

5   Spoon evenly into a greased shallow 1¾-quart baking dish. Interleave the mozzarella and tomatoes over the top, adding the olives and anchovies and a sprinkling of herbes de Provence and black pepper. Sprinkle the bread crumbs around the edge of the dish and trickle a little oil over.

6   Bake in the heated oven 25 minutes.

## 137

# seafood tossed with spaghetti, lemon, & arugula

PREPARATION TIME 5 minutes COOKING TIME 10 minutes SERVES 4

18 ounces FRESH SPAGHETTI

1 pound 7 ounces GOOD-QUALITY MARINATED
SEAFOOD SALAD*

3½ ounces ARUGULA

GRATED ZEST AND JUICE OF 1 LEMON

4 tablespoons CHOPPED PARSLEY

3 tablespoons PINE NUTS, LIGHTLY TOASTED

FRESHLY GROUND BLACK PEPPER

1  Cook and drain the pasta according to the package directions.
2  Return to the hot pan, toss in the seafood salad and return the pan to medium heat. Heat 2 to 3 minutes, tossing occasionally, until piping hot. Add the arugula with the lemon zest and juice and parsley. When it wilts, serve sprinkled with the toasted pine nuts and black pepper.

*  If prepared marinated seafood salad is not available, toss 1 pound 7 ounces cooked mixed seafood with a few tablespoons virgin olive oil, a dash white wine vinegar, and a small handful chopped mixed herbs.

## 138

# linguine with red clam sauce

PREPARATION TIME 5 minutes COOKING TIME 30 minutes SERVES 4

1 SMALL ONION, FINELY CHOPPED

2 GARLIC CLOVES, CRUSHED

VIRGIN OLIVE OIL

1 CAN (14-oz.) CHERRY TOMATOES

2 pounds CLAMS

¾ cup MEDIUM-BODIED DRY WHITE WINE

12 ounces LINGUINE

HANDFUL OF FLAT-LEAF PARSLEY, CHOPPED

1  Fry the onion and garlic in a little oil in a skillet until translucent and soft. Add the tomatoes, bring to a boil, then simmer 15 to 20 minutes until thickened to a sauce.
2  Meanwhile, put the clams and wine in a large, heavy casserole, cover, and cook over high heat, shaking the pan occasionally about 5 minutes until the shells open; discard any that remain closed. Using a slotted spoon, transfer the clams to a bowl.
3  Strain the cooking juices, then boil to reduce by half, then add to the tomato sauce.
4  Meanwhile, cook and drain the linguine according to the package directions. Toss with the sauce, clams, and parsley.

## 139

# quick tagliatelle with shrimp & red pesto

PREPARATION TIME 10 minutes COOKING TIME 10 minutes SERVES 4

12 OUNCES **TAGLIATELLE**
3 **GARLIC CLOVES, THINLY SLICED**
**PINCH OF DRIED CHILI FLAKES**
**VIRGIN OLIVE OIL**
12 OUNCES **RAW JUMBO SHRIMP, SHELLED**
2 TABLESPOONS **RED PESTO (SEE PAGE 19)**

**ZEST AND JUICE OF 1 LEMON**
1 TABLESPOON **CAPERS (OPTIONAL)**
4 TABLESPOONS **MIXED CHOPPED BASIL**
    **AND FLAT-LEAF PARSLEY**
**SALT AND FRESHLY GROUND BLACK PEPPER**

1   Cook and drain the pasta according to the package directions.
2   Meanwhile, cook the garlic and chili in a little oil until softened. Add the shrimp and cook, stirring,
    2 to 3 minutes until they turn pink. Remove the pan from the heat immediately to avoid overcooking
    and toughening the shrimp.
3   Toss the tagliatelli with 1 to 2 tablespoons oil, the red pesto, lemon zest and juice, capers
    (if using), the herbs, shrimp, and seasoning. Serve straightaway.

## 140

# tonnarelli with shrimp, clams, & arugula

PREPARATION TIME 5 minutes COOKING TIME 10 minutes SERVES 4

13 OUNCES **TONNARELLI**
3 **GARLIC CLOVES, FINELY CHOPPED**
**PINCH OF DRIED CHILI FLAKES**
**VIRGIN OLIVE OIL**
⅓ CUP **MEDIUM-BODIED DRY WHITE WINE**
2 POUNDS **CLAMS**

9 OUNCES **COOKED MEDIUM SHRIMP, SHELLED**
4 OUNCES **ARUGULA**
**EXTRA-VIRGIN OLIVE OIL, TO SERVE**

1   Cook and drain the pasta according to the package directions, giving it 1 minute less than specified on
    the package; reserve ½ cup of the cooking water.
2   Meanwhile, fry the garlic and chili in a little oil in a large skillet about 2 minutes. Pour in the wine,
    then add the clams. Cook about 2 minutes until they open; discard any that remain closed.
    Add the shrimp and arugula.
3   Add the pasta to the pan, adding the reserved cooking water, if necessary, to moisten and
    heat together about 1 minute. Serve with extra-virgin olive oil trickled over.

# 141
# seafood linguine en papillote

PREPARATION TIME 5 minutes COOKING TIME 35 minutes SERVES 4 to 6

18 ounces LINGUINE

2 GARLIC CLOVES, CRUSHED

OLIVE OIL

1 CAN (14-oz.) CHERRY TOMATOES

2 tablespoons SUN-DRIED TOMATO PASTE

SALT AND FRESHLY GROUND BLACK PEPPER

1½ pounds COOKED MIXED SEAFOOD,
  SUCH AS SHELLED SHRIMP, MUSSELS,
  HALVED JUMBO SHRIMP, CANNED TUNA

6 ounces COOKED CLAMS

1½–2 tablespoons CAPERS

LEAVES FROM A SMALL BUNCH OF
  FLAT-LEAF PARSLEY, CHOPPED

1. Heat the oven to 375°F. Lightly oil four to six 14-inch squares waxed paper.
2. Cook the linguine 1 minute less than specified on the package, then drain well.
3. Meanwhile, fry the garlic in a little oil 1 minute. Stir in the canned tomatoes, tomato paste, and seasoning and simmer 5 minutes. Toss with the pasta, seafood, capers, and parsley.
4. Place one portion in the middle of each of the pieces of waxed paper. Fold the edges loosely over the pasta mixture and twist the edges together to seal tightly. Place on a baking sheet and bake in the heated oven 20 to 25 minutes until hot throughout.

## 142
# rotelle with tuna & arugula

PREPARATION TIME 10 minutes COOKING TIME 10 minutes SERVES 4

12 OUNCES ROTELLE*
2 CANS (7-oz.) TUNA IN OIL
1 RED ONION, CHOPPED

GRATED ZEST AND JUICE OF 1 LEMON
½ CUP SLICED PITTED GREEN OLIVES
4 OUNCES ARUGULA

1   Cook and drain the pasta according to the package directions.
2   Meanwhile, drain the oil from the tuna into a skillet and fry the onion until tender.
    Add the flaked tuna, lemon zest and juice, olives, and two-thirds of the arugula.
    Season and warm through, then toss with the pasta and remaining arugula.

*   Conchiglie, fusilli, farfalle, or gnocchi can also be used.

## 143
# fettuccine with smoked salmon, dill, & ricotta

PREPARATION TIME 5 minutes COOKING TIME 10 minutes SERVES 4

14 OUNCES FETTUCCINE
3 EGGS
½ CUP RICOTTA
SALT AND FRESHLY GROUND BLACK PEPPER

2 TABLESPOONS CHOPPED DILL
4 OUNCES SMOKED SALMON, CUT INTO STRIPS
SALMON EGGS (KETA), TO SERVE (OPTIONAL)

1   Cook the pasta according to the package directions.
2   Meanwhile, work the eggs into the ricotta, using a fork. Season with a pinch of salt, if liked
    (the smoked salmon will make the dish salty) and plenty of black pepper.
3   Drain the pasta well and immediately and quickly toss with the eggs and ricotta to make a creamy
    sauce (place over very low heat if necessary). Then toss lightly with the dill and smoked salmon.
    Serve garnished with salmon eggs, if liked.

## 144
# penne with cauliflower, anchovies, & garlic

PREPARATION TIME 5 minutes COOKING TIME 10 minutes SERVES 4

3½ CUPS CAULIFLOWER FLOWERETS
1 POUND DRIED PENNE
2 LARGE GARLIC CLOVES, FINELY CHOPPED
PINCH OF CRUSHED CHILI FLAKES
4 ANCHOVY FILLETS, CHOPPED

6 TABLESPOONS EXTRA-VIRGIN OLIVE OIL
2 TABLESPOONS CHOPPED FLAT-LEAF PARSLEY
SALT AND FRESHLY GROUND BLACK PEPPER

1   Boil the cauliflower until tender; drain well.
2   Meanwhile, cook and drain the pasta following the package directions.
3   While the pasta is cooking, fry the garlic, chili, and anchovies in the oil in a large skillet, stirring
    occasionally until the anchovies dissolve and the garlic is golden; do not let it burn. Add the cauliflower.
    Using a fork, stir thoroughly so the flowerets are coated in the oil, quickly breaking them up and
    reducing some to a puree. Toss thoroughly with the pasta, parsley, and seasoning.

## 145
# cavatelli with crab, avocado, & fresh tomatoes

PREPARATION TIME 10 minutes COOKING TIME 10 minutes SERVES 4

12 OUNCEES **CAVATELLI**\*
2 GARLIC CLOVES, FINELY CHOPPED
PINCH OF CHILI FLAKES
2 TABLESPOONS **VIRGIN OLIVE OIL**
4 VINE-RIPENED TOMATOES, SEEDED AND CHOPPED
6 OUNCES **FRESH OR FROZEN MIXED WHITE**
AND BROWN CRABMEAT

2 TABLESPOONS **FINELY CHOPPED FLAT-LEAF PARSLEY,**
PLUS EXTRA FOR GARNISH
2 TABLESPOONS **LEMON JUICE**
1 AVOCADO, DICED
SMALL BUNCH OF SLIM SCALLIONS,
FINELY CHOPPED
SALT AND FRESHLY GROUND BLACK PEPPER

1   Cook and drain the pasta according to the package directions.
2   Meanwhile, fry the garlic and chili in the oil 1 minute, then add the tomatoes, crabmeat, parsley, and lemon juice and heat slowly until just warmed through.
3   Toss with the pasta, avocado, scallions, and seasoning. Serve sprinkled with flat-leaf parsley.

\*   Radiatori, fusilli, riccioli, or taglioni can also be used.

## 146
# shrimp & pasta al forno

PREPARATION TIME 10 minutes COOKING TIME 50 minutes SERVES 4

ABOUT 1½ cups LEEKS, THINLY SLICED
1 pound WELL-FLAVORED TOMATOES, QUARTERED
OLIVE OIL
SALT AND FRESHLY GROUND BLACK PEPPER
10 ounces PENNE RIGATE OR RIGATONI
4 ounces SHELLED COOKED SHRIMP
1½ tablespoons COARSELY CHOPPED
  FLAT-LEAF PARSLEY

⅓ cup VEGETABLE OR FISH STOCK
⅔ cup HEAVY CREAM
¾ cup GRATED BUFFALO MOZZARELLA
2 tablespoons FRESHLY GRATED PARMESAN
1 THICK SLICE CRUSTLESS BREAD, MADE
  INTO CRUMBS

1  Heat the oven to 400°F.
2  Spread leeks and tomatoes in a small roasting pan and trickle a little oil over. Season and stir together, then roast in the heated oven 30 minutes.
3  Meanwhile, cook and drain the pasta according to the package directions, giving it 1 minute less than specified on the package. Tip into the roasting pan with the shrimp and parsley and stir in the stock. Season and trickle the cream ovre. Sprinkle the cheese and bread crumbs over and return to the oven 15 to 20 minutes until the top is crisp and golden.

## 147
# orecchiette with smoked mussels, spinach, & cashews

PREPARATION TIME 5 minutes COOKING TIME 10 minutes SERVES 4

9 ounces PASTA SHELLS
3 PLUMP GARLIC CLOVES, FINELY CHOPPED
12 ounces BABY SPINACH
½ cup VIRGIN OLIVE OIL
2 CANS (3½-oz.) SMOKED MUSSELS, DRAINED

1 RED BELL PEPPER, BROILED, PEELED, AND SLICED
  (SEE PAGE 67)
⅓ cup CASHEW NUTS, LIGHTLY TOASTED
FRESHLY GROUND BLACK PEPPER
LEMON WEDGES, TO SERVE

1  Cook and drain the pasta according to the package directions.
2  Meanwhile, stir-fry the garlic and spinach in the oil in a deep skillet or wok set over high heat 1 minute.
3  Gently stir in the mussels, red bell pepper, and nuts and season with black pepper. Heat briefly until warmed through, shaking the pan occasionally, then toss with the pasta. Serve with lemon wedges.

## 148
# roast vegetable, seafood, & pasta salad

PREPARATION TIME 15 minutes, plus cooling time COOKING TIME 30 to 40 minutes SERVES 4 to 6

1 ZUCCHINI, CUT INTO 1½-INCH CHUNKS
1 SMALL EGGPLANT, CUT INTO 1½-INCH CHUNKS
1 FENNEL BULB, CUT INTO 1½-INCH PIECES
1 ONION, CUT INTO 1½-INCH CHUNKS
1 RED BELL PEPPER, CUT INTO 1½-INCH CHUNKS
3 GARLIC CLOVES, CHOPPED
1 SPRIG OF ROSEMARY

2 SPRIGS OF THYME
VIRGIN OLIVE OIL
4 RIPE TOMATOES, QUARTERED
9 OUNCES PASTA SHAPES
8 OUNCES PREPARED MIXED SEAFOOD
½ CUP BLACK OLIVES

1 Heat the oven to 400°F.
2 Put the vegetables, except the tomatoes, in a large roasting pan with the garlic and herbs. Trickle a little oil over, stir together to coat the vegetables, and spread them out. Roast in the top of the heated oven 30 to 40 minutes until tender and charred in patches, adding the tomatoes after 15 minutes; discard the herbs.
3 About 15 minutes before the vegetables are ready, cook and drain the pasta according to the package directions. Combine with the vegetables, seafood, and olives. Serve warm.

## 149
# green fettuccine & lobster with vodka-cream sauce

PREPARATION TIME 5 minutes COOKING TIME 10 minutes SERVES 4

2 GARLIC CLOVES, FINELY CHOPPED
4 LARGE SCALLIONS, CHOPPED
2 TABLESPOONS VIRGIN OLIVE OIL
1–2 TABLESPOONS SUN-DRIED TOMATO PASTE
2 TABLESPOONS VODKA
¾ CUP HEAVY CREAM

ABOUT 2 CUPS CHOPPED COOKED LOBSTER MEAT
12 OUNCES GREEN FETTUCCINE
SALT AND FRESHLY GROUND BLACK PEPPER
CHOPPED FRESH DILL, TO SERVE

1 Fry the garlic and scallionss in the oil in a skillet for 2 minutes. Stir in the tomato paste until it is amalgamated with the oil, then stir in the vodka and bring to a boil. Add the cream and simmer until beginning to thicken slightly. Add the lobster and remove from the heat if pasta is not ready.
2 Meanwhile, cook and drain the pasta according to the package directions, reserving ½ cup of the cooking water.
3 If necessary, just before the pasta is cooked, reheat the sauce over low heat, stirring occasionally, until warmed through. Season and toss with the pasta, adding enough of the reserved cooking water to moisten, if necessary. Serve sprinkled with dill.

## 150
# seafood spaghetti with saffron

PREPARATION TIME 10 minutes COOKING TIME 20 minutes SERVES 4 to 6

2 LEEKS, THINLY SLICED
1 ONION, FINELY CHOPPED
2 GARLIC CLOVES, FINELY CHOPPED
VIRGIN OLIVE OIL
12 ounces DRIED SPAGHETTI
¾ cup MEDIUM-BODIED
  DRY WHITE WINE

⅔ cup CRÈME FRAÎCHE
4 tablespoons CHOPPED FLAT-LEAF PARSLEY,
  PLUS EXTRA TO GARNISH
LARGE PINCH OF SAFFRON THREADS, CRUSHED
8 ounces LARGE SHRIMP, SHELLED
2 pounds MUSSELS
6 ounces SHUCKED SCALLOPS

1   Fry the leeks, onion, and garlic in a little olive oil 3 to 4 minutes. Cover and cook slowly about
    10 minutes until very soft.
2   Cook and drain the spaghetti according to the package directions.
3   Meanwhile, add the wine, crème fraîche, parsley, and saffron to the vegetables. Bubble for a few minutes,
    then add all the shrimp and mussels. Re-cover the pan and cook, shaking the pan frequently, about
    3 minutes until the mussels open; discard any that remain closed. Add the scallops and poach
    about 2 minutes. Toss with the pasta and serve with plenty of parsley sprinkled over.

## 151
# puffed spinach & anchovy bake

PREPARATION TIME 15 minutes COOKING TIME 50 minutes SERVES 4

6 ounces PASTA
12 ounces SPINACH
4 EGGS, SEPARATED
2 CANS (2-oz.) ANCHOVY FILLETS, DRAINED AND VERY
  FINELY CHOPPED
ABOUT 2 teaspoons WHOLEGRAIN MUSTARD

WHITE SAUCE
2 tablespoons UNSALTED BUTTER
3 tablespoons ALL-PURPOSE FLOUR
1¼ cups MILK

1   Heat the oven to 375°F.
2   Cook and drain the pasta according to the package directions, but allowing 2 minutes less than specified.
3   Meanwhile, cook the spinach in a covered pan until wilted; drain well and squeeze dry.
4   Make a simple white sauce (see page 17) with the butter, flour, and milk. Off the heat, stir in the egg
    yolks, spinach, anchovies, pasta, and mustard to taste.
5   Whisk the egg whites until stiff but not dry. Stir 2 spoonfuls into the sauce, then gently fold in the
    remainder in 3 batches. Transfer to a greased baking dish.
6   Bake in the heated oven about 40 minutes.

## 152
# tagliarini with crab & fennel

PREPARATION TIME 10 minutes COOKING TIME 10 minutes SERVES 4

I FENNEL BULB, VERY THINLY SLICED CROSSWISE
   USING A MANDOLINE OR FOOD PROCESSOR
2 TEASPOONS FENNEL SEEDS, CRUSHED
I GARLIC CLOVE, FINELY CHOPPED
SMALL KNOB OF UNSALTED BUTTER
10 OUNCES TAGLIARINI

8 OUNCES FRESH MIXED WHITE AND
   BROWN CRABMEAT
GRATED ZEST AND JUICE OF I LEMON
SALT AND FRESHLY GROUND BLACK PEPPER
1½ TABLESPOONS CHOPPED FRESH HERB FENNEL

1   Cook the sliced fennel, fennel seeds, and garlic in a little butter and 2 tablespoons water in a covered heavy pan, shaking the pan occasionally, until the fennel is tender. If necessary, add a little dry white wine or water to prevent sticking.

2   Meanwhile, cook and drain the pasta according to the package directions, reserving a little of the cooking water.

3   While the pasta is cooking, stir the crabmeat and lemon zest and juice into the fennel and heat slowly to warm though. Season.

4   Combine the crab sauce with the pasta, adding a little of the cooking water, if necessary, to moisten. Serve with the herb fennel scattered over.

## 153
# fusilli lunghi with shrimp, fennel, & tomatoes

PREPARATION TIME 10 minutes COOKING TIME 20 minutes SERVES 4

I GARLIC CLOVE, FINELY CHOPPED
VIRGIN OLIVE OIL
2 LARGE FENNEL BULBS (12 OUNCES TOTAL), THINLY
   SLICED CROSSWISE, FEATHERY TOPS RESERVED
4 TABLESPOONS MEDIUM-BODIED DRY WHITE WINE
14 OUNCES FUSILLI LUNGHI

1¾ CUPS PEELED, SEEDED, AND CHOPPED
   WELL-FLAVORED PLUM TOMATOES
I TEASPOON OREGANO
12 OUNCES MEDIUM RAW SHRIMP, SHELLED
SALT AND FRESHLY GROUND BLACK PEPPER
FRESHLY GRATED PARMESAN TO SERVE (OPTIONAL)

1   Cook the garlic in a little oil in a large skillet until just beginning to change color. Stir in the fennel, then add the wine. Cover the pan and cook slowly about 15 minutes until the fennel is tender.

2   Meanwhile, cook and drain the pasta according to the package directions.

3   When the fennel is tender, uncover the pan and boil until the liquid evaporates. Add the tomatoes and oregano and cook until the tomato liquid has almost evaporated. Stir in the shrimp and cook about 2 to 3 minutes until they just turn to pink. Season and toss with the pasta. Serve with the reserved feathery tops sprinkled over, and accompanied by Parmesan, if liked.

## 154
# crab in conchiglie with red pesto sauce

PREPARATION TIME 10 minutes COOKING TIME 30 minutes SERVES 4

20 LARGE CONCHIGLIE

2 SHALLOTS, FINELY CHOPPED

1 GARLIC CLOVE, FINELY CHOPPED

SMALL KNOB OF UNSALTED BUTTER

2 TABLESPOONS DRY WHITE VERMOUTH

1 POUND FRESH MIXED WHITE AND
   BROWN CRABMEAT

½ OUNCE FRESH BASIL LEAVES, FINELY SHREDDED

SALT AND FRESHLY GROUND BLACK PEPPER

5 TABLESPOONS RED PESTO (SEE PAGE 19)

5 TABLESPOONS LIGHT CREAM

2–3 TABLESPOONS FRESH BREAD CRUMBS

3 TABLESPOONS FRESHLY GRATED PARMESAN

VIRGIN OLIVE OIL

1   Heat the oven to 425°F.
2   Cook the conchiglie according to the package directions but giving them 1 minute less than
    specified. Drain, rinse in cold water, and drain again; leave upside down to drain on a cloth.
3   Fry the shallots and garlic in the butter until soft but not colored. Add the vermouth and boil
    until it almost evaporates. Remove from the heat and stir in the crab, basil, and seasoning.
    Divide between the pasta shells and place upright in a single layer in a shallow baking dish.
4   Stir the pesto into the cream. Add black pepper and pour around the shells. Sprinkle the bread
    crumbs and cheese over. Trickle a little oil over and bake in the heated oven 15 minutes.
    Uncover and bake 5 minutes longer.

## 155
# taglioni with seared scallops, pancetta, & tomatoes

PREPARATION TIME 10 minutes COOKING TIME 10 minutes SERVES 4

¾ CUP CUBED PANCETTA

2 GARLIC CLOVES, CRUSHED AND COARSELY CHOPPED

5 LARGE, RIPE, WELL-FLAVORED PLUM TOMATOES,
   CORED, SEEDED, AND COARSELY CHOPPED

LEAVES FROM A LARGE HANDFUL OF
   FLAT-LEAF PARSLEY, CHOPPED

LEAVES FROM A FEW SPRIGS OF TARRAGON, CHOPPED

SALT AND FRESHLY GROUND BLACK PEPPER

12–20 SHUCKED SCALLOPS, DEPENDING ON SIZE

14 OUNCES TAGLIONI

1   Fry the pancetta in a large nonstick skillet until lightly colored. Add the garlic and cook 2 minutes.
    Stir in the tomatoes and cook 2 to 3 minutes, theb add the herbs and seasoning.
    Draw the pan partly off the heat so the sauce cooks very slowly.
2   Season the scallops, then sear in a hot ridged griddle pan, or a heated heavy skillet about
    1½ minutes, undisturbed. Turn them over and cook a 1 to 2 minutes longer so they remain
    tender and juicy.
3   While the scallops are cooking, cook and drain the taglioni according to the package directions.
    Toss the pasta with the sauce and serve topped with the scallops.

## 156
# fettuccine with jumbo shrimp, tomatoes, & basil

PREPARATION TIME 10 minutes COOKING TIME 5 minutes SERVES 4

1½ POUNDS **WELL-FLAVORED PLUM TOMATOES,
QUARTERED LENGTHWISE**
**EXTRA-VIRGIN OLIVE OIL**
2 TABLESPOONS **FINELY SHREDDED BASIL,
PLUS EXTRA TO SERVE**
ABOUT 1 TABLESPOON **BALSAMIC VINEGAR**

**SALT AND FRESHLY GROUND BLACK PEPPER**
18 OUNCES **HEADLESS RAW JUMBO SHRIMP, SHELLED**
2 **PLUMP GARLIC CLOVES, CRUSHED**
1 POUND **FRESH FETTUCCINE**

1  Cut away the tomato "cores," if tough. Scoop the seeds and juice into a strainer set over a bowl. When all the juice has drained through, discard the seeds. Dice the flesh and add to the bowl with 1 tablespoon oil, the basil, and vinegar and seasoning to taste. Warm through over a saucepan of simmering water, stirring occasionally.
2  Stir-fry the shrimp in some oil in a large nonstick skillet 2 minutes. Add the garlic and stir-fry until the shrimp turn pink; remove immediately from the heat.
3  While the shrimp are cooking, cook and drain the pasta according to the package directions. Toss with the shrimp, tomatoes, and juices. Serve sprinkled with finely shredded basil.

# conchiglie with seafood sauce

PREPARATION TIME 10 minutes COOKING TIME 20 minutes SERVES 4 to 6

2 ONIONS, CHOPPED

1¾ cups MEDIUM-BODIED DRY WHITE WINE

2 POUNDS MUSSELS

2 GARLIC CLOVES, FINELY CHOPPED

OLIVE OIL

1⅓ cups SLICED CREMINI MUSHROOMS

PINCH OF CRUSHED CHILI FLAKES

1 POUND RAW SHRIMP, SHELLED

4 OUNCES SHUCKED SCALLOPS

14 OUNCES CONCHIGLIE

LEAVES FROM A SMALL BUNCH OF
    FLAT-LEAF PARSLEY, CHOPPED

1 Put half the onions and the wine into a large pan, bring to the boil and add the mussels. Cover and simmer about 4 minutes until the shells open; discard any that remain closed. Remove the mussels from the shells; reserve the liquid.

2 Meanwhile, fry the remaining onion and the garlic in a little oil until soft. Add the mushrooms and chili and cook until the moisture evaporates.

3 Strain in the liquid from the mussels. Boil until reduced to 1 cup. Add the shrimp, cook 1 minute, then add the scallops and simmer slowly 2 minutes longer or until they turn white and the shrimp turn pink. Add the mussels and reheat slowly.

4 Meanwhile, cook and drain the pasta according to the package directions. Toss with the shellfish sauce and the parsley.

FISH & SHELLFISH

# tagliatelle with scallops, red bell peppers, & basil

PREPARATION TIME 10 minutes COOKING TIME 10 minutes SERVES 4

8 LARGE SCALLOPS, SHUCKED

2 LARGE RED BELL PEPPERS, QUARTERED
    LENGTHWISE

4 TABLESPOONS VIRGIN OLIVE OIL

1 POUND TAGLIATELLE

½ JUICY LEMON

SMALL HANDFUL OF BASIL LEAVES, SHREDDED

SALT AND FRESHLY GROUND BLACK PEPPER

1 Separate the corals from the scallops. Slice the bodies in half horizontally; set corals and slices aside.

2 Lay the peppers skin-side up on a baking sheet or broiler rack and broil until the skin is charred and blackened. Working over a bowl, peel off the skins and slice the flesh. Combine the flesh with any juices that are in the bowl and 2 tablespoons oil in a small saucepan and warm through slowly.

3 Meanwhile, cook and drain the pasta according to the package directions.

4 Just before the pasta is ready, cook the scallops and corals on a heated hot, ridged griddle pan (or heated very hot broiler) 1 minute per side until the flesh just becomes opaque: take care not to overcook the scallops. Squeeze lemon juice over them.

5 Toss the pepper, basil, remaining oil, and seasoning with the pasta and serve with the scallops on top.

## 159

# linguine with seafood, saffron, & tomatoes

PREPARATION TIME 10 minutes COOKING TIME 20 minutes SERVES 4

2 SHALLOTS, FINELY CHOPPED

2 GARLIC CLOVES, FINELY CHOPPED

PINCH OF CRUSHED CHILI FLAKES

SMALL KNOB OF UNSALTED BUTTER

¾ CUP MEDIUM-BODIED
  DRY WHITE WINE

1 CAN (15-oz.) CRUSHED PLUM TOMATOES

PINCH OF SAFFRON THREADS, CRUSHED

1½ POUNDS MUSSELS

14 OUNCES LINGUINE

8 OUNCES LARGE RAW SHRIMP, SHELLED

6 OUNCES FRESH SHUCKED SCALLOPS

3 TABLESPOONS CHOPPED FLAT-LEAF PARSLEY

SALT AND FRESHLY GROUND BLACK PEPPER

1   Fry the shallots, garlic, and chili flakes in a little butter in a large saucepan until soft. Add the wine and boil until it almost evaporates.

2   Stir in the tomatoes and saffron and simmer 15 minutes. Add the mussels; cover the pan, and simmer 3 to 4 minutes, shaking the pan occasionally, until the mussels open; discard any that remain closed. Remove the mussels from the pan and remove some or all of the top shells, if liked.

3   Cook and drain the linguine according to the package directions.

4   Meanwhile, add the shrimp to the pan and poach slowly for 1½ minutes, then add the scallops and cook 1½ to 2 minutes or so longer until the shrimp just turn pink and the scallops just become white; take care not overcook. Return the mussels to the pan, add the parsley and seasoning, and warm through. Toss with the pasta and sauce.

*   Squid can be used, if preferred; remove the tentacles to cook separately, and thinly slice the bodies. Add with the shrimp.

## 160

# tagliatelle & jumbo shrimp with red bell pepper sauce

PREPARATION TIME 5 minutes COOKING TIME 20 minutes SERVES 4

4 PLUMP RED BELL PEPPERS

6 UNPEELED WHOLE GARLIC CLOVES

SALT AND FRESHLY GROUND BLACK PEPPER

14 OUNCES TAGLIATELLE

VIRGIN OLIVE OIL FOR FRYING

1 POUND JUMBO SHRIMP

1 TABLESPOON BALSAMIC VINEGAR

LEAVES FROM A SMALL BUNCH OF
  FLAT-LEAF PARSLEY, CHOPPED

1   Broil the peppers and garlic until the peppers blacken, blister, and are soft, and the garlic cloves are soft. Remove the papery skins from the garlic and put the cloves in a blender or food processor. Holding the peppers over a bowl to catch the juices, peel off the skins and discard the seeds and cores. Add the peppers and any juices in the bowl to the blender or food processor and mix to a nubbly puree; season and set aside.

2   Cook and drain the pasta according to the package directions.

3   Meanwhile, heat a little oil in a large skillet. Add the shrimp and fry quickly until they just color; take care not to overcook. Pour in the red pepper sauce, add the balsamic vinegar, and parsley and heat through slowly. Toss with the pasta and serve.

# shellfish spaghetti with sun-blush tomatoes

PREPARATION TIME 10 minutes COOKING TIME 15 minutes SERVES 4 to 6

1 SHALLOT, FINELY CHOPPED

4 GARLIC CLOVES, SLICED

PINCH OF CHILI FLAKES

4 TABLESPOONS VIRGIN OLIVE OIL

⅔ CUP MEDIUM-BODIED DRY WHITE WINE

12 PEELED RAW MEDITERRANEAN SHRIMP, WITH HEADS AND TAILS LEFT ON

1 POUND SQUID, SLICED BUT TENTACLES LEFT WHOLE

2 POUNDS MUSSELS

14 OUNCES SPAGHETTI

12 SUN-BLUSH TOMATOES OR PLUMP SUN-DRIED TOMATOES

SALT AND FRESHLY GROUND BLACK PEPPER

SHREDDED BASIL LEAVES, TO SERVE

1   Fry the shallots, garlic, and chili in a little oil in saucepan until soft but not colored. Pour in the wine and bubble 2 minutes. Add the shrimp, cover, and cook slowly 2 minutes. Add the squid, cook 1 to 2 minutes until the shrimp change color and the squid is just cooked; remove them both with a slotted spoon.

2   Add the mussels to the pan, cover, and cook 3 to 4 minutes, shaking the pan frequently, until the shells open; discard any that remain closed. Strain off and reserve the liquid.

3   Meanwhile, cook the spaghetti according to the package directions, but giving it 1 minute less than specified; drain and return to the pan. Add the reserved liquid, the shrimp, mussels, squid, and sun-blush tomatoes, plus any cooking juices. Toss lightly and heat through 1 minute. Season.
Serve with plenty of basil scattered over.

FISH & SHELLFISH

## 162
# crab & shrimp ravioli

PREPARATION TIME 45 minutes COOKING TIME 4 to 8 minutes SERVES 4

2-EGG QUANTITY OF PASTA (SEE PAGE 10)
8 OUNCES MIXED COOKED FRESH WHITE CRABMEAT
   AND SHELLED SHRIMP
¼ CUP RICOTTA, STRAINED
2 SCALLIONS, FINELY CHOPPED

SALT AND FRESHLY GROUND BLACK PEPPER
4 TABLESPOONS UNSALTED BUTTER
JUICE OF 1 SMALL LEMON
CHOPPED FENNEL, FOR SPRINKLING

1   While the pasta is resting, mix the crabmeat and shrimp with the ricotta, the scallions, and seasoning.
2   Make the ravioli with the pasta dough and filling (see page 11).
3   Cook the ravioli in gently boiling water, in batches, about 4 minutes per batch; drain well.
4   Meanwhile, melt the butter with the lemon juice in a small pan over low heat.
    Serve with the butter poured over the ravioli and sprinkled with fennel.


## 163
# conchiglie with shrimp sauce

PREPARATION TIME 10 minutes COOKING TIME 10 minutes SERVES 4

14 OUNCES CONCHIGLIE
2 GARLIC CLOVES, FINELY CHOPPED
1 RED BELL PEPPER, SEEDED AND FINELY CHOPPED
4 SCALLIONS, CHOPPED

OLIVE OIL
1¼ POUNDS MEDIUM RAW SHRIMP, SHELLED
LEAVES FROM A SMALL BUNCH OF FLAT-LEAF
   PARSLEY, FINELY CHOPPED

1   Cook and drain the pasta according to the package directions, reserving ½ cup of the cooking water.
2   Meanwhile, fry the garlic, red pepper, and scallions in a little oil in a large skillet for a couple of minutes.
    Stir in the shrimp and cook 2 to 3 minutes until they turn pink. Toss with the pasta and parsley, adding
    enough cooking water, if necessary, to moisten and serve.


## 164
# spaghetti with squid, tomatoes, & herbs

PREPARATION TIME 10 minutes COOKING TIME 10 minutes SERVES 4

14 OUNCES SPAGHETTI
3 GARLIC CLOVES, THINLY SLICED
5 TABLESPOONS VIRGIN OLIVE OIL
12 OUNCES PREPARED SQUID, TENTACLES DETACHED,
   BODIES THINLY SLICED

8 OUNCES WELL-FLAVORED CHERRY TOMATOES,
   QUARTERED
2 TABLESPOONS LEMON JUICE
2 TABLESPOONS MIXED FINELY CHOPPED FLAT-LEAF
   PARSLEY, OREGANO, AND BASIL
SALT AND FRESHLY GROUND BLACK PEPPER

1   Cook and drain the pasta according to the package directions.
2   Meanwhile, fry the garlic in 3 tablespoons of the oil until turning golden. Add the squid and cook quickly
    2 to 3 minutes until just turning opaque, stirring. Scoop out into a covered bowl.
3   Add the tomatoes to the pan and warm slowly, shaking the pan occasionally so the tomatoes do not
    break up too much. Add the lemon juice, herbs, and seasoning and return the squid to the pan.
    Toss with the pasta and remaining oil, then serve.

## 165
# fettucine with scallops, buttered pine nuts, & shredded lettuce

PREPARATION TIME 5 minutes COOKING TIME 10 minutes SERVES 2

7 OUNCES **FETTUCINE**
I **GARLIC CLOVE, CRUSHED, WITH A PINCH OF SALT**
2 OUNCES **OF UNSALTED BUTTER, DICED**
3 TABLESPOONS **PINE NUTS**
I2 **BAY SCALLOPS**

**FRESHLY GROUND BLACK PEPPER**
**OUTER LEAVES OF 2 SMALL SOFT LETTUCES, TORN**
  **INTO WIDE STRIPS**
**LEMON WEDGES, TO SERVE (OPTIONAL)**

I   Cook and drain the pasta according to the package instructions.
2   Meanwhile, fry the garlic in the butter I minute. Add the scallops and pine nuts and cook 1-2 minutes until the scallops are just beginning to turn opaque. Season lightly with pepper and toss in the lettuce.
3   Drain the pasta and toss with the scallops, lettuce, and pine nuts. Serve with lemon wedges, if liked.

## 166
# linguine with squid, basil, & chili

PREPARATION TIME 10 minutes COOKING TIME 5 minutes SERVES 4

10 OUNCES **CLEANED SQUID**
3 **GARLIC CLOVES, THINLY SLICED**
I **RED CHILI, SEEDED AND FINELY CHOPPED**
**VIRGIN OLIVE OIL**

I–2 TEASPOONS **LEMON JUICE**
**SALT AND FRESHLY GROUND BLACK PEPPER**
I POUND **FRESH LINGUINE**
3 TABLESPOONS **SHREDDED BASIL LEAVES**

I   Remove and reserve the tentacles from the squid. Slice the bodies into rings. Stir-fry the tentacles and rings, the garlic, and chili in a little oil in a large skillet over high heat about 3 minutes until the squid turns white; toss with the lemon juice and seasoning.
2   Meanwhile, cook and drain the linguine. Toss with the squid and basil and serve.

## 167
# spaghetti with swordfish, lemon, capers, & arugula

PREPARATION TIME 10 minutes COOKING TIME 10 minutes SERVES 4

14 OUNCES **SPAGHETTI**
3 **GARLIC CLOVES, THINLY SLICED**
**PINCH OF CRUSHED CHILI FLAKES**
4 TABLESPOONS **VIRGIN OLIVE OIL**
12 OUNCES **SWORDFISH STEAKS, CUT ACROSS INTO**
  STRIPS ABOUT ¾ INCH **WIDE**

**LEAVES FROM A BUNCH OF FLAT-LEAF PARSLEY,**
  **FINELY CHOPPED**
I TABLESPOON **CAPERS**
I TABLESPOON **LEMON JUICE**
**SALT AND FRESHLY GROUND BLACK PEPPER**

I   Cook and drain the pasta according to the package directions.
2   Meanwhile, fry the garlic and chili in the oil 2 minutes. Add the swordfish strips and parsley and cook quickly about 2 minutes on each side, until the fish is just cooked through; take care not to overcook. Add the capers and lemon juice and seasoning and toss with the pasta.

## 168
# bucatini with squid, shrimp, lemon, parsley, & garlic

PREPARATION TIME 10 minutes COOKING TIME 10 minutes SERVES 4

14 ounces **BUCATINI**
3 **GARLIC CLOVES, THINLY SLICED**
4 tablespoons **VIRGIN OLIVE OIL**
12 ounces **PREPARED SQUID, TENTACLES DETACHED,**
  **BODIES THINLY SLICED**

12 **LARGE RAW SHRIMP, SHELLED**
**GRATED ZEST AND JUICE OF ½ LEMON**
**SMALL HANDFUL OF FLAT-LEAF PARSLEY**
  **LEAVES, CHOPPED**
**SALT AND FRESHLY GROUND BLACK PEPPER**

1   Cook and drain the pasta according to the package directions.
2   Meanwhile, fry the garlic in 3 tablespoons oil until turning golden. Scoop out with a slotted spoon into a covered bowl. Add the squid in batches to the pan and cook 1 to 2 minutes per batch, stirring until it just changes color. Scoop out and add to the garlic. Fry the shrimp until they just turn pink.
3   Add the lemon zest and juice and return the squid and any juices that have collected. Warm through slowly. Toss with the pasta, remaining oil, parsley, and seasoning.

## 169
# taglioni with crab sauce

PREPARATION TIME 10 minutes COOKING TIME 10 minutes SERVES 4

10 ounces **TAGLIONI**
1 **GARLIC CLOVE, FINELY CHOPPED**
**PINCH OF CHILI FLAKES**
**GRATED ZEST OF 1 LEMON**
5 **SCALLIONS, THINLY SLICED DIAGONALLY**
**VIRGIN OLIVE OIL**
1 cup **MEDIUM-BODIED DRY WHITE WINE**

⅔ cup **FRESH OR FROZEN BROWN CRABMEAT, THAWED**
1⅓ cups **FRESH OR FROZEN MIXED CRABMEAT,**
  **THAWED**
1–2 teaspoons **LEMON JUICE**
**SALT AND FRESHLY GROUND BLACK PEPPER**
2½ tablespoons **FINELY CHOPPED FLAT-LEAF PARSLEY,**
  **PLUS EXTRA TO GARNISH**

1   Cook and drain the pasta according to the package directions, reserving ½ cup of the cooking water.
2   Meanwhile, cook the garlic, chili flakes, lemon zest, and scallions slowly in a little oil 1½ minutes.
3   Pour in the wine and boil, uncovered, until most of the wine evaporates. Stir in the crabmeat and lemon juice and seasoning to taste; warm through briefly. Toss with the pasta and parsley, adding enough of the reserved water to moisten, if necessary. Sprinkle parsley over and serve.

# 170
# tuna & broccoli bake

PREPARATION TIME 10 minutes COOKING TIME 35 minutes SERVES 4

8 OUNCES **FUSILLI**
1 CUP **BROCCOLI DIVIDED INTO SMALL FLOWERETS**
1 CUP **TALEGGIO OR FONTINA, GRATED**
1 CAN (7-OZ.) **TUNA, DRAINED AND FLAKED**
1 LARGE (OR 2 HALVES) **BROILED RED PEPPER IN OIL, DRAINED AND SLICED**

2½ CUPS **MILK**
3 **EXTRA-LARGE EGGS, BEATEN**
**SALT AND FRESHLY GROUND BLACK PEPPER**
2 TABLESPOONS **FRESH BREAD CRUMBS**

1   Heat the oven to 350°F.
2   Cook and drain the pasta according to the package directions but giving it 1 minute less than specified; add the broccoli for the last 2 to 3 minutes.
3   Combine the pasta and broccoli with half of the cheese, then tip half of the mixture into a greased baking dish. Scatter the tuna and red pepper over. Cover with the remaining pasta mixture.
4   Beat the milk with the eggs and seasoning. Pour into the dish; it should flow through the pasta, but if not, ease the pasta apart. Scatter the remaining cheese and the bread crumbs over, making sure any protruding broccoli is covered.
5   Bake in the heated oven about 25 minutes until just set and golden.

# 171
# cavatelli with mussels, tomatoes, & chili

PREPARATION TIME 5 minutes COOKING TIME 15 minutes SERVES 4

4 TABLESPOONS **MEDIUM-BODIED DRY WHITE WINE**
2 POUNDS **MUSSELS**
2 **GARLIC CLOVES, FINELY CHOPPED**
1 SMALL **CHILI, SEEDED AND FINELY CHOPPED**
3 TABLESPOONS **VIRGIN OLIVE OIL**

10 OUNCES **WELL-FLAVORED CHERRY TOMATOES**
**LEAVES FROM A SMALL BUNCH OF FLAT-LEAF PARSLEY, CHOPPED**
**SALT AND FRESHLY GROUND BLACK PEPPER**
14 OUNCES **CAVATELLI**

1   Put the wine and mussels in a large saucepan, cover, and cook over medium heat 3 to 4 minutes, shaking the pan frequently, until the shells open; discard any that remain closed. Remove the shells from half of the mussels, then strain and reserve the liquid.
2   Meanwhile, fry the garlic and chili in the oil in a large skillet about 2 minutes until soft but not colored. Halve some of the tomatoes, then add all the tomatoes to the pan and fry until beginning to soften but still retain their shape. Add the parsley, all the mussels, the reserved cooking liquid, and seasoning and heat through slowly.
3   Meanwhile, cook and drain the pasta according to the package directions. Toss with the mussel sauce.

# meat &
# poultry

Meat sauces for pasta tend to come from the middle to north of Italy, especially from the region of Emilia-Romagna, the source of abundant supplies of hams, pancetta, salami, and fresh sausages. And, of course, there's the well-known Bolognese sauce, or ragù alla Bolognese to give it its correct name. Contrary to the norm outside Italy, the rich, intensely flavored sauce should be served with tagliatelle, not spaghetti. This chapter also features plenty of lasagne recipes, such as chicken with leek and sausage with eggplant. As well as the popular beef-filled version of cannelloni, there is a lighter recipe using pork, spinach, and ricotta, plus a version with a chicken and prosciutto filling. Meat, particularly cured meats, are often combined with vegetables, as in Tagliatelle with Prosciutto, Peas, and Lemon.

172

# tagliolini with meatballs & tomato sauce

PREPARATION TIME 10 minutes*, plus soaking time COOKING TIME 35 minutes* SERVES 4

1 SLICE STALE FIRM WHITE BREAD, CRUSTS REMOVED

2 TABLESPOONS MILK

1 ONION, FINELY CHOPPED

1 GARLIC CLOVE, FINELY CHOPPED

OLIVE OIL

12 OUNCES LEAN GROUND BEEF

1 EGG, BEATEN

2 TABLESPOONS FRESHLY GRATED PARMESAN, PLUS
   EXTRA TO SERVE (OPTIONAL)

4 TABLESPOONS CHOPPED FLAT-LEAF PARSLEY

SALT AND FRESHLY GROUND BLACK PEPPER

PLAIN FLOUR

FRESH TOMATO SAUCE (SEE PAGE 18) OR WINTER
   TOMATO SAUCE (SEE PAGE 19), WARM

14 OUNCES TAGLIOLINI

1   Crumble the bread into the milk and leave to soak 10 minutes.

2   Meanwhile, fry the onion and garlic in a little oil until very soft and pale gold. Transfer to paper towels to drain and cool.

3   Put the beef into a large bowl and break it up. Squeeze the milk from the bread crumbs and add the soaked crumbs to the beef with the onion, garlic, egg, Parmesan, half the parsley, and seasoning; combine thoroughly. With floured hands, form into walnut-size balls.

4   Fry the balls in oil, in batches, if necessary, so the pan is not crowded, until golden. Pour in the warm sauce, turn over gently a few times so they are well coated, and cook together slowly 15 to 20 minutes.

5   Meanwhile, cook and drain the pasta. Toss with the sauce, top with the meatballs, and serve with the Parmesan.

*   Assumes the sauce is already made.

## 173
# prosciutto & basil frittata
# with roast tomatoes

PREPARATION TIME 5 minutes COOKING TIME 15 to 20 minutes SERVES 4

9 OUNCES **CHERRY TOMATOES**
1 TABLESPOON **BALSAMIC VINEGAR**
**VIRGIN OLIVE OIL**
**SALT AND FRESHLY GROUND BLACK PEPPER**
½ CUP **MACARONI**
⅔ CUP **LIGHT OR WHIPPING CREAM**
4 **EGGS**

**LEAVES FROM A BUNCH OF BASIL, SHREDDED**
3 SLICES **PROSCIUTTO, SHREDDED**
3 OUNCES **FONTINA OR TALEGGIO CHEESE,
FINELY CHOPPED**
**SMALL BUNCH OF ARUGULA**

1  Heat the oven to 400°F.
2  Put the tomatoes in a roasting pan and stir with the balsamic vinegar, a little oil, and seasoning; spread in a single layer. Roast in the heated oven 15 to 20 minutes until soft; stir a couple of times.
3  Meanwhile, cook the pasta according to the package directions and drain well.
4  Combine the cream, eggs, and basil briefly in a blender, add to the cooked pasta with the prosciutto and seasoning and stir together.
5  Heat a little oil in a large nonstick skillet. Pour in the prosciutto mixture to make an even layer and cook slowly until the frittata is set most of the way through but still creamy on top.
6  Scatter the cheese over evenly and place under a heated broiler until golden. Slide the frittata onto a large plate. Serve topped with the roast tomatoes and any pan juices and the arugula.

## 174
# sardinian ragù

PREPARATION TIME 10 minutes COOKING TIME 2 hours SERVES 4

1 POUND **LEAN SHOULDER OF LAMB, CUT INTO
¾-INCH CUBES**
**SEASONED FLOUR**
**OLIVE OIL**
1 **LARGE ONION, CHOPPED**
4 **GARLIC CLOVES, CHOPPED**
**LEAVES FROM 1 SMALL SPRIG OF ROSEMARY, FINELY
CHOPPED**

¾ CUP **FULL-BODIED DRY WHITE WINE**
1 **BOUQUET GARNI**
1 TEASPOON **GROUND CINNAMON**
**SALT AND FRESHLY GROUND BLACK PEPPER**
⅔ CUP **PITTED GREEN OLIVES**
10 OUNCES **GARGANELLI**

1  Heat the oven to 350°F.
2  Toss the lamb in seasoned flour to coat lightly, then fry in batches in a little oil in a heavy flameproof casserole until evenly brown; remove with a slotted spoon.
3  Add the onion to the pan, and more oil, if necessary, and fry until brown. Add the garlic and rosemary and fry 1 minute, then stir in the wine to dislodge the sediment. Add the bouquet garni, cinnamon, seasoning, fried lamb, and enough water to just cover the meat. Cover and heat until the liquid bubbles at the edges.
4  Cook the casserole in the heated oven 1½ to 2 hours until the lamb is very tender. Stir in the olives 10 minutes before the end. If there is too much liquid, uncover the casserole toward the end of the cooking; if the casserole is too dry, stir in a little more wine or water.
5  Meanwhile, cook and drain the pasta according to the package directions. Toss with the lamb ragù.

## 175
# tortiglioni with lamb ragù

PREPARATION TIME 10 minutes, plus soaking time COOKING TIME 2 to 2½ hours SERVES 4

½ OUNCE **DRIED PORCINI**
I **ONION, CHOPPED**
I **CARROT, FINELY CHOPPED**
**OLIVE OIL**
3 **GARLIC CLOVES, FINELY CHOPPED**
2 TEASPOONS **FENNEL SEEDS, LIGHTLY CRUSHED**
I **SPRIG OF ROSEMARY**

12 OUNCES **LEAN GROUND LAMB**
½ CUP **RED WINE**
I CAN (15-OZ.) **CRUSHED TOMATOES**
3 TABLESPOONS **CHOPPED OREGANO**
**SALT AND FRESHLY GROUND BLACK PEPPER**
14 OUNCES **TORTIGLIONI**\*
**FRESHLY GRATED PARMESAN, TO SERVE**

1   Soak the porcini in about ½ cup boiling water 15 minutes.
2   Meanwhile, cook the onion and carrot in a little oil in a large skillet until softened and lightly colored, adding the garlic about 2 minutes before the end.
3   Stir in the fennel seeds and rosemary for 1 minute. Increase the heat, add the lamb, and cook until light brown, stirring to break it up. Stir in the wine and bubble very slowly until reduced by half.
4   Lift the mushrooms from the liquid (reserve the liquid) and chop them.
5   Add the tomatoes, oregano, and mushrooms to the lamb and strain in the mushroom liquid. Cook, uncovered, over very low heat at least 1½ hours, preferably 2 hours, stirring occasionally, until the lamb is very tender and the sauce no longer watery. If necessary, add a little more wine or water during cooking. Discard the rosemary; season.
6   Cook and drain the pasta according to the package directions and toss with the sauce. Serve with grated Parmesan.

\*   Rigatoni can also be used.

## 176
# sedani with tomatoes, sausages, & mushrooms

PREPARATION TIME 10 minutes COOKING TIME 40 minutes SERVES 4

I **ONION, FINELY CHOPPED**
**VIRGIN OLIVE OIL**
2 CUPS **SLICED CREMINI MUSHROOMS**
2 **PLUMP GARLIC CLOVES, FINELY CHOPPED**
9 OUNCES **FRESH ITALIAN (OR FRENCH) SAUSAGES, SKINNED AND CRUMBLED**
**PINCH OF CHILI FLAKES**
I–I¼ TEASPOONS **DRIED OREGANO**
I CAN (14-OZ.) **CHERRY TOMATOES**

I TABLESPOON **SUN-DRIED TOMATO PASTE**
½ CUP **HEAVY CREAM (OPTIONAL)**
**SALT AND FRESHLY GROUND BLACK PEPPER**
10 OUNCES **SEDANI OR OTHER LARGE PASTA TUBES**
**CHOPPED PARSLEY AND FRESHLY GRATED PARMESAN, TO SERVE**

1   Fry the onion in a little oil in a large skillet until soft. Add the mushrooms and garlic and fry briskly until the mushrooms brown.
2   Stir in the sausages to break them up and cook until light brown. Add the chili, oregano, tomatoes, and tomato paste. Simmer slowly 15 to 20 minutes until thick, stirring occasionally. Stir in the cream, if using, and heat through gently; season.
3   Meanwhile, cook and drain the pasta according to the package directions. Toss with the sauce, sprinkle with parsley, and serve accompanied by Parmesan.

# pappardelle with steak & mushrooms

PREPARATION TIME 10 minutes COOKING TIME 15 minutes SERVES 4

I ONION, HALVED AND THINLY SLICED

4 TABLESPOONS UNSALTED BUTTER

I GARLIC CLOVE, FINELY CHOPPED

3¼ CUPS MIXED MUSHROOMS, WILD IF POSSIBLE, HALVED, QUARTERED, OR SLICED, ACCORDING TO SIZE

I POUND SIRLOIN STEAK, CUT ACROSS THE GRAIN INTO STRIPS

2 TABLESPOONS DRY MARSALA

3 TABLESPOONS CRÈME FRAÎCHE

SALT AND FRESHLY GROUND BLACK PEPPER

LEMON JUICE

I POUND FRESH PAPPARDELLE

SMALL HANDFUL OF MIXED FLAT-LEAF PARSLEY AND TARRAGON, CHOPPED

1   Fry the onion in half the butter until soft and lightly colored, adding the garlic the last 2 minutes. Add the mushrooms and cook, stirring frequently, until light brown and tender. Remove the vegetables with a slotted spoon and keep warm.

2   Add the remaining butter to the cooking juices and fry the steak strips briskly, keeping them moving, 2 to 3 minutes until sealed on the outside but still pink in the middle.

3   Add the marsala to the pan and boil until almost evaporated. Stir the crème fraîche into the pan, return the mushrooms, and bring to a boil. Simmer gently to thicken slightly. Season, adding lemon juice, to taste.

4   Cook the pappardelle according to the package directions and drain, reserving ½ cup of the cooking water. Toss the pasta with the meat and mushroom sauce; include some of the reserved water, if necessary, to moisten. Serve sprinkled with parsley and tarragon.

MEAT & POULTRY

## 178
# tagliatelle with steak & onions

PREPARATION TIME 10 minutes COOKING TIME 15 minutes SERVES 4

2 LARGE RED ONIONS, THICKLY SLICED
VIRGIN OLIVE OIL
SCANT ¾ CUP HALF-FAT CRÈME FRAÎCHE
9 OUNCES TAGLIATELLE

2 x 7-OUNCE STEAKS
SALT AND FRESHLY GROUND BLACK PEPPER
LEAVES FROM A SMALL HANDFUL OF FLAT-LEAF
  PARSLEY, CHOPPED

1   Cook the onions, stirring frequently, in a little oil in large heavy nonstick skillet 8 to 10 minutes until soft and golden. Stir in the crème fraîche and heat through slowly.
2   Meanwhile, cook and drain the pasta according to the package directions, reserving ½ cup of the cooking water.
3   At the same time, season the steaks and cook on a hot ridged griddle pan 2 to 3 minutes per side until brown but still pink inside; transfer to a plate and leave to rest.
4   Cut the steaks into strips across the grain. Add to the onions, with any juices that have collected on the plate, and the parsley and seasoning. After a minute or so, toss with the pasta, and enough of the reserved water, if necessary to moisten.

## 179
# fettuccine with mushrooms, pancetta, & wine

PREPARATION TIME 10 minutes COOKING TIME 10 minutes SERVES 4

14 OUNCES FETTUCCINE
4 OUNCES PANCETTA, CUT INTO STRIPS
SMALL KNOB OF UNSALTED BUTTER
1 GARLIC CLOVE, VERY THINLY SLICED
5 CUPS SLICED CREMINI MUSHROOMS
5 TABLESPOONS MEDIUM-BODIED DRY WHITE WINE

½ CUP HEAVY CREAM
SALT AND FRESHLY GROUND BLACK PEPPER
4 TABLESPOONS FRESHLY GRATED PARMESAN,
  PLUS EXTRA TO SERVE

1   Cook and drain the pasta according to the package directions, reserving ½ cup of the cooking water.
2   Meanwhile, fry the pancetta in the butter in a large skillet until crisp. Add the garlic and mushrooms and fry about 5 minutes, until lightly colored, stirring frequently.
3   Pour in the wine and bubble until it evaporates, then add the cream and simmer slowly for a couple of minutes until lightly thickened; season. Toss with the pasta and Parmesan, adding reserved water, as necessary, to moisten.

## 180
# sedani with beef ragù

PREPARATION TIME 10 minutes COOKING TIME 20 minutes SERVES 4

12 ounces RUMP STEAK, CUT ACROSS INTO
  2-inch STRIPS
OLIVE OIL
1 ONION, FINELY CHOPPED
2 GARLIC CLOVES, THINLY SLICED
1 CAN (15-oz.) CRUSHED PLUM TOMATOES

1 teaspoon DRIED OREGANO
14 PITTED BLACK OLIVES, SLICED
2 tablespoons CAPERS
1 tablespoon FLAT-LEAF PARSLEY
SALT AND FRESHLY GROUND BLACK PEPPER
14 ounces SEDANI*

1  Fry the steak in a little oil in a large skillet about 3 minutes until brown; remove with
  a slotted spoon.
2  Add the onion to the pan and fry until soft and light brown, adding the garlic 2 minutes before the
  end of cooking. Stir in the tomatoes and oregano and simmer over fairly high heat, stirring occasionally,
  about 10 minutes until thick. Add the olives, capers, parsley, and seasoning.
3  Meanwhile, cook and drain the pasta according to the package directions. Toss with the beef sauce.

*  Penne rigate, macaroni rigate, or strozzapreti can also be used.

## 181
# bucatini with prosciutto, radicchio, capers, & lemon

PREPARATION TIME 10 minutes COOKING TIME 10 minutes SERVES 4

14 ounces BUCATINI*
9 THIN SLICES OF PROSCIUTTO, CUT ACROSS INTO
  THIN SLICES
VIRGIN OLIVE OIL
2 GARLIC CLOVES, FINELY CHOPPED

1 HEAD OF RADICCHIO, THINLY SLICED
2 tablespoons CAPERS
JUICE OF 1 LEMON, OR TO TASTE
SALT AND FRESHLY GROUND BLACK PEPPER
FRESHLY GRATED PARMESAN, TO SERVE

1  Cook and drain the pasta according to the package directions, reserving ½ cup of the cooking water.
2  Meanwhile, fry the prosciutto in olive oil until golden. Add the garlic, radicchio, and capers.
  As soon as the radicchio wilts, add the lemon juice and remove from the heat.
  Season lightly with salt but plenty of black pepper. Toss with the pasta, adding
  reserved cooking water to moisten. Serve with freshly grated Parmesan.

*  Tagliatelle can also be used.

## 182
# tonnarelli with pork & mushrooms

PREPARATION TIME 10 minutes COOKING TIME 10 minutes SERVES 4

10 OUNCES **PORK, CUT ACROSS INTO**
  1-INCH-**WIDE STRIPS**
**VIRGIN OLIVE OIL**
3¼ CUPS **SLICED CREMINI MUSHROOMS**
2 **GARLIC CLOVES, FINELY CHOPPED**

2–3 TEASPOONS **THYME**
2 TABLESPOONS **LEMON JUICE**
**SALT AND FRESHLY GROUND BLACK PEPPER**
14 OUNCES **TONNARELLI**

1  Fry the pork strips in some olive oil in a large pan about 4 minutes, stirring frequently, until they have changed color.
2  Add the mushrooms, garlic, and thyme and continue to cook, stirring frequently, until the mushrooms are tender and the pork is cooked. Stir in the lemon juice and seasoning, using plenty of black pepper.
3  Meanwhile, cook and drain the pasta according to the package directions. Toss with the sauce and 2 to 3 tablespoons virgin olive oil.

## 183
# penne with chorizo, arugula, & tomatoes

PREPARATION TIME 5 minutes COOKING TIME 10 minutes SERVES 2

6 OUNCES **PENNE**
4-OUNCE **PIECE OF CHORIZO, CHOPPED**
**OLIVE OIL**
9 OUNCES **CHERRY OR BABY PLUM TOMATOES, HALVED**
  **LENGTHWISE**

2 TEASPOONS **BALSAMIC VINEGAR**
2 TABLESPOONS **TAPENADE**
2 OUNCES **ARUGULA**
**FRESHLY GROUND BLACK PEPPER**

1  Cook the penne according to the package directions.
2  Meanwhile, fry the chorizo in a little olive oil in a nonstick skillet 2 to 3 minutes. Add the tomatoes and vinegar and cook until the tomatoes just begin to collapse.
3  Drain the penne and stir in the tapenade, then the arugula, chorizo mixture, and black pepper.

## 184
# tagliatelle with chicken & sage

PREPARATION TIME 10 minutes COOKING TIME 10 minutes SERVES 4

14 OUNCES **TAGLIATELLE**
2 **SHALLOTS, FINELY CHOPPED**
**KNOB OF UNSALTED BUTTER**
11 OUNCES **CHICKEN BREAST, CUT ACROSS**
  **INTO STRIPS**

1 **GARLIC CLOVE, CUT INTO THIN SLIVERS**
8 **SMALL SAGE LEAVES, SHREDDED**
4 TABLESPOONS **MEDIUM-BODIED DRY WHITE WINE**
**SALT AND FRESHLY GROUND BLACK PEPPER**
**FRESHLY GRATED PARMESAN, TO SERVE**

1   Cook and drain the pasta according to the package directions, reserving ½ cup of the cooking water.
2   Meanwhile, fry the shallots in the butter until transparent. Add the chicken and fry until golden on
    the outside and just cooked through, but do not overcook. Add the garlic and sage for the final
    2 minutes or so of cooking. Pour in the wine and bubble a couple of minutes, then season.
3   Toss the chicken mixture with the pasta and enough of the reserved water to moisten.
    Serve with plenty of grated Parmesan.

## 185
# tagliatelle alla bolognese

PREPARATION TIME 5 minutes COOKING TIME 10 minutes* SERVES 4

3-EGG QUANTITY **TAGLIATELLE (SEE PAGE 10) OR**
  14 OUNCES **DRIED TAGLIATELLE**

1 QUANTITY **RAGÙ (SEE PAGE 16)**
½ CUP **FRESHLY GRATED PARMESAN**

1   Bring a large saucepan of water for cooking fresh pasta to a boil, or cook and drain dried pasta
    according to the package directions.
2   Meanwhile, reheat the sauce over low heat, stirring frequently and adding a little water, if necessary,
    to prevent the sauce sticking.
3   Cook and drain fresh pasta. Toss with the ragù and Parmesan.

*   Assumes that the sauce is already made.

## 186
# cavatappi with pork ragù

PREPARATION TIME 10 minutes COOKING TIME 30 minutes SERVES 4

1 SMALL ONION, FINELY CHOPPED
OLIVE OIL
2 GARLIC CLOVES, FINELY CHOPPED
3¼ CUPS SLICED CREMINI MUSHROOMS
12 OUNCES PORK, CUT INTO VERY SMALL PIECES
2 OUNCES PROSCIUTTO, CHOPPED
⅔ CUP MEDIUM-BODIED DRY WHITE WINE

2 TABLESPOONS CHOPPED FLAT-LEAF PARSLEY
SALT AND FRESHLY GROUND BLACK PEPPER
13 OUNCES CAVATAPPI*
FRESHLY GRATED PARMESAN, TO SERVE

1 Fry the onion in a little oil until soft. Add the garlic and mushrooms and cook 2 minutes, then stir in the pork and prosciutto. Cook, stirring, until light brown.
2 Add the wine and bubble for a couple of minutes, then add the parsley. Cover and simmer slowly about 20 minutes; season.
3 Meanwhile, cook and drain the pasta according to the package directions. Toss with the ragù and serve with freshly grated Parmesan.

* Conchiglie, bucatini, or tagliatelle can also be used.

114

## 187
# penne with sausages & mushrooms

PREPARATION TIME 10 minutes COOKING TIME 15 minutes SERVES 4

1 ONION, FINELY CHOPPED
2 GARLIC CLOVES, FINELY CHOPPED
PINCH OF CHILI FLAKES
9 OUNCES GOOD-QUALITY SPICY FRESH ITALIAN (OR FRENCH) SAUSAGES, SKINS REMOVED
VIRGIN OLIVE OIL
5 CUPS SLICED CREMINI MUSHROOMS
1 TABLESPOON THYME

SALT AND FRESHLY GROUND BLACK PEPPER
14 OUNCES PENNE
3 TABLESPOONS UNSALTED BUTTER, DICED
LEAVES FROM A SMALL HANDFUL OF FLAT-LEAF PARSLEY
½ CUP FRESHLY GRATED PARMESAN, PLUS EXTRA TO SERVE

1 Fry the onion, garlic, chili, and sausagemeat in a little oil until light brown, stirring frequently to break up the sausagemeat. Add the mushrooms and thyme and cook until the liquid from the mushrooms evaporates but do not let them become too dry; season.
2 Meanwhile, cook and drain the penne according to the package directions, reserving ¼ cup of the cooking water.
3 Off the heat, add the butter to the mushrooms, then toss with the pasta, parsley, and Parmesan, and enough of the reserved cooking water to moisten.

# 188
# elicoidali, sausages, & bell peppers al forno

PREPARATION TIME 10 minutes COOKING TIME 35 to 40 minutes SERVES 4

11 OUNCES **ELICOIDALI***
1 **CHILI, SEEDED AND SLICED INTO RINGS**
2 CUPS **PASSATA (BOTTLED STRAINED PUREED TOMATOES)**
5 OUNCES **DRAINED BROILED RED AND YELLOW PEPPERS SLICES IN OIL**

5 OUNCES **BUFFALO MOZZARELLA, TORN INTO PIECES**
5 TABLESPOONS **TORN BASIL LEAVES**
**SALT AND FRESHLY GROUND BLACK PEPPER**
9 OUNCES **WELL-FLAVORED ITALIAN (OR FRENCH) SAUSAGES, SKINS REMOVED**

1   Heat the oven to 400°F.
2   Cook and drain the pasta according to the package directions, but cooking it 1 to 2 minutes less than specified. Reserve about 4 tablespoons of the cooking water.
3   Stir the reserved cooking water into the passata, then slowly combine with the pasta, peppers, cheese, basil, and seasoning.
4   Using damp hands, form the sausagemeat into 12 golf ball-size balls. Gently stir into the pasta. Transfer to a large gratin dish and bake in the heated oven 25 to 30 minutes until the sausage balls are cooked and the cheese is bubbling.

*   Penne rigate can also be used.

# 189
# strozzapreti with sausages, onions, & bell peppers

PREPARATION TIME 10 minutes COOKING TIME 35 minutes SERVES 4 to 6

14 OUNCES **WELL-FLAVORED ITALIAN (OR FRENCH) SAUSAGES**
1 **LARGE ONION, HALVED LENGTHWAYS AND SLICED**
**VIRGIN OLIVE OIL**

2 EACH **RED AND YELLOW BELL PEPPERS, BROILED, PEELED, AND SLICED (SEE PAGE 67)**
**SALT AND FRESHLY GROUND BLACK PEPPER**
14 OUNCES **STROZZAPRETI**
2 TABLESPOONS **SHREDDED BASIL**

1   Heat the oven to 350°F.
2   Put the sausages into a shallow baking dish, pour a little water around them, and bake in the heated oven 25 minutes.
3   Meanwhile, fry the onion in some oil until soft and brown. Stir in the peppers and seasoning; remove from the heat.
4   Slice the sausages while they are still in the dish, using a knife and fork or scissors. Stir in the onion and peppers and return to the oven 10 minutes.
5   During this time, cook and drain the pasta according to the package directions. Toss with the sausage mixture and the basil.

## 190
# orecchiette with cauliflower, chorizo, & black olives

PREPARATION TIME 10 minutes COOKING TIME 10 minutes SERVES 4

14 OUNCES **ORECCHIETTE**
1 **SMALL TO MEDIUM CAULIFLOWER, DIVIDED**
   **INTO FLOWERETS**
1 **ONION, CHOPPED**

7-OUNCE **PIECE OF CHORIZO, CHOPPED**
**OLIVE OIL**
24 **OIL-CURED PITTED BLACK OLIVES, HALVED**
**CHOPPED FLAT-LEAF PARSLEY, TO SERVE**

1   Cook and drain the pasta according to the package directions.
2   Meanwhile, boil the cauliflower until just tender. Drain, reserving about ½ cup of the cooking water. About 1 minute before the pasta is cooked, add half of the cauliflower, to warm through.
3   While the cauliflower is cooking, fry the onion and chorizo in a little olive oil until the onion is soft and transparent. Stir in the remaining cauliflower 2 to 3 minutes. Toss with the pasta and olives and add enough reserved cooking water, if necessary, to moisten. Serve sprinkled with parsley.

## 191

# tagliatelle with prosciutto, peas, & lemon

PREPARATION TIME 10 minutes COOKING TIME 10 minutes SERVES 4

10 ounces **TAGLIATELLE**
2 **SHALLOTS, FINELY CHOPPED**
**SMALL KNOB OF UNSALTED BUTTER**
1 cup **SHELLED FRESH, OR FROZEN, PEAS**
¾ cup **CRÈME FRAÎCHE**
4 tablespoons **MILK OR LIGHT CREAM**

**FINELY GRATED ZEST AND JUICE OF 1 LEMON, PLUS**
   **EXTRA LEMON ZEST TO SERVE**
3 tablespoons **FRESHLY GRATED PARMESAN**
8 **SLICES OF PROSCIUTTO, CUT INTO STRIPS**
2 tablespoons **SHREDDED BASIL**
**SALT AND FRESHLY GROUND BLACK PEPPER**
**PARMESAN SHAVINGS, TO SERVE**

1   Cook and drain the pasta according to the package directions.
2   Meanwhile, soften the shallots in the butter, without browning. Add the peas, crème fraîche, milk or cream, and lemon zest and juice and heat through slowly.
3   Toss with the pasta, Parmesan, prosciutto, basil, and seasoning, using not too much salt but plenty of black pepper. Sprinkle with lemon zest and serve topped with Parmesan shavings.

## 192

# mediterranean chicken & pasta al forno

PREPARATION TIME 15 minutes COOKING TIME 1 hour SERVES 4

12 ounces **SKINLESS, BONELESS CHICKEN THIGHS,**
   **THICKLY SLICED ACROSS**
**VIRGIN OLIVE OIL**
1 **SMALL ONION, CHOPPED**
2 **GARLIC CLOVES, FINELY CHOPPED**
1 tablespoon **THYME LEAVES**
¼ cup **DRY WHITE VERMOUTH**
1 CAN (15-oz.) **CRUSHED PLUM TOMATOES**
1¼ cups **PASSATA (STRAINED PUREED TOMATOES)**
2 tablespoons **SUN-DRIED TOMATO PASTE**

**SALT AND FRESHLY GROUND BLACK PEPPER**
¾ cup **RICOTTA**
5 tablespoons **PESTO (SEE PAGE 18)**
4 ounces **CONCHIGLIE***
⅓ cup **PITTED BLACK OLIVES**

### WHITE SAUCE

2 tablespoons **UNSALTED BUTTER,**
3 tablespoons **ALL-PURPOSE FLOUR**
1¾ cups **MILK**

1   Fry the chicken thighs in a little oil, turning frequently, until just cooked; take care not to overcook. Remove with a slotted spoon.
2   Fry the onion in the oil until soft, then add the garlic and thyme and fry 2 minutes. Pour in the vermouth and bubble a couple of minutes or so, then add the tomatoes, passata, and sun-dried tomato paste. Simmer 15 to 20 minutes until reduced by about one third; season.
3   Meanwhile, make the simple white sauce (see page 17), and leave to simmer gently 10 to 15 minutes. Off the heat, whisk the ricotta and pesto into the white sauce.
4   Heat the oven to 400°F.
5   While the sauce is cooking, cook and drain the pasta according to package directions but for 1½ minutes less than usual. Combine with the chicken, olives, and tomato sauce. Transfer to a large, shallow baking dish. Spoon the white sauce over and bake in the oven about 30 minutes until golden.
   Leave to stand 5 minutes before serving.

\*   Other pasta shapes such as farfalle, fusilli, or macaroni can also be used.

## 193
# vermicelli, chorizo, & mozzarella torta

PREPARATION TIME 5 minutes  COOKING TIME 20 minutes  SERVES 4

10 OUNCES **VERMICELLI**
3–4 TABLESPOONS **OLIVE OIL**
7 OUNCES **BUFFALO MOZZARELLA, VERY THINLY SLICED**
8–12 **BASIL LEAVES**
4 OUNCES **CHORIZO, VERY FINELY SLICED**
**PINCH OF CHILI FLAKES**

**SALT AND FRESHLY GROUND BLACK PEPPER**
**3 EXTRA-LARGE EGGS, BEATEN**
**BROILED RED PEPPERS (SEE PAGE 67),**
   **TO SERVE (OPTIONAL)**

1  Cook and drain the vermicelli according to the package directions. Rinse under running cold water and leave to cool.

2  Pour a little oil into a large skillet, preferably nonstick, and spread an even layer of half the vermicelli on the bottom. Top with the mozzarella, basil leaves, chorizo, and then the remaining vermicelli.

3  Season the eggs and add the chili flakes. Pour over the vermicelli in the pan, prodding the pasta with a fork to allow the eggs to seep through to the bottom. Cook over medium heat 8 minutes until the underneath is golden.

4  Put a large plate over the top. Flip the pan over so the torta falls on to the plate. Add a little more oil to the pan and slide the torta back in. Cook 5 to 6 minutes longer until the other side is golden. Flip out of the pan on to a warm serving plate. Serve in large wedges, accompanied by broiled peppers, if liked.

# penne rigate with sausages al forno

PREPARATION TIME 10 minutes COOKING TIME 30 minutes SERVES 4 to 6

12 OUNCES LAGUENGA OR OTHER FRESH
  ITALIAN SAUSAGES
OLIVE OIL
1 ONION, FINELY CHOPPED
2 GARLIC CLOVES, CHOPPED
½ CUP MEDIUM-BODIED DRY WHITE WINE
2 CANS (15-oz.) CRUSHED TOMATOES
6 SUN-DRIED TOMATOES IN OIL, DRAINED AND SLICED

12 PITTED BLACK OLIVES, SLICED
2 TABLESPOONS CHOPPED FRESH OREGANO
2 TABLESPOONS CHOPPED FLAT-LEAF PARSLEY
SALT AND FRESHLY GROUND BLACK PEPPER
14 OUNCES PENNE RIGATE
1½ CUPS GRATED MOZZARELLA
½ CUP SHAVED PARMESAN

1   Heat the oven to 400°F.
2   Fry the sausages in a little oil in a large skillet until light brown; remove and slice.
3   Fry the onion and garlic in the pan until soft and lightly colored. Pour in the wine and bubble until reduced by about two-thirds, then stir in the tomatoes. Add the sausage slices, sun-dried tomatoes, and olives and cook, uncovered, about 15 minutes until just lightly reduced. Add the herbs and seasoning.
4   Meanwhile, cook the pasta according to the package directions but about 2 minutes less than specifed, then drain.
5   Tip the pasta into a large, greased baking dish and stir in the tomato mixture. Scatter the mozzarella over and then the Parmesan. Bake in the heated oven about 15 minutes until bubbling. Leave to stand 5 minutes before serving.

# tonnarelli with meatballs & broiled tomato sauce

PREPARATION TIME 15 minutes*, plus 30 minutes chiling COOKING TIME 10 minutes* SERVES 4

3 SLICES CRUSTLESS BREAD, CRUMBLED
2 TABLESPOONS MILK
8 OUNCES GROUND PORK
¾ CUP FINELY CHOPPED MORTADELLA
1 GARLIC CLOVE, FINELY CHOPPED
2 TABLESPOONS FINELY CHOPPED FLAT-LEAF PARSLEY
1 EGG, BEATEN

2 TABLESPOONS FRESHLY GRATED PARMESAN, PLUS
  EXTRA TO SERVE
SALT AND FRESHLY GROUND BLACK PEPPER
OLIVE OIL
14 OUNCES TONNARELLI**
1 QUANTITY BROILED TOMATO SAUCE (SEE PAGE 18),
  WARM

1   Soak the bread in the milk for a few minutes until it is no longer dry. Combine with the pork, mortadella, garlic, parsley, egg, Parmesan, and seasoning. With wet hands, break off walnut-size pieces and roll into balls. Cover and chill 30 minutes to firm up.
2   Fry the balls in batches in a large skillet in a little oil 4 to 5 minutes per batch, until brown and crisp, turning the balls over a couple of times.
3   Meanwhile, cook and drain the pasta according to the package directions. Toss with the meatballs and warmed sauce. Serve sprinkled with Parmesan.

\*   Assumes sauce is already made.
\*\*  Bucatini, spaghetti, or bigoli can also be used.

## 196
# light tagliatelle alla bolognese

PREPARATION TIME 5 minutes COOKING TIME 40 to 50 minutes SERVES 4

I LARGE ONION, CHOPPED
OLIVE OIL
2 GARLIC CLOVES, CHOPPED
8 OUNCES LEAN GROUND BEEF
HEAPED ½ CUP RED LENTILS
2 CUPS BEEF OR VEGETABLE STOCK
I CAN (15-oz.) CRUSHED TOMATOES

2–3 TABLESPOONS SUN-DRIED TOMATO PASTE
1–1½ TABLESPOONS DIJON MUSTARD
2–3 TEASPOONS HERBES DE PROVENCE
SALT AND FRESHLY GROUND BLACK PEPPER
9 OUNCES TAGLIATELLE
FRESHLY GRATED PARMESAN, TO SERVE (OPTIONAL)

1   Fry the onion in a little oil in a heavy skillet or flameproof casserole until soft and golden, adding the garlic the final 2 minutes of cooking.
2   Stir in the meat to break it up and cook, stirring occasionally, until it changes color. Add the lentils, stock, tomatoes, tomato paste, mustard, herbs, and seasoning. Heat just to simmering point, then cook very slowly 30 to 40 minutes until the beef is tender. Add a little more liquid if it becomes too dry.
3   About 10 minutes before the sauce is ready, cook and drain the tagliatelle, according to the package directions. Toss lightly with the sauce and serve with freshly grated Parmesan, if liked.

## 197
# spiced chicken tortellini

PREPARATION TIME 55 to 65 minutes COOKING TIME 15 to 20 minutes SERVES 4

5 OUNCES SKINLESS CHICKEN BREAST, CUT INTO
   ½-INCH PIECES
VIRGIN OLIVE OIL
2 OUNCES SPICY SALAMI, FINELY CHOPPED
⅔ CUP RICOTTA
I EGG YOLK

½ CUP FRESHLY GRATED PARMESAN
SALT AND FRESHLY GROUND BLACK PEPPER
2-EGG QUANTITY PASTA DOUGH (SEE PAGE 10)
¾ CUP LIGHT CREAM
2–3 TEASPOONS PESTO (SEE PAGE 18), TO TASTE

1   Cook the chicken in a little oil over fairly low heat, stirring, until just cooked through. Using a slotted spoon, transfer to paper towels to drain.
2   Chop the chicken finely in a food processor using the pulse button; do not reduce to a paste. Tip into a bowl and mix with the salami, ricotta, egg yolk, Parmesan, and seasoning.
3   Make tortellini with the pasta dough and filling (see page 11). Bring a large saucepan of water to a boil for cooking the tortellini.
4   Meanwhile, warm the cream and pesto, to taste, in a small pan over a low heat.
5   Cook the tortellini, in batches, if necessary, in gently simmering water 4 to 5 minutes. Drain well and serve with the pesto sauce.

## 198
# penne with chicken, leeks, & gorgonzola

PREPARATION TIME 10 minutes COOKING TIME 15 minutes SERVES 4

SCANT I CUP THINLY SLICED SLIM LEEKS

2 GARLIC CLOVES, FINELY CHOPPED

SMALL KNOB OF UNSALTED BUTTER

2 SKINLESS CHICKEN BREAST HALVES, CUT ACROSS
   INTO THIN STRIPS

⅔ CUP MEDIUM-BODIED DRY WHITE WINE

⅔ CUP CRÈME FRAÎCHE

SALT AND FRESHLY GROUND BLACK PEPPER

14 OUNCES PENNE

⅔ CUP DICED GORGONZOLA

FRESHLY GRATED PARMESAN, TO SERVE

1   Fry the leeks and garlic in the butter until soft. Add the chicken and continue cooking, stirring
    occasionally, until the chicken changes color.
2   Pour in the wine and boil until reduced by half, then add the crème fraîche and bubble until slightly
    thickened; season.
3   Meanwhile, cook and drain the penne according to the package directions. Toss with the Gorgonzola and
    sauce; return to a low heat if the cheese does not start to melt. Serve with freshly grated Parmesan.

## 199
# bigoli with lamb, tomatoes, & olives

PREPARATION TIME 10 minutes COOKING TIME 25 minutes SERVES 4

10 OUNCES LEAN LAMB, SUCH AS END OF LEG, CUT
   ACROSS INTO ½-INCH-WIDE STRIPS

VIRGIN OLIVE OIL

2 GARLIC CLOVES, FINELY CHOPPED

I TEASPOON DRIED OREGANO

I CAN (15-oz.) CRUSHED TOMATOES

10 PITTED KALAMATA OLIVES, CHOPPED

2 TABLESPOONS CAPERS

2 TABLESPOONS CHOPPED FLAT-LEAF PARSLEY

SALT AND FRESHLY GROUND BLACK PEPPER

14 OUNCES BIGOLI*

1   Fry the lamb in a little olive oil in a large skillet 3 to 4 minutes until evenly brown, adding the garlic
    and oregano the last 1½ to 2 minutes.
2   Stir in the tomatoes, olives, and capers. Heat until just simmering, then simmer very slowly about
    15 minutes, stirring occasionally, until the sauce thickens slightly and the lamb is tender.
    Add the parsley and seasoning.
3   Meanwhile, cook and drain the pasta according to the package directions.
    Toss with the sauce.

*   Penne can also be used.

## 200
# chicken & leek lasagne

PREPARATION TIME 10 minutes COOKING TIME 1 hour SERVES 6 to 8

1 QUART **GOOD CHICKEN STOCK**
⅔ CUP **DRY WHITE VERMOUTH**
1 POUND **BONELESS, SKINLESS CHICKEN LEGS**
   (OR BREASTS, IF PREFERRED)
**BOUQUET GARNI OF 3 THYME SPRIGS,**
   **1 BAY LEAF TORN ACROSS, AND 2 SAGE LEAVES**
7 OUNCES **SPINACH LASAGNE**
2 CUPS **THICKLY SLICED LEEKS**
2 **GARLIC CLOVES, FINELY CHOPPED**

⅓ CUP **UNSALTED BUTTER**
⅓ CUP **ALL-PURPOSE FLOUR**
¼ CUP **FRESHLY GRATED PARMESAN**
1¼ CUPS **GRATED FONTINA**
⅓ CUP **RICOTTA**
⅔ CUP **LIGHT CREAM**
**SALT AND FRESHLY GROUND BLACK PEPPER**
3 TABLESPOONS **PINE NUTS**

1   Combine the stock and vermouth. Poach the chicken legs in the stock-vermouth mixture with the bouquet garni in a covered pan about 10 minutes, until lightly cooked. Lift out with a slotted spoon and cut into bite-size pieces; reserve the liquid and bouquet garni.
2   Cook the lasagne, even if using the no-precook type (see page 15), and spread on a dish towel to dry.
3   Heat the oven to 400°F.
4   Meanwhile, fry the leeks and garlic in 4 tablespoons of the butter, over fairly low heat until tender and pale gold in color; remove with a slotted spoon.
5   Add the remaining butter to the pan and make a simple white sauce (see page 17) with the flour and reserved liquid; discard the bouquet garni. Off the heat, whisk in two-thirds of the Parmesan, three-quarters of the fontina, the ricotta, and the cream. Season, using plenty of black pepper.
6   Spoon a little of the sauce into a large shallow baking dish. Cover with a layer of lasagne, followed by chicken, leeks, a sprinkling of Parmesan, and then sauce. Continue layering to finish with lasagne, sauce, and the last of the Parmesan and fontina. Sprinkle the pine nuts over. Bake in the heated oven about 35 minutes until golden. Leave to stand 10 minutes before serving.

## 201
# cavatappi with pancetta, bell peppers, & tomatoes

PREPARATION TIME 10 minutes COOKING TIME 15 minutes SERVES 4

1 **ONION, FINELY CHOPPED**
**VIRGIN OLIVE OIL**
3 OUNCES **PANCETTA, CUT INTO STRIPS**
1 **GARLIC CLOVE, FINELY CHOPPED**
**PINCH OF CHILI FLAKES**
1 TEASPOON **OREGANO**
4 TABLESPOONS **CHOPPED FLAT-LEAF PARSLEY**

1 **LARGE RED BELL PEPPER, SLICED**
1½ CUPS **SEEDED AND CHOPPED WELL-FLAVORED**
   **PLUM TOMATOES, PEELED**
2 TABLESPOONS **CAPERS**
⅓ CUP **QUARTERED PITTED GREEN OLIVES**
12 OUNCES **CAVATAPPI**
½ CUP **FRESHLY GRATED PARMESAN**

1   Fry the onion in a little oil until soft and golden. Add the pancetta, garlic, chili, oregano, and half the parsley, then cook until the pancetta is crisp but not brown.
2   Add the pepper and cook 5 to 6 minutes until tender, then add the tomatoes and cook 5 minutes longer, stirring occasionally, until they are no longer watery. Stir in the remaining parsley, the capers, and olives.
3   Meanwhile, cook and drain the pasta according to the package directions. Toss with the Parmesan and vegetable sauce.

# 202
# chicken-stuffed pasta shells

PREPARATION TIME 15 minutes COOKING TIME 35 minutes SERVES 4

3¼ CUPS **SLICED CREMINI MUSHROOMS**
1 **ONION, FINELY CHOPPED**
1½ CUPS **FINELY CHOPPED ZUCCHINI**
1 **RED BELL PEPPER, FINELY CHOPPED**
4 OUNCES **SKINLESS CHICKEN BREAST HALF,**
   **FINELY CHOPPED**
¼ CUP **FRESH BREAD CRUMBS**
2 TABLESPOONS **CHOPPED FLAT-LEAF PARSLEY**
**SALT AND FRESHLY GROUND BLACK PEPPER**
3 TABLESPOONS **CHICKEN STOCK**
16 **LARGE PASTA SHELLS, ABOUT 2¼ INCHES LONG**

**RED BELL PEPPER AND TOMATO SAUCE**
2 **LARGE RED BELL PEPPERS (ABOUT 8 OUNCES EACH)**
1 **GARLIC CLOVE, CHOPPED**
2 **SCALLIONS, CHOPPED**
1 CUP **SEEDED AND CHOPPED WELL-FLAVORED**
   **TOMATOES**
**LEAVES FROM A SMALL BUNCH OF BASIL, SHREDDED**

1   Fry the mushrooms, onion, zucchini, and pepper in a little oil over medium heat, stirring occasionally, until soft. Mix in the chicken and cook 5 minutes longer. Add the bread crumbs, parsley, and seasoning, and moisten with chicken stock. Bring to a boil and set aside.
2   Cook the pasta shells according to package directions but for 1 minute less than specified, and drain well.
3   Meanwhile, make the sauce by cooking the peppers, garlic, scallions and tomatoes 15 to 20 minutes until thick; puree until almost smooth. Add the basil and seasoning.
4   Heat the oven to 425°F.
5   Fill the pasta shells with the chicken mixture and arrange in a single layer in a shallow baking dish. Pour the sauce around, cover, and bake in the heated oven 15 minutes or so until heated through.

## 203
# garganelle with chicken & watercress sauce

PREPARATION TIME 10 minutes COOKING TIME 10 minutes SERVES 4

2 SHALLOTS, FINELY CHOPPED

2 CUPS BONELESS CHICKEN CUT INTO ½-INCH STRIPS

VIRGIN OLIVE OIL

LEAVES FROM A BUNCH OF MIXED HERBS, CHOPPED

3–4 TABLESPOONS BALSAMIC VINEGAR, TO TASTE

SALT AND FRESHLY GROUND BLACK PEPPER

14 OUNCES GARGANELLE

6 OUNCES WATERCRESS, COARSE STEMS DISCARDED

1 GARLIC CLOVE, CHOPPED

JUICE OF ½ LEMON

3 TOMATOES, SEEDED AND CHOPPED

1   Fry the shallots and chicken in a little olive oil in a large nonstick skillet 3 to 4 minutes. Add the herbs and balsamic vinegar and cook 2 to 3 minutes, stirring, until the chicken is cooked through and flecked in pale gold; season.

2   Meanwhile, cook and drain the pasta according to the package directions, reserving ½ cup of the cooking water.

3   While the pasta is cooking, blanch the watercress in boiling water 30 seconds. Drain well and puree with the garlic and 4 tablespoons virgin olive oil. Season and add lemon juice to taste.

4   Shortly before the pasta is ready, add the tomatoes to the chicken and heat slowly. Toss with the pasta and watercress sauce. Add some of the reserved cooking water, to moisten, if necessary.

## 204
# bucatini with sausages & pancetta

PREPARATION TIME 10 minutes COOKING TIME 25 minutes SERVES 4

4 ounces CHOPPED PANCETTA
OLIVE OIL
I ONION, CHOPPED
I FLESHY RED BELL PEPPER, CHOPPED
2 GARLIC CLOVES, CHOPPED
6 ounces TASTY FRESH ITALIAN (OR FRENCH)
  SAUSAGES, SKINNED AND CRUMBLED

I CAN (15-oz.) CRUSHED PLUM TOMATOES
2 TABLESPOONS CHOPPED MIXED PARSLEY, SAGE, AND
  THYME, PLUS EXTRA TO SERVE
14 ounces BUCATINI
FRESHLY GRATED PARMESAN, TO SERVE

I   Fry the pancetta in a little oil until brown. Remove with a slotted spoon and drain on paper towels.
2   Fry the onion in the oil until beginning to color, adding the red bell pepper toward the end. Stir in the garlic for I minute, then add the sausagemeat, stirring to break it up. Cook, stirring, 3 to 4 minutes, then add the tomatoes, pancetta, and herbs. Simmer slowly, stirring occasionally, about 15 minutes until lightly thickened.
3   Meanwhile, cook and drain the pasta according to the package directions. Toss the pasta with the sauce and serve with the Parmesan.

## 205
# tagliatelle with bresaola, peas, & leeks

PREPARATION TIME 10 minutes COOKING TIME 10 minutes SERVES 4

14 ounces TAGLIATELLE
I SMALL LEEK, HALVED LENGTHWISE, THEN THINLY
  SLICED
SMALL KNOB OF UNSALTED BUTTER
1½ cups SMALL FROZEN PEAS, THAWED

4 ounces BRESAOLA SLICES, CUT ACROSS INTO STRIPS
SALT AND FRESHLY GROUND BLACK PEPPER
4 TABLESPOONS FRESHLY GRATED PARMESAN, PLUS
  EXTRA TO SERVE

I   Cook and drain the pasta according to the package directions, reserving ½ cup of the cooking water.
2   Meanwhile fry the leek in the butter until soft. Add the peas and bresaola and cook about 2 minutes, until warmed through; season, using plenty of pepper. Toss with the pasta and Parmesan, adding reserved water as necessary. Serve with additional Parmesan.

## 206
# taglioni with prosciutto, peas, & parsley

PREPARATION TIME 10 minutes COOKING TIME 15 minutes SERVES 4

14 ounces TAGLIONI
HEAPED I cup FROZEN PEAS
4 SLICES PROSCIUTTO, CUT ACROSS INTO STRIPS
5 TABLESPOONS UNSALTED BUTTER, DICED

2 TABLESPOONS FINELY CHOPPED FLAT-LEAF PARSLEY
½ cup FRESHLY GRATED PARMESAN
SALT AND FRESHLY GROUND BLACK PEPPER

I   Cook and drain the pasta according to the package directions, adding the peas the last 2 to 3 minutes.
2   Toss with the prosciutto, butter, parsley, most of the Parmesan, and seasoning. Serve with the remaining Parmesan.

## 207
# conchiglie with chicken, cherry tomato, & herb sauce

PREPARATION TIME 10 minutes, plus 1 hour marinating COOKING TIME 20 minutes SERVES 4

12 ounces SKINLESS CHICKEN, CUT INTO
 BITE-SIZE PIECES
4 tablespoons DRY ITALIAN VERMOUTH
1 teaspoon FINELY CHOPPED ROSEMARY
LEAVES FROM 3 SPRIGS OF THYME
SALT AND FRESHLY GROUND BLACK PEPPER
1 ONION, FINELY CHOPPED

⅓ cup CHOPPED SALAMI
OLIVE OIL
1 CAN (14-oz.) CHERRY TOMATOES
1 tablespoon BALSAMIC VINEGAR
PINCH OF CHILI FLAKES
10 ounces CONCHIGLIE
FRESHLY GRATED PARMESAN, TO SERVE (OPTIONAL)

1   Stir the chicken with the vermouth, herbs, and black pepper; cover and set aside 1 hour.
2   Fry the onion and salami in a little oil until the onion is tender and pale gold. Scoop the chicken from the vermouth and fry quickly, stirring, until the color changes. Stir in the vermouth, tomatoes, vinegar, and chili flakes. Simmer slowly about 15 minutes until the chicken is cooked through and the sauce slightly thickened; season.
3   About 10 minutes before the chicken is done, cook and drain the pasta according to the package directions. Toss with the sauce and serve with a little freshly grated Parmesan, if liked.

## 208
# pasta with pork, spinach, & lemon

PREPARATION TIME 10 minutes COOKING TIME 15 minutes SERVES 4

14 ounces PORK TENDERLOIN
VIRGIN OLIVE OIL
2 GARLIC CLOVES, FINELY CHOPPED
1¼ cups MEDIUM-BODIED DRY WHITE WINE
1 tablespoon FINELY CHOPPED ROSEMARY
½ cup HEAVY CREAM
1½ pounds BABY SPINACH

14 ounces FRESH PAPPARDELLE
JUICE OF 1½ LARGE OR 2 SMALL LEMONS, TO TASTE
¾ cup FRESHLY GRATED PARMESAN, PLUS EXTRA
 TO SERVE
SALT AND FRESHLY GROUND BLACK PEPPER

1   Cover the pork with plastic wrap and flatten with a meat bat, rolling pin, or the bottom of a heavy pan; cut into thick strips, then fry quickly in a little oil in a large, heavy skillet until brown. Remove and keep warm.
2   Fry the garlic 1 minute, then add the wine and rosemary and boil until reduced by at least half. Pour in the cream and heat through. Return the pork to the pan.
3   Meanwhile, bring a pan of water for the pasta to a boil. Cook the spinach in a large pan, stirring or shaking the pan occasionally, until it wilts and excess water evaporates.
4   Cook and drain the pasta. Toss with the spinach, pork, and cooking juices, the lemon juice, Parmesan, and seasoning. Serve with additional Parmesan.

## 209
# chicken & walnut cannelloni

PREPARATION TIME 15 minutes COOKING TIME 35 minutes SERVES 4

12 CANNELLONI TUBES
6 ounces COOKED SKINLESS CHICKEN, GROUND
½ cup WALNUT HALVES, LIGHTLY TOASTED AND FINELY
  CHOPPED
½ cup RICOTTA
½ cup COTTAGE CHEESE, STRAINED
2–3 teaspoons FINELY CHOPPED FLAT-LEAF PARSLEY
SALT AND FRESHLY GROUND BLACK PEPPER

½ QUANTITY FRESH TOMATO SAUCE (SEE PAGE 18)
  OR WINTER TOMATO SAUCE (SEE PAGE 19)
2 tablespoons FRESHLY GRATED PARMESAN

BÉCHAMEL SAUCE
1½ tablespoons BUTTER
3 tablespoons ALL-PURPOSE FLOUR
1¾ cups MILK

1  Heat the oven to 350°F.
2  Cook and drain the cannelloni tubes according to the package directions.
3  Meanwhile, make the béchamel sauce (see page 17).
4  Combine the chicken with all but 1 tablespoon walnuts, the ricotta, cottage cheese, parsley, and seasoning. Divide between the cannelloni tubes.
5  Spread a little of the tomato sauce in the bottom of a large gratin dish. Lay the filled tubes on top and cover with the remaining sauce. Scatter the Parmesan and reserved walnuts over. Cover and bake in the heated oven 15 minutes, then uncover and bake 20 minutes longer until the top is browned.

## 210
# chicken & spinach pasticcio

PREPARATION TIME 15 minutes COOKING TIME 45 minutes SERVES 4 to 6

18 ounces SPINACH
4 ounces TAGLIATELLE
18 ounces BONELESS SKINLESS CHICKEN LEGS, VERY
  FINELY CHOPPED
OLIVE OIL
2 PLUMP GARLIC CLOVES, CHOPPED
PINCH OF CHILI FLAKES

1½ tablespoons SUN-DRIED TOMATO PASTE
¾ cup FRESHLY GRATED PARMESAN

BÉCHAMEL SAUCE
1½ tablespoons UNSALTED BUTTER
3 tablespoons ALL-PURPOSE FLOUR
1½ cups MILK

1  Heat the oven to 400°F.
2  Cook the spinach in a covered pan until wilted, shaking the pan occasionally; drain and squeeze out surplus moisture.
3  Meanwhile, cook and drain the pasta according to the package directions, but for 1 minute less than the recommended time.
4  While the pasta is cooking, fry the chicken in a little oil 2 to 3 minutes. Add the garlic and chili flakes and fry 2 minutes longer, stirring in the tomato paste just before the end. Spoon evenly into a large, shallow baking dish. Cover with the spinach.
5  While the chicken is cooking, make the béchamel sauce (see page 17). Gently combine with the pasta and pour over the spinach. Sprinkle the cheese over the top and bake in the heated oven 20 to 25 minutes until golden brown. Leave to stand 5 minutes before serving.

## 211
# lumache with prosciutto, arugula, & capers

PREPARATION TIME 10 minutes COOKING TIME 10 to 15 minutes SERVES 4

14 ounces LUMACHE

2 SHALLOTS, FINELY CHOPPED

2 GARLIC CLOVES, FINELY CHOPPED

LEAVES FROM 2 SMALL SPRIGS OF SAGE, FINELY SHREDDED

OLIVE OIL

4 ounces PROSCIUTTO, CUT ACROSS INTO STRIPS

1 CAN (14-oz.)CHERRY TOMATOES

1 CAN (15-oz.) GARBANZO BEANS, DRAINED AND RINSED

FRESHLY GROUND BLACK PEPPER

2 HANDFULS OF YOUNG ARUGULA

⅓ cup CRUMBLED FETA

1   Cook and drain the lumache according to the package directions.

2   Meanwhile, fry the shallots, garlic, and sage in a little oil about 4 minutes until the shallots are soft and translucent. Add the prosciutto halfway through the cooking.

3   Add the tomatoes and garbanzo beans, bring to a boil, then simmer about 10 minutes until the sauce thickens slightly. Season with black pepper (the salt in the prosciutto and feta should make extra salt unnecessary). Toss with the pasta, arugula, and feta.

## 212
# strappiozi with sausages, mixed bell peppers, & tomatoes

PREPARATION TIME 10 minutes COOKING TIME 10 minutes SERVES 4

6 ounces GOOD-QUALITY FRESH ITALIAN (OR FRENCH) SAUSAGES, CUT INTO ½-INCH SLICES

VIRGIN OLIVE OIL

1 SMALL ONION, THINLY SLICED

1 PLUMP RED BELL PEPPER, SLICED

1 PLUMP YELLOW OR ORANGE BELL PEPPER, SLICED

2 LARGE, RIPE WELL-FLAVORED TOMATOES, SEEDED AND CHOPPED

SALT AND FRESHLY GROUND BLACK PEPPER

14 ounces STRAPPIOZI

2 tablespoons FRESHLY GRATED PARMESAN, PLUS EXTRA TO SERVE

1   Fry the sausages in a little oil until brown; transfer to paper towels to drain. Fry the onion in the oil until pale golden brown. Add the peppers and cook until soft but not colored.

2   At the same time, in another pan, cook the tomatoes in a little oil about 10 minutes. Add to the peppers, with the sausages, and cook together, stirring frequently, 1 minute; season.

3   Meanwhile, cook and drain the pasta according to the package directions. Toss with the sausage sauce and Parmesan and serve with additional Parmesan.

## 213
# agnolotti with asparagus & prosciutto

PREPARATION TIME 5 minutes COOKING TIME 15 minutes SERVES 6

1½ POUNDS ASPARAGUS
½ CUP CRÈME FRAÎCHE
SALT AND FRESHLY GROUND BLACK PEPPER
2 SHALLOTS, FINELY CHOPPED
1 TABLESPOON UNSALTED BUTTER

3 OUNCES PROSCIUTTO, CUT ACROSS INTO STRIPS
1 QUANTITY HERB AND CHEESE AGNOLOTTI (SEE
   PAGE 12), OR BOUGHT FILLED PASTA SHAPE
FRESH SHAVINGS OF PARMESAN, TO SERVE

1   Cut off the asparagus tips and reserve. Cook the remaining stems in boiling water until just tender.
    Drain well, pat dry, and puree with a little of the crème fraîche, then mix in the remaining crème
    fraîche and season.
2   Fry the shallots in the butter until soft but not colored. Add the prosciutto for a couple of minutes, then
    stir in the asparagus puree and warm through very gently.
3   Cook the agnolotti, in batches if necessary, in simmering water, adding the asparagus tips for the final
    2 to 3 minutes. Drain well and combine with the asparagus purée. Serve sprinkled with Parmesan.

## 214
# conchiglie with broccoli, walnuts, & pancetta

PREPARATION TIME 10 minutes COOKING TIME 15 minutes SERVES 4

1 POUND BROCCOLI FLORETTES
12 OUNCES CONCHIGLIE
7 OUNCES PANCETTA, SLICED ACROSS
VIRGIN OLIVE OIL
2 PLUMP GARLIC CLOVES, CHOPPED

SCANT ½ CUP LIGHTLY TOASTED AND CHOPPED
   WALNUT HALVES
SALT AND FRESHLY GROUND BLACK PEPPER
FRESHLY GRATED PARMESAN, TO SERVE

1   Bring enough water to a boil for cooking the pasta. Add the broccoli and boil 3 to 4 minutes until
    just tender; remove with a slotted spoon. Cook the pasta in the water according to the package directions.
2   Meanwhile, fry the pancetta in a little oil until crisp. Add the garlic and cook 1 minute, then stir in the
    broccoli, walnuts, and seasoning. Stir slowly 2 to 3 minutes to warm through.
3   Drain the pasta, reserving some of the cooking water. Toss the pasta with the broccoli sauce and enough
    cooking water to moisten. Sprinkle some freshly grated Parmesan over and serve with extra Parmesan.

## 215
# campanelli with chicken, prosciutto, & basil

PREPARATION TIME 10 minutes COOKING TIME 15 minutes SERVES 4

4 SKINLESS CHICKEN BREAST HALVES, THINLY SLICED ACROSS THE GRAIN

VIRGIN OLIVE OIL

6 OUNCES PROSCIUTTO SLICES, SLICED ACROSS

⅔ CUP MEDIUM-BODIED DRY WHITE WINE

⅔ CUP CHICKEN STOCK

⅔ CUP HEAVY CREAM

12 OUNCES CAMPANELLI

1½–2 TABLESPOONS LEMON JUICE

3 TABLESPOONS SHREDDED BASIL

SALT AND FRESHLY GROUND BLACK PEPPER

1   Stir-fry the chicken in 2 batches in a little oil until just cooked through; do not overcrowd the pan or overcook; remove with a slotted spoon.
2   Fry the prosciutto in the oil 2 to 3 minutes; remove. Pour the wine and stock into the pan and boil until reduced by half. Add the cream and simmer until syrupy.
3   Meanwhile, cook and drain the pasta according to the package directions.
4   Return the chicken and prosciutto to the pan and add the lemon juice, basil, and seasoning. Warm through slowly. Toss with the pasta and serve.

## 216
# fettuccine with peas, prosciutto, & sage

PREPARATION TIME 10 minutes COOKING TIME 5 minutes SERVES 4

½ cup LIGHT CREAM
1 EXTRA-LARGE EGG YOLK
1 cup SHELLED FRESH, OR FROZEN PEAS
3–4 OUTER LETTUCE LEAVES, SHREDDED
1 GARLIC CLOVE, FINELY CHOPPED

VIRGIN OLIVE OIL
8–10 SMALL SAGE LEAVES, FINELY SHREDDED
3 SLICES OF PROSCIUTTO, SLICED INTO RIBBONS
18 ounces FRESH FETTUCCINE
SALT AND FRESHLY GROUND BLACK PEPPER

1   Stir the cream into the egg yolk; set aside.
2   Boil the peas until just tender, adding the lettuce leaves immediately before the peas are ready; drain.
3   While the peas are cooking, fry the garlic in about 2 tablespoons oil 1 minute.
    Add the sage and prosciutto and cook 1 minute longer.
4   Meanwhile, cook and drain the pasta. Toss immediately with the egg yolk mixture, the peas
    and lettuce, and seasoning. Serve with the sage and prosciutto scattered over.

## 217
# tagliatelle with peas, prosciutto, & basil

PREPARATION TIME 10 minutes COOKING TIME 10 minutes SERVES 4

14 ounces TAGLIATELLE
1½ cups SHELLED SMALL FRESH PEAS
6 tablespoons UNSALTED BUTTER
4 ounces PROSCIUTTO, CUT ACROSS INTO STRIPS

2 tablespoons SHREDDED BASIL
6 tablespoons FRESHLY GRATED PARMESAN,
    PLUS EXTRA TO SERVE
SALT AND FRESHLY GROUND BLACK PEPPER

1   Cook and drain the pasta according to the package directions.
2   Meanwhile, boil the peas about 5 minutes until just tender. Drain and then fry slowly in the butter with
    the prosciutto 2 to 3 minutes, stirring frequently. Toss with the pasta, basil, cheese, and seasoning.
    Serve with extra Parmesan.

## 218
# pappardelle with lamb & rosemary

PREPARATION TIME 10 minutes, COOKING TIME 15 minutes SERVES 4

9 ounces BONELESS LAMB STEAKS, CUT ACROSS
    INTO 1-inch-wide STRIPS
OLIVE OIL
2 GARLIC CLOVES, CRUSHED
3½ cups SLICED CREMINI MUSHROOMS
1 teaspoon FINELY CHOPPED ROSEMARY

½ cup MEDIUM-BODIED DRY WHITE WINE
6 tablespoons HEAVY CREAM
SALT AND FRESHLY GROUND BLACK PEPPER
14 ounces PAPPARDELLE
FINELY GRATED LEMON ZEST AND CHOPPED
    FLAT-LEAF PARSLEY, TO SERVE

1   Fry the lamb in a little oil in a large skillet, stirring frequently, until sealed on the outside. Add the garlic,
    mushrooms, and rosemary and cook, stirring, until the mushrooms are tender. Pour in the wine and
    bubble until reduced by two-thirds. Stir in the cream; season.
2   Meanwhile, cook and drain the pasta according to the package directions, reserving ½ cup of the cooking
    liquid. Toss with the lamb and mushroom sauce, adding enough reserved pasta liquid to moisten,
    if necessary. Sprinkle with lemon zest and parsley and serve.

## 219
# fusilli with turkey, mortadella, & mozzarella

PREPARATION TIME 10 minutes COOKING TIME 50 minutes SERVES 4

1 ONION, CHOPPED
1 RED BELL PEPPER, CHOPPED
2 cups DICED TURKEY BREAST
4-ounce PIECE OF MORTADELLA, CHOPPED
4 tablespoons MEDIUM-BODIED DRY WHITE WINE
2 GARLIC CLOVES, CRUSHED
1 CAN (15-oz.) CRUSHED TOMATOES

6 SUN-DRIED TOMATOES IN OIL, DRAINED (OIL
  RESERVED) AND SLICED
1 teaspoon DRIED OREGANO
1 teaspoon DRIED THYME
SALT AND FRESHLY GROUND BLACK PEPPER
10 ounces FUSILLI
8 ounces BUFFALO MOZZARELLA, SLICED
2 tablespoons FRESHLY GRATED FONTINA

1  Fry the onion and red pepper in a little of the sun-dried tomato oil in a heavy-bottomed pan until soft.
2  Add the turkey and mortadella and fry, stirring frequently, until the turkey changes color. Pour in the
   wine, add the garlic, all the tomatoes and herbs, heat to just on simmering point, and cook slowly
   about 15 minutes, stirring occasionally, until the turkey is just cooked; do not overcook. Season.
3  Heat the oven to 375°F.
4  Cook the fusilli for 1 minute less than specified. Drain and mix with the sauce. Spread half in a gratin
   dish. Cover with half the mozzarella, followed by the remaining pasta mixture. Top with the rest
   of the mozzarella and the fontina.
5  Bake in the heated oven 20 to 25 minutes until bubbling and the top is brown.
   Leave to stand 5 minutes before serving.

## 220
# lumache with chicken, eggplant, & oregano

PREPARATION TIME 10 minutes COOKING TIME 25 minutes SERVES 4

1 ONION, FINELY CHOPPED
OLIVE OIL
2 GARLIC CLOVES, FINELY CHOPPED
12 ounces CHICKEN BREASTS OR BONELESS LEGS
  OR THIGHS, CUT INTO ½-INCH CUBES
1 SMALL EGGPLANT, CUT INTO ½-INCH CUBES
1 CAN (14-oz.) CHERRY TOMATOES

2 tablespoons SUN-DRIED TOMATO PASTE
12 PITTED KALAMATA OLIVES, HALVED
LEAVES FROM A SMALL BUNCH OF OREGANO,
  CHOPPED
12 ounces LUMACHE*
SALT AND FRESHLY GROUND BLACK PEPPER

1  Fry the onion in a little oil until soft and transparent. Add the garlic and fry 1 minute, then stir in the
   chicken. Cook over fairly high heat, stirring, until turning golden on the outside. Transfer the mixture from
   the pan with a slotted spoon; set aside.
2  Add a little more oil to the pan and fry the eggplant until brown. Add the tomatoes and tomato paste
   and bring to a boil. Lower the heat, return the chicken mixture to the pan with the olives, oregano, and
   seasoning. Cover and simmer about 15 minutes.
3  Meanwhile, cook and drain the pasta according to the package directions. Toss with the chicken sauce.

*  Conchiglie, farfalle, fusilli, or sedani can also be used.

## 221
# tagliatelle with chicken, zucchini, & red bell pepper

PREPARATION TIME 10 minutes COOKING TIME 30 minutes SERVES 4

4 SKINLESS CHICKEN BREAST HALVES, 4–5 OUNCES
    EACH
1 SMALL RED BELL PEPPER, FINELY CHOPPED
2 TABLESPOONS CAPERS
2 TABLESPOONS FINELY CHOPPED MIXED FLAT-LEAF
    PARSLEY, THYME, AND OREGANO
SALT AND FRESHLY GROUND BLACK PEPPER

2 TABLESPOONS VIRGIN OLIVE OIL
2 TABLESPOONS DRY WHITE VERMOUTH
2 SMALL ZUCCHINI, SLICED
14 OUNCES TAGLIATELLE
1½ TABLESPOONS FINELY CHOPPED FLAT-LEAF PARSLEY
FRESHLY GRATED PARMESAN

1    Heat the oven to 375°F.
2    Lay the chicken breasts in a single layer on a piece of foil that is large enough
to enclose them. Scatter the red pepper, capers, herbs, and seasoning over.
Fold up the sides of the foil and pour the oil and vermouth over. Twist the
foil edges tightly together to seal, place on a baking sheet, and bake in
the heated oven 30 minutes until the chicken is cooked through.
3    Meanwhile, fry the zucchini in a little oil until soft and becoming
flecked with brown.
4    About 10 minutes before the chicken is ready, cook and drain
the tagliatelle according to the package directions.
5    Carefully remove the chicken from the foil (keep the cooking juices)
and slice across the grain.
6    Toss the pasta with the chicken and reserved juices, the parsley
and zucchini. Serve accompanied by freshly grated Parmesan.

133

## 222
# macaroni, beef, & beans

PREPARATION TIME 10 minutes COOKING TIME 30 minutes SERVES 4 to 6

I ONION, FINELY CHOPPED
I CARROT, FINELY CHOPPED
OLIVE OIL
3 GARLIC CLOVES, CHOPPED
9 ounces LEAN GROUND BEEF
4 cups BEEF STOCK
BOUQUET GARNI OF 2 SAGE LEAVES, SPRIG OF
   ROSEMARY, AND 2 THYME SPRIGS

I CAN (15-oz.) CRUSHED PLUM TOMATOES
2–3 tablespoons SUN-DRIED TOMATO PASTE
I CAN (14-oz.) BORLOTTI BEANS, DRAINED AND
   RINSED
1½ cups MACARONI
SALT AND FRESHLY GROUND BLACK PEPPER
FRESHLY GRATED PECORINO AND CHOPPED
   FLAT-LEAF PARSLEY, TO SERVE

1  Fry the onion and carrot in a little oil in a large pan until soft. Stir in the garlic and the beef and cook until light brown, stirring to break it up.
2  Pour in the stock, stirring, then add the bouquet garni, tomatoes, tomato paste and beans. Heat until just beginning to simmer, then stir in the macaroni and cook, uncovered, 18 to 20 minutes until the macaroni is tender and the liquid reduced to make a soupy stew.
3  Discard the bouquet garni, season, and serve sprinkled with pecorino and flat-leaf parsley.

## 223
# ravioli with squash & prosciutto

PREPARATION TIME 45 minutes COOKING TIME I hour SERVES 4

2-EGG QUANTITY PASTA DOUGH (SEE PAGE 10)
SMALL KNOB OF UNSALTED BUTTER
LEAVES FROM A SMALL BUNCH OF MIXED HERBS,
   SUCH AS PARSLEY, BASIL, TARRAGON, AND
   OREGANO, CHOPPED
FRESHLY GRATED PARMESAN, TO SERVE

FILLING
I-pound PIECE OF BUTTERNUT SQUASH
VIRGIN OLIVE OIL
2 tablespoons HEAVY CREAM
I EGG YOLK
3 ounces PROSCIUTTO, FINELY CHOPPED
½ cup GRATED PROVOLONE
1½ tablespoons SHREDDED BASIL
1½ tablespoons FINELY CHOPPED FLAT-LEAF PARSLEY
SALT AND FRESHLY GROUND BLACK PEPPER

1  While the pasta dough is resting for 30 minutes, make the filling. Heat the oven to 375°F. Brush the squash flesh with a little oil and bake in the heated oven about I hour until soft. Cool slightly and then scrape the flesh into a bowl, then add the cream and mash with a potato masher or a fork. Mix in the egg yolk, prosciutto, provolone, herbs, and seasoning.
2  Make the ravioli with the dough and filling (see page 11).
3  Cook the ravioli in simmering water, in batches, if necessary, about 4 minutes per batch; drain well.
4  Meanwhile, melt the butter with the herbs. Toss lightly with the ravioli. Serve with Parmesan.

## 224
# gnocchi with chicken ragù

PREPARATION TIME 10 minutes COOKING TIME 25 to 30 minutes SERVES 4

1 RED ONION, FINELY CHOPPED

2 GARLIC CLOVES, FINELY CHOPPED

VIRGIN OLIVE OIL

2 SKINLESS CHICKEN BREAST FILLETS, CUT INTO
BITE-SIZE PIECES

1 RED BELL PEPPER, BROILED, PEELED, AND SLICED
(SEE PAGE 67)

1 YELLOW BELL PEPPER, BROILED, PEELED, AND
SLICED (SEE PAGE 67)

LEAVES FROM 3 SPRIGS OF THYME

1 CAN (15-oz.) CRUSHED PLUM TOMATOES

SCANT ½ CUP RED WINE

HANDFUL OF PITTED GREEN AND BLACK OLIVES

1 TABLESPOON CAPERS

SALT AND FRESHLY GROUND BLACK PEPPER

14 OUNCES GNOCCHI

CHOPPED FLAT-LEAF PARSLEY, TO SERVE

1   Fry the onion and garlic in a little oil until soft and pale gold. Add the chicken, peppers, and thyme and fry quickly, stirring, until the chicken changes color.
2   Stir in the tomatoes and wine and simmer gently about 15 minutes until the chicken is cooked through and the sauce slightly thickened. Add the olives and capers; season.
3   Meanwhile, cook and drain the pasta according to the package directions. Toss with the sauce and sprinkle with plenty of parsley.

## 225
# elicoidali with artichokes, bell peppers, zucchini, & prosciutto

PREPARATION TIME 10 minutes COOKING TIME 45 minutes SERVES 4 to 6

1 CAN (14-oz.) ARTICHOKES, DRAINED

1 PLUMP RED BELL PEPPER, THICKLY SLICED

4 WELL-FLAVORED PLUM TOMATOES, QUARTERED

1 ZUCCHINI, HALVED LENGTHWISE AND SLICED

3 GARLIC CLOVES, THINLY SLICED

SPRIG OF ROSEMARY

3 THYME SPRIGS

SALT AND FRESHLY GROUND BLACK PEPPER

VIRGIN OLIVE OIL

6 SLICES OF PROSCIUTTO, CUT ACROSS INTO STRIPS

2 TABLESPOONS PINE NUTS

12 OUNCES ELICOIDALI*

FRESHLY GRATED PECORINO, TO SERVE

1   Heat the oven to 400°F.
2   Put all the vegetables and herb sprigs into a large roasting pan. Sprinkle seasoning over and trickle with oil. Stir to insure the vegetables are evenly coated. Roast in the heated oven about 45 minutes until the vegetables are soft and are light brown, stirring a couple of times. Add the prosciutto and pine nuts after 20 to 25 minutes.
3   Meanwhile, cook and drain the pasta according to the package directions.
4   Discard the herb sprigs from the roasting pan. Toss the remaining ingredients, including the cooking juices in the pan, with the pasta. Serve with pecorino.

*   Rigatoni or penne can also be used.

## 226
# bucatini with pancetta, tomatoes, olives, & herbs

PREPARATION TIME 10 minutes COOKING TIME 10 minutes SERVES 4

3 ounces PANCETTA, CUT ACROSS INTO STRIPS
OLIVE OIL
2 GARLIC CLOVES, FINELY CHOPPED
1 CAN (15-oz.) CRUSHED PLUM TOMATOES
2 tablespoons MIXED CHOPPED OREGANO, THYME,
  PARSLEY, AND SAGE

12 KALAMATA OLIVES, SLICED OFF THE PITS
SALT AND FRESHLY GROUND BLACK PEPPER
14 ounces BUCATINI
FRESHLY GRATED PARMESAN, TO SERVE

1   Fry the pancetta in a little oil until just golden. Add the garlic and fry 1 to 2 minutes.
    Stir in the tomatoes, herbs, and olives and simmer about 15 minutes until thick; season.
2   Meanwhile, cook and drain the pasta according to the package directions.
    Toss with the sauce and serve with Parmesan.

## 227
# conchiglie with pancetta, peas, & ricotta

PREPARATION TIME 10 minutes COOKING TIME 10 minutes SERVES 4

14 ounces CONCHIGLIE
4 ounces PANCETTA, CUT ACROSS INTO STRIPS
VIRGIN OLIVE OIL
HEAPED 1 cup FROZEN PEAS

⅔ cup CRUMBLED RICOTTA
3 tablespoons FRESHLY GRATED PARMESAN
FRESHLY GROUND BLACK PEPPER

1   Cook and drain the pasta according to the package directions.
2   Meanwhile, fry the pancetta in a little olive oil until light brown and the fat runs, but do not allow it to
    become crisp. Add the peas and cook 1 to 2 minutes, stirring. Toss with the pasta, ricotta,
    Parmesan, and black pepper.

## 228
# tonnarelli with radicchio, rosemary, & prosciutto

PREPARATION TIME 10 minutes COOKING TIME 10 minutes SERVES 4

12 ounces **TONNARELLI**
2 **GARLIC CLOVES, CHOPPED**
**LEAVES FROM A SMALL SPRIG OF ROSEMARY,**
  **FINELY CHOPPED**
**EXTRA-VIRGIN OLIVE OIL**

6 **SLICES OF PROSCIUTTO, SLICED**
1 **LARGE HEAD OF RADICCHIO, SHREDDED**
½ cup **FRESHLY GRATED PARMESAN**
**SALT AND FRESHLY GROUND BLACK PEPPER**

1   Cook and drain the pasta according to the package directions, reserving ½ cup of the cooking water.
2   Meanwhile, fry the garlic and rosemary in a little oil 1 minute. Add half the prosciutto and half the radicchio and fry briskly until beginning to wilt. Toss with the pasta, remaining prosciutto and radicchio, the Parmesan, and seasoning. Add enough of the reserved cooking water to moisten and serve.

## 229
# lumache with pancetta & artichokes

PREPARATION TIME 10 minutes COOKING TIME 10 minutes SERVES 4

14 ounces **LUMACHE**
6 ounces **PANCETTA, CUT ACROSS INTO STRIPS**
2 **GARLIC CLOVES, FINELY CHOPPED**
9½ ounces **BROILED ARTICHOKES IN OIL,**
  **DRAINED AND OIL RESERVED, HALVED**

2½ tablespoons **FLAT-LEAF PARSLEY, FINELY CHOPPED**
**FRESHLY GRATED PARMESAN, TO SERVE**

1   Cook and drain the pasta according to the package directions.
2   Meanwhile, fry the pancetta in 2 tablespoons of the reserved oil until brown. Stir in the garlic 1 minute, then add the artichokes and parsley. Cover and heat slowly, shaking the pan occasionally, until warmed through. Toss with the pasta and serve with the Parmesan.

## 230
# penne with mushrooms
# & frazzled prosciutto

PREPARATION TIME 10 minutes COOKING TIME 10 minutes SERVES 4

6 OUNCES THINLY SLICED PROSCIUTTO
OLIVE OIL
2 SHALLOTS, SLICED
2 GARLIC CLOVES, FINELY CHOPPED
3¼ CUPS SLICED CEPS OR CREMINI MUSHROOMS

3 TABLESPOONS MIXED CHOPPED FLAT-LEAF PARSLEY
    AND TARRAGON
SALT AND FRESHLY GROUND BLACK PEPPER
14 OUNCES PENNE
3 TABLESPOONS CRÈME FRAÎCHE
FRESHLY GRATED PARMESAN, TO SERVE

1   Briefly fry the prosciutto slices in a little oil in a large skillet over high heat; cooking in batches,
    if necessary, so the pan is not crowded; remove and keep warm.
2   Cook the shallots and garlic in the pan until soft but not colored. Add the mushrooms and herbs
    and cook until soft and the liquid evaporates; season.
3   Meanwhile, cook and drain the pasta according to the package directions, reserving ½ cup of the cooking
    water. Toss with the crème fraîche, mushroom mixture, and reserved cooking water to moisten,
    as necessary. Top with the prosciutto and serve with Parmesan.

## 231
# fusilli lunghi chicken with
# avocado & green pesto sauce

PREPARATION TIME 10 minutes COOKING TIME 15 minutes SERVES 4 to 6

1 POUND FUSILLI LUNGHI*
2 SHALLOTS, FINELY CHOPPED
1 TABLESPOON VIRGIN OLIVE OIL
1 POUND CHICKEN BREASTS, CUT ACROSS
    INTO STRIPS
½ CUP CRÈME FRAÎCHE

¾ CUP PESTO (SEE PAGE 18)
1 LARGE, OR 1½ AVOCADO(S), CUT INTO ½-INCH PIECES
SALT AND FRESHLY GROUND BLACK PEPPER
FRESHLY GRATED PARMESAN, TO SERVE

1   Cook and drain the pasta according to the package directions.
2   Meanwhile, fry the shallots until transparent. Add the chicken and fry until golden on the outside
    and just cooked through, but do not overcook.
3   Stir in the crème fraîche, pesto, and avocado and heat through. Season and toss with the pasta.
    Serve with the Parmesan.

*   Farfalle, conchiglie, lumache, or cavatappi can also be used.

## 232
# lasagne al forno

PREPARATION TIME 15 minutes* COOKING TIME 35 minutes* SERVES 4 to 6

10–12 LASAGNE SHEETS
1 QUANTITY RAGU (SEE PAGE 16)
1 CUP CRUMBLED RICOTTA

9 OUNCES BUFFALO MOZZARELLA,
THINLY SLICED OR GRATED
3 TABLESPOONS FRESHLY GRATED PARMESAN

1   Heat the oven to 400°F.
2   Cook, drain, and rinse the lasagne, even if using the no-precook type (see page 15).
    Spread on a dish towel to dry.
3   Arrange a layer of lasagne over the bottom of over a large, shallow baking dish
    (about 12 x 8 x 3 inches). Spread with some of the ragù. Scatter over about one-third
    of the ricotta and mozzarella, followed by a layer of some of the ragù. Reserve some of the
    ragù for the top and repeat the layering of lasagne, ricotta and mozzarella, then ragù, to make
    4 layers of pasta and 3 of filling. Finish with a layer of ragù and sprinkle the Parmesan over.
4   Bake in the heated oven about 25 minutes until the top is crisp and golden and the lasagne
    heated throughout. Leave to stand 5 minutes before serving.

*   Assumes the ragù is already made.

## 233
# strozzapreti with cauliflower, pancetta, & parsley

PREPARATION TIME 10 minutes COOKING TIME 15 to 20 minutes SERVES 4

15 OUNCES CAULIFLOWER, DIVIDED INTO FLOWERETS
14 OUNCES STROZZAPRETI*
4 OUNCES PANCETTA, CUT INTO THIN STRIPS
VIRGIN OLIVE OIL
2 PLUMP GARLIC CLOVES, CRUSHED

PINCH OF CHILI FLAKES
SALT AND FRESHLY GROUND BLACK PEPPER
2 TABLESPOONS FINELY CHOPPED FLAT-LEAF PARSLEY
4 TABLESPOONS FRESHLY GRATED PARMESAN,
PLUS EXTRA TO SERVE

1   Boil or steam the cauliflower until tender. Cut into ½-inch pieces.
2   Meanwhile, cook and drain the pasta according to the package directions, reserving ½ cup of the water.
3   At the same time, fry the pancetta in a little oil until brown but not crisp. Add the garlic and chili
    to cook the last 1 to 2 minutes. Stir in the cauliflower pieces, season, and fry, stirring occasionally,
    until light brown. Add the parsley shortly before the cauliflower is ready.
4   Toss with the pasta and cheese, and moisten with a little of the reserved water, if necessary.
    Serve with freshly grated Parmesan.

*   Farfalle or fusilli can also be used.

## 234

# penne rigate with spinach, prosciutto, & crumbled goat cheese

PREPARATION TIME 5 minutes COOKING TIME 10 minutes SERVES 4 to 5

I POUND **PENNE RIGATE**
2 **GARLIC CLOVES, CRUSHED**
**VIRGIN OLIVE OIL**
2½ OUNCES **PROSCIUTTO, CUT ACROSS INTO STRIPS**

8 OUNCES **BABY SPINACH**
8 OUNCES **GOAT CHEESE, CRUMBLED**
**FRESHLY GROUND BLACK PEPPER**

I    Cook and drain the pasta according to the package directions.
2    Meanwhile, fry the garlic in a little oil I minute, then add the prosciutto and cook 2 minutes longer before adding the spinach. Cook, stirring frequently, until it just wilts. Season and toss with the pasta and goat cheese so most of the cheese melts; heat slowly, if necessary. Serve with freshly ground black pepper.


## 235

# orecchiette with peas, pancetta, & sage

PREPARATION TIME 10 minutes COOKING TIME 10 minutes SERVES 4

14 OUNCES **ORECCHIETTE**
1½ CUPS **FRESH PEAS**
7 OUNCES **PANCETTA, FINELY CHOPPED**
I **ONION, FINELY CHOPPED**
**OLIVE OIL**

I **GARLIC CLOVE, FINELY CHOPPED**
10 **SAGE LEAVES, VERY FINELY SLIVERED, PLUS EXTRA**
    **FOR GARNISH**
3 TABLESPOONS **FRESHLY GRATED PARMESAN, PLUS**
    **EXTRA TO SERVE**

I    Cook and drain the pasta according to the package directions, adding the peas the last 5 minutes; drain, reserving a little of the cooking water.
2    Meanwhile, fry the pancetta and onion in a little oil over low heat until the pancetta and onion are both golden and the onion is soft. Add the garlic and sage and fry 2 to 3 minutes, then toss with the pasta, Parmesan, and 2 to 3 tablespoons of the cooking water. Serve scattered with extra sage and Parmesan.


## 236

# eliche with prosciutto, bell peppers, & peas

PREPARATION TIME 10 minutes COOKING TIME 10 minutes SERVES 4

13 OUNCES **ELICHE**
½ CUP **SHELLED YOUNG PEAS, OR FROZEN**
    **PEAS, THAWED**
4 OUNCES **PROSCIUTTO, FINELY CHOPPED**
**SMALL KNOB OF UNSALTED BUTTER**
**SALT AND FRESHLY GROUND BLACK PEPPER**

¾ CUP **RICOTTA**
2 **LARGE, FLESHY RED BELL PEPPERS, BROILED,**
    **PEELED, AND CHOPPED (SEE PAGE 67)**
4 TABLESPOONS **FRESHLY GRATED PARMESAN, PLUS**
    **EXTRA TO SERVE**

I    Cook and drain the pasta according to the package directions, reserving ½ cup of the cooking water.
2    Meanwhile, cook fresh peas in boiling water 3 to 4 minutes until just tender; drain.
3    Fry the prosciutto briefly in the butter and then stir in the cooked fresh, or thawed frozen, peas and cook I minute. Season, taking care with the salt.
4    Blend I to 2 tablespoons of the reserved water into the ricotta. Toss with the pasta and vegetables and Parmesan.

## 237
# fusilli lunghi with asparagus & prosciutto

PREPARATION TIME 10 minutes COOKING TIME 15 minutes SERVES 4

12 OUNCES **SLIM ASPARAGUS SPEARS**
14 OUNCES **FUSILLI LUNGHI**
4 OUNCES **PROSCIUTTO, CUT INTO STRIPS**
2 TABLESPOONS **CHOPPED FLAT-LEAF PARSLEY**

**SMALL KNOB OF UNSALTED BUTTER**
**SALT AND FRESHLY GROUND BLACK PEPPER**
½ **LEMON**
ABOUT 5 TABLESPOONS **FRESHLY GRATED PARMESAN**

1  Bring a saucepan of water large enough for the pasta to a boil. Add the asparagus and cook 3 to 4 minutes until almost tender. Remove with a slotted spoon and drain on paper towels.
2  Return the water to a boil, add the pasta and cook, then drain according to the package directions, reserving ½ cup of the cooking water.
3  Meanwhile, heat the asparagus, prosciutto, and parsley in the butter, stirring occasionally until warm. Season and squeeze some lemon juice over. Toss with the pasta and freshly grated Parmesan, adding reserved cooking water, as necessary, to moisten.

## 238
# tagliatelle with turkey, marsala, & mushrooms

PREPARATION TIME 10 minutes COOKING TIME 15 minutes SERVES 4

4 TURKEY SCALLOPS, TOTAL WEIGHT
  ABOUT 1 POUND
4 TABLESPOONS UNSALTED BUTTER
1½ CUPS SLICED CREMINI MUSHROOMS
½ CUP MARSALA

½ CUP HEAVY CREAM
SQUEEZE OF LEMON JUICE
SALT AND FRESHLY GROUND BLACK PEPPER
14 OUNCES TAGLIATELLE
CHOPPED FLAT-LEAF PARSLEY, TO SERVE

1   Lay the turkey scallops between 2 sheets of plastic wrap. Using a heavy-bottomed saucepan, beat them just to flatten but don't overdo it. Cut across the grain into 3 or 4 pieces each.
2   Heat half the butter in a large skillet and fry the turkey, in batches so the pan is not crowded, about 1 minute on each side; remove and keep warm.
3   Add the remaining butter to the pan and cook the mushrooms, stirring, about 2 minutes until tender and their liquid evaporates. Stir in the marsala to dislodge the sediment and boil until reduced by half. Add the cream and boil until thickened slightly. Season with lemon juice, salt, and pepper.
4   Meanwhile, cook and drain the pasta according to the package directions.
5   Just before the pasta is ready, return the turkey to the pan and heat through gently. Toss with the pasta and serve sprinkled with parsley.

## 239
# chifferi with lentils & pancetta

PREPARATION TIME 10 minutes COOKING TIME 30 minutes SERVES 4 to 6

1¼ CUPS UMBRIAN (OR PUY) LENTILS
½ ONION, HALVED THROUGH THE ROOT END
1 ROSEMARY SPRIG
1 SAGE SPRIG
18 OUNCES CHIFFERI*
4 OUNCES PANCETTA, CUT ACROSS INTO FINE STRIPS
3 GARLIC CLOVES, CHOPPED

VIRGIN OLIVE OIL
4 LARGE WELL-FLAVORED TOMATOES, SEEDED
  AND CHOPPED
HANDFUL OF FLAT-LEAF PARSLEY, CHOPPED
EXTRA-VIRGIN OLIVE OIL, TO SERVE
FRESHLY GRATED PARMESAN, TO SERVE

1   Bring the lentils, onion, and herbs to a boil in 3 quarts water, then simmer 15 to 20 minutes until the lentils are tender. Return to a boil, add the pasta, stir, and cook until al dente, stirring occasionally.
2   Meanwhile, fry the pancetta and garlic in a little oil until the pancetta is light brown. Add the tomatoes and parsley and fry 3 to 4 minutes until the tomatoes are soft but not disintegrated completely.
3   Drain the pasta and lentils, reserving about ½ cup of the cooking water; discard the onion and herbs. Toss the pasta and lentils with the tomato mixture, adding enough of the reserved water to moisten. Serve with extra-virgin olive oil trickled into each portion and with freshly grated Parmesan.

\*   Pipe rigate or gnocchi can also be used.

## 240
# lasagne alla bolognese

PREPARATION TIME 15 minutes* COOKING TIME 35 minutes* SERVES 4 to 6

10–12 LASAGNE SHEETS
I QUANTITY RAGÙ (SEE PAGE 16)
3 TABLESPOONS FRESHLY GRATED PARMESAN

BÉCHAMEL SAUCE
3 CUPS MILK
5 TABLESPOONS BUTTER
6 TABLESPOONS ALL-PURPOSE FLOUR

1 Heat the oven to 400°F.
2 Cook, drain, and rinse the lasagne, even if using the no-precook type (see page 15).
  Spread on a dish towel to dry.
3 Make the béchamel sauce (see page 17).
4 Arrange a layer of lasagne over the bottom of over a large, shallow baking dish
  (about 12 x 8 x 3 inches). Next, spread a thin layer of béchamel over the bottom of the dish,
  followed by lasagne, then ragù (reserving some for the top). Add another layer of béchamel, followed
  by a layer of lasagne. Repeat the layering to make 4 layers of pasta and 3 of filling. Finish with
  a layer of ragù and sprinkle the Parmesan over.
5 Bake in the heated oven about 25 minutes until the top is crisp and golden and the lasagne
  heated throughout. Leave to stand 5 minutes before serving.

* Assumes the béchamel and ragù are already made.

## 241
# cannelloni with sausages & broccoli

PREPARATION TIME 10 minutes COOKING TIME 40 minutes SERVES 4

6 OUNCES LASAGNE SHEETS
8 OUNCES BROCCOLI
2½ CUPS MILK
ABOUT I CUP FRESH BREAD CRUMBS
GRATED ZEST AND JUICE OF I LEMON
I POUND FRESH ITALIAN PORK SAUSAGES,
  SKINS REMOVED

SALT AND FRESHLY GROUND BLACK PEPPER
3½ TABLESPOONS UNSALTED BUTTER
4 TABLESPOONS ALL-PURPOSE FLOUR
4 OUNCES PROVOLONE, GRATED
4 TABLESPOONS FRESHLY GRATED PARMESAN

1 Heat the oven to 400°F.
2 Cook, drain, and rinse the lasagne, even if using the no-precook type (see page 15). Spread on a dish
  towel to dry.
3 Meanwhile, boil the broccoli until completely tender, then chop coarsely and puree with 3 tablespoons
  of the milk. Combine with the bread crumbs, lemon zest and juice, and the sausagemeat; season.
4 Make a simple white sauce (see page 17) with the butter, flour, and remaining milk. Off the heat,
  stir in the provolone.
5 If the lasagne sheets are large, cut them in half across. Divide the sausage and broccoli mixture between
  the sheets and roll up. Place, seam side down, in a single layer in a greased large shallow baking dish.
  Pour the cheese sauce over and sprinkle with the Parmesan.
6 Bake in the heated oven about 30 minutes until golden and bubbling.

## 242
# chicken & prosciutto cannelloni on spinach & mushrooms

PREPARATION TIME 15 minutes COOKING TIME 50 minutes SERVES 6

12 ounces **BONELESS CHICKEN**
**BOUQUET GARNI OF 1 BAY LEAF, 2 THYME SPRIGS,**
  **1 ROSEMARY SPRIG, AND 4 PARSLEY SPRIGS**
1 **ONION, SLICED**
8 ounces **CANNELLONI TUBES**
2 **GARLIC CLOVES, FINELY CHOPPED**
**KNOB OF UNSALTED BUTTER**
3¼ cups **SLICED CREMINI MUSHROOMS**
1½ pounds **SPINACH, CHOPPED**

**SALT AND FRESHLY GROUND BLACK PEPPER**
2 tablespoons **ALL-PURPOSE FLOUR**
⅔ cup **HEAVY CREAM**
⅔ cup **MEDIUM-BODIED DRY WHITE WINE**
6 ounces **PROSCIUTTO**
5 ounces **PROVOLONE, GRATED**
2 tablespoons **FRESHLY GRATED PARMESAN**

1  Put the chicken, herbs, and onion into a pan with scant 2 cups water. Cover and bring to a simmer. Lower the heat so the water barely moves and poach the chicken about 15 minutes; lift out the chicken. Strain and measure the stock; you will need 1¼ cups. If necessary, boil to reduce to the correct amount.
2  Meanwhile, cook and drain the cannelloni tubes (see page 15) and spread on a dish towel to dry.
3  Heat the oven to 375°F. Grease a shallow 11 x 9-inch baking dish.
4  Cook the garlic in a little butter 1 minute. Add the mushrooms and cook 5 minutes longer until soft, stirring. Add the spinach and cook until wilted, stirring occasionally. Season and spread the spinach mixture in the baking dish.
5  Make a white sauce with a knob of butter, the flour, measured stock, cream, and wine (see page 17).
6  Finely chop the chicken with the prosciutto. Season, using little salt but plenty of black pepper, and beat in ⅔ cup of the white sauce. Divide between the cannelloni tubes and place in a single layer on the spinach mixture. Add all but 2 tablespoons of the provolone to the remaining sauce. Pour over the tubes and sprinkle with the remaining provolone and the Parmesan.
7  Bake in the heated oven 30 to 35 minutes until golden.

## 243
# pork & spinach cannelloni

PREPARATION TIME 10 minutes COOKING TIME 35 minutes SERVES 4

9 ounces **SPINACH**
2 **GARLIC CLOVES, FINELY CHOPPED**
**OLIVE OIL**
14 ounces **GROUND PORK**
4-ounce **PIECE OF MORTADELLA, FINELY CHOPPED**
1 cup **RICOTTA, BEATEN UNTIL SMOOTH**

2 tablespoons **PINE NUTS, LIGHTLY TOASTED**
**SALT AND FRESHLY GROUND BLACK PEPPER**
9 ounces **FRESH LASAGNE SHEETS**
1 **QUANTITY CHEESE SAUCE (SEE PAGE 17)**
3 tablespoons **FRESHLY GRATED PARMESAN**

1  Heat the oven to 350°F.
2  Cook the spinach in a covered pan, shaking it occasionally. Drain well, pressing out surplus water; chop.
3  Fry the garlic in a little oil 1 minute in a large skillet, then stir in the pork 4 to 5 minutes. Stir in the mortadella, spinach, ricotta, pine nuts, and seasoning; remove from the heat.
4  Cook and drain the lasagne sheets (see page 15) and spread on a dish towel to dry.
5  Spread a small amount of the cheese sauce in the bottom of a greased shallow baking dish.
6  Divide the filling between the lasagne sheets, spreading it along one edge, about ½ inch in. Roll over to form tubes and place seam side down in the baking dish. Pour the remaining sauce over, sprinkle the Parmesan over and bake in the heated oven 20 to 25 minutes until bubbling and brown.

# 244

# cannelloni with beef, roast shallots, & garlic

PREPARATION TIME 5 minutes COOKING TIME 50 minutes SERVES 4

| | |
|---|---|
| 1 HEAD OF GARLIC, DIVIDED INTO CLOVES | ⅔ cup RED WINE |
| 5 SHALLOTS | 1½ TABLESPOONS THYME |
| VIRGIN OLIVE OIL | ABOUT 8 LASAGNE SHEETS |
| ½ ounce DRIED MUSHROOMS | 2 TABLESPOONS SUN-DRIED TOMATO PASTE |
| ½ cup VEGETABLE STOCK, BOILING | 1¼ cups LIGHT CREAM |
| 18 ounces LEAN GROUND BEEF | ½ cup FRESHLY GRATED FONTINA |

1. Heat the oven to 350°F.
2. Put the garlic and shallots in a small roasting pan, trickle some oil over, and stir so the shallots and garlic are evenly coated. Bake in the heated oven 25 minutes until soft. Leave the oven on, increasing the temperature to 400°F.
3. When the garlic and shallots are cool enough to handle, pop the flesh from the skins of the garlic cloves, peel the shallots, and then mash them together
4. Meanwhile, soak the mushrooms in the boiling stock 20 minutes; drain (strain and reserve the stock) and chop finely.
5. Cook the meat a little oil in a skillet, stirring to break up the meat until it browns. Add the mushroom liquid, mushrooms, wine, and thyme and cook slowly until most of the liquid evaporates, but it should not be too dry. Stir in the mashed garlic and shallots.
6. Cook the lasagne, even if using the no-precook type (see page 15), and lay the separate sheets flat on a dish towel. Spoon the meat mixture along one long edge, roll up to enclose the filling, and cut each tube in half.
7. Using a greased, shallow baking dish, layer half the tubes, seam side down, half the sauce and half the cheese; repeat the layering.
8. Stir the sun-dried tomato paste into the cream, pour over the cannelloni, cover with foil, and bake in the heated oven 10 minutes. Bake uncovered 10 to 15 minutes longer until light brown.

# 245

# braised lamb shanks with pasta

PREPARATION TIME 10 minutes COOKING TIME 1½ hours SERVES 6

| | |
|---|---|
| 6 SMALL LAMB SHANKS | 8 SUN-DRIED TOMATOES, SLICED |
| OLIVE OIL | 1 CAN (14-oz.) CHERRY TOMATOES |
| 1 LARGE ONION, HALVED AND THINLY SLICED | 2½ cups RED WINE |
| 3 GARLIC CLOVES, FINELY CHOPPED | 2½ cups VEGETABLE STOCK |
| 2 SMALL CARROTS, SLICED | BOUQUET GARNI OF 1 BAY LEAF AND SEVERAL |
| 2 CELERY STALKS, SLICED | THYME SPRIGS |
| 1 ounce DRIED PORCINI MUSHROOMS, FINELY SNIPPED | ⅔ cup ELBOW MACARONI |

1. Heat the oven to 325°F.
2. Fry the lamb shanks in batches in olive oil in a large, flameproof casserole until light brown. Set aside.
3. Add the onion, garlic, carrot, and celery to the casserole, adding more oil if necessary, and fry until soft and golden. Add the dried mushrooms, sun-dried tomatoes, cherry tomatoes, wine, stock, and herbs and simmer 10 minutes. Put the shanks on top, cover with a tight-fitting lid, and cook in the heated oven about 1¼ hours until the lamb is very tender and falling off the bone.
4. Remove the lamb from the casserole, cover, and keep warm. Bring the casserole to a boil, add the pasta, and simmer until al dente. Serve with the lamb.

## 246
# baked rigatoni alla bolognese

PREPARATION TIME 5 minutes* COOKING TIME 30 minutes SERVES 4 to 6

1 POUND **RIGATONI**
6 TABLESPOONS **FRESHLY GRATED PARMESAN**
1 QUANTITY **RAGÙ (SEE PAGE 16), WARMED**
**VIRGIN OLIVE OIL**

**BÉCHAMEL SAUCE**
2 CUPS **MILK**
3½ TABLESPOONS **UNSALTED BUTTER**
4 TABLESPOONS **ALL-PURPOSE FLOUR**
**FLAVORINGS (SEE PAGE 17)**

1  Heat the oven to 400°F.
2  Cook the rigatoni 2 minutes less than specified on the package, then drain well.
3  Meanwhile, make the béchamel sauce (see page 17).
4  Toss the pasta with 4 tablespoons of the cheese, then the ragù and béchamel sauce. When well mixed, spread evenly in a gratin dish, sprinkle the remaining Parmesan over and trickle a little oil over.
5  Bake in the heated oven 15 to 20 minutes until the top is brown. Leave to stand 5 minutes before serving.

*  Assumes the ragù is already made.

## 247
# pennette with chicken livers & marsala

PREPARATION TIME 10 minutes COOKING TIME 10 minutes SERVES 4

14 ounces PENNETTE
2 GARLIC CLOVES, FINELY CHOPPED
4 teaspoons FINELY CHOPPED SMALL SAGE LEAVES
2 tablespoons OLIVE OIL
2½ tablespoons UNSALTED BUTTER

12 ounces CHICKEN LIVERS, CUT INTO SMALL PIECES
4 tablespoons MARSALA
4 tablespoons MEDIUM-BODIED DRY WHITE WINE
SALT AND FRESHLY GROUND BLACK PEPPER
FRESHLY GRATED PARMESAN, TO SERVE

1   Cook and drain the pasta according to the package directions, reserving about ½ cup of the water.
2   Meanwhile, fry the garlic and sage in a little oil and the butter 2 minutes. Add the chicken livers and fry briskly, stirring, 1 to 2 minutes until the outside changes color.
3   Pour in the marsala and wine and continue to cook briskly to thicken slightly. Season and toss with the pasta. Sprinkle with freshly grated Parmesan and add enough of the reserved cooking water, if necessary, to moisten. Serve with extra Parmesan.

## 248
# tagliatelle with pancetta, arugula, & gorgonzola

PREPARATION TIME 10 minutes COOKING TIME 10 minutes SERVES 4

14 ounces TAGLIATELLE
6 ounces PANCETTA, CHOPPED
VIRGIN OLIVE OIL
2 GARLIC CLOVES, FINELY CHOPPED
4 tablespoons HEAVY CREAM

SALT AND FRESHLY GROUND BLACK PEPPER
6 ounces GORGONZOLA, VERY FINELY CHOPPED
4 ounces ARUGULA
¼ cup WALNUT HALVES, CHOPPED

1   Cook and drain the tagliatelle according to the package directions, reserving ½ cup of the cooking water.
2   Meanwhile, brown the pancetta in a little oil. Add the garlic, fry 1 minute, then add the cream. Warm through without boiling before seasoning and tossing with the pasta, cheese, and arugula. Add enough of the reserved cooking water, if necessary, to moisten. Serve with the walnuts scattered over.

## 249
# bucatini with pancetta, tomatoes, & chilies

PREPARATION TIME 10 minutes COOKING TIME 30 minutes SERVES 4

1 ONION, FINELY CHOPPED
4 ounces PANCETTA, CUT INTO STRIPS
VIRGIN OLIVE OIL
1 GARLIC CLOVE, FINELY CHOPPED
PINCH OF CHILI FLAKES, TO TASTE
5 tablespoons MEDIUM-BODIED DRY WHITE WINE

2 CANS (15-oz.) CRUSHED PLUM TOMATOES
SALT AND FRESHLY GROUND BLACK PEPPER
14 ounces BUCATINI
3 tablespoons FRESHLY GRATED PARMESAN, PLUS
    EXTRA TO SERVE

1   Fry the onion and pancetta in a little oil until the pancetta is brown but not crisp, and the onion is soft and turning golden. Add the garlic and chilies toward the end of the cooking. Pour in the wine and bubble until it evaporates by about three-quarters. Add the tomatoes and simmer until thick; season.
2   Meanwhile, cook and drain the pasta according to the package directions. Toss with the sauce and cheese and serve with additional cheese.

# cannelloni with spinach & prosciutto filling

PREPARATION TIME 15 minutes COOKING TIME 35 minutes SERVES 4

1½ POUNDS **SPINACH**
6 **LASAGNE SHEETS, ABOUT 7 X 3** INCHES
4 OUNCES **FONTINA, GRATED**
12 **THIN SLICES PROSCIUTTO**
3 TABLESPOONS **FRESHLY GRATED PARMESAN**
1 **QUANTITY BROILED TOMATO SAUCE (SEE**
  **PAGE 18), WARM**

**WHITE SAUCE**
3½ TABLESPOONS **UNSALTED BUTTER**
½ CUP **ALL-PURPOSE FLOUR**
1¼ CUPS **MILK**

1  Heat the oven to 400°F.
2  Cook the spinach in a covered pan over a medium heat until wilted. Drain well, squeeze out surplus moisture, and chop finely.
3  Cook, drain, and rinse the lasagne, even if using the no-precook type (see page 15). Halve each sheet across and spread on a dish towel to dry.
4  Meanwhile, make the simple white sauce (see page 17) with the butter, flour, and milk. Stir in the fontina and spinach.
5  Lay a slice of prosciutto on each lasagne sheet, top with the spinach sauce and roll up. Place, seam side down and just touching, in a single layer in a greased large, shallow baking dish. Pour the white sauce over, sprinkle with the Parmesan, and bake in the heated oven about 30 minutes until heated through. Serve with the broiled tomato sauce.

# turkey meatballs al forno

PREPARATION TIME 10 minutes COOKING TIME 1 hour SERVES 6

12 OUNCES **ZITI**\*
3 POUNDS **WELL-FLAVORED TOMATOES, SEEDED AND**
  **CHOPPED**
3 **GARLIC CLOVES, FINELY CHOPPED**
**LEAVES FROM A BUNCH OF BASIL, SHREDDED**
**SALT AND FRESHLY GROUND BLACK PEPPER**
18 OUNCES **GROUND TURKEY**

**LEAVES FROM 4 FLAT-LEAF PARSLEY SPRIGS,**
  **FINELY CHOPPED**
1 CUP **FRESHLY GRATED PARMESAN**
1 **EGG, BEATEN**
**JUICE OF** ½ **LEMON**
**OLIVE OIL, FOR FRYING**

1  Cook and drain the pasta according to the package directions, giving it 2 minutes less than specified.
2  Meanwhile, simmer the tomatoes and two-thirds of the garlic in a pan 10 to 15 minutes until most of the liquid evaporates (don't let it become too thick). Add the basil and puree the sauce; season.
3  While the sauce is cooking, combine the ground turkey, parsley, one-quarter of the Parmesan, the egg, lemon juice, remaining garlic, and seasoning, preferably using your hands. With wet hands, form the mixture into balls approximately ¾ inch in diameter.
4  Heat the oven to 375°F.
5  Fry the meatballs in batches in a little oil in a large skillet, 2 to 4 minutes until brown on the outside but still pink in the middle; drain on paper towels.
6  Gently stir the pasta into the sauce and spoon one-third of the mixture into a deep baking dish, such as a soufflé dish. Add a layer of half the turkey balls and sprinkle with one-third of the remaining Parmesan. Top with another third of the pasta mixture, then the remaining meatballs and half the rest of the Parmesan. Finish with the last of the pasta and sprinkle the last of the Parmesan over.
7  Bake in the heated oven 30 to 40 minutes until heated through, then leave to stand 5 minutes before serving.

\*  Rigatoni can also be used.

## 252
# sausage & eggplant lasagne

PREPARATION TIME 20 minutes COOKING TIME 50 minutes SERVES 6

9 OUNCES **LASAGNE SHEETS**
9 OUNCES **SPICY FRESH ITALIAN SAUSAGES**
13 OUNCES **EGGPLANTS, CUT INTO ¼-INCH SLICES**
**OLIVE OIL**
**SALT AND FRESHLY GROUND BLACK PEPPER**
¾ CUP **FRESHLY GRATED PARMESAN**
6 OUNCES **BUFFALO MOZZARELLA, SLICED**
13 OUNCES **WELL-FLAVORED TOMATOES, SLICED**

**WHITE SAUCE**
3¼ CUPS **MILK**
4½ TABLESPOONS **BUTTER**
3 TABLESPOONS **ALL-PURPOSE FLOUR**
I BAY LEAF, TORN ACROSS

1   Heat the oven to 350°F.
2   Cook, drain, and rinse the lasagne, even if using the no-precook type (see page 15). Spread on a dish towel to dry.
3   Meanwhile, broil the sausages until evenly brown. Drain on paper towels and then slice thinly.
4   Lay the eggplant slices in a single layer on a large baking sheet (you may need to use two sheets), brush lightly with oil, and season. Broil until tender and brown on both sides.
5   While the eggplants are cooking, make the white sauce (see page 17), adding the bay leaf to the milk. Discard the bay leaf when the sauce is ready, then add three-quarters of the Parmesan.
6   Spread a thin layer of the sauce over the bottom of a large, shallow baking dish. Cover with a layer of lasagne sheets and arrange half the eggplant and sausage slices on top. Add another layer of sauce, one of lasagne, and then half the mozzarella. Cover with half the tomatoes, another layer of lasagne sheets, the remaining eggplants and sausages, more sauce, lasagne, and the rest of the mozzarella and tomatoes. Finish with a generous layer of cheese sauce. Sprinkle the remaining Parmesan over.
7   Bake in the heated oven about 30 minutes until bubbling and brown.

## 253
# gnocchi with borlotti beans & pancetta

PREPARATION TIME 10 minutes COOKING TIME 15 minutes SERVES 4

I ONION, CHOPPED

2 GARLIC CLOVES, CHOPPED

VIRGIN OLIVE OIL

4 OUNCES PANCETTA, CHOPPED

1¼ CUPS CANNED CRUSHED PLUM TOMATOES

I CUP COOKED OR CANNED BORLOTTI BEANS

3 TABLESPOONS HEAVY CREAM

3 TABLESPOONS CHOPPED FRESH BASIL

SALT AND FRESHLY GROUND BLACK PEPPER

14 OUNCES GNOCCHI

EXTRA-VIRGIN OLIVE OIL AND

    FRESHLY GRATED PARMESAN, TO SERVE

1   Fry the onion and garlic in a little oil in a heavy skillet until soft. Add the pancetta and cook until beginning to color. Stir in the tomatoes and beans and bubble 5 minutes, then add the cream; cook slowly until heated through. Mash the beans coarsely, or use a hand blender. Stir in the basil and seasoning.

2   Meanwhile, cook and drain the gnocchi according to the package directions, reserving a little of the cooking water.

3   Add sufficient of the cooking water to loosen the sauce, if necessary, then toss with the pasta. Serve with extra-virgin olive oil and Parmesan.

150

## 254
# tortellini with spinach, ricotta, & prosciutto

PREPARATION TIME 50 to 60 minutes COOKING TIME 10 to 15 minutes SERVES 4

2-EGG QUANTITY PASTA DOUGH (SEE PAGE 10)

2 OUNCES PROSCIUTTO, CUT INTO STRIPS

I POUND SPINACH

¾ CUP RICOTTA

I EGG YOLK

SALT AND FRESHLY GROUND BLACK PEPPER

KNOB OF UNSALTED BUTTER

2 GARLIC CLOVES, HALVED

PARMESAN SHAVINGS, TO SERVE

1   While the dough is resting, fry the prosciutto a couple of minutes.

2   Meanwhile, cook the spinach in a covered pan over medium heat, until it wilts and is soft. Drain well and press out surplus moisture; chop finely. Combine with the prosciutto, ricotta, egg yolk, and seasoning.

3   Make tortellini with the pasta and filling (see page 11).

4   Heat the butter in a small pan with the garlic over medium heat 3 to 4 minutes, until the garlic just turns golden; discard the garlic. Keep the butter warm over very low heat.

5   Cook the tortellini, in batches if necessary, in simmering water 3 to 4 minutes until puffy. Remove with a slotted spoon, drain well, and pour the butter over. Serve with Parmesan shavings scattered over.

## 255
# mushroom & salami al forno

PREPARATION TIME 5 minutes COOKING TIME 35 minutes SERVES 4

1 ONION, HALVED AND THINLY SLICED
1 LEEK, THINLY SLICED
3 GARLIC CLOVES, THINLY SLICED
OLIVE OIL, FOR FRYING
1 CUP DICED SALAMI
8 OUNCES RIGATONI

5 CUPS SLICED CREMINI MUSHROOMS
2 TABLESPOONS CHOPPED FLAT-LEAF PARSLEY
¾ CUP HEAVY CREAM
SALT AND FRESHLY GROUND BLACK PEPPER
3 TABLESPOONS BREAD CRUMBS
2 TABLESPOONS FRESHLY GRATED PARMESAN

1   Heat the oven to 400°F.
2   Fry the onion, leek, and garlic in olive oil in a skillet until soft and turning golden. Stir in the salami and cook 2 minutes.
3   Meanwhile, cook and drain the pasta according to the package directions, allowing 1 minute less than specified. Remove the vegetables and salami from the pan with a slotted spoon and add to the pasta.
4   Fry half the mushrooms in the pan over high heat 2 minutes.; scoop out and add to the pasta. Repeat with the remaining mushrooms, adding the cream as well to the pasta. Season and toss everything together so the cream coats the other ingredients. Transfer to a baking dish, sprinkle the bread crumbs and Parmesan mixed together over, and bake in the heated oven 20 minutes.

## 256
# tagliatelle with chicken, lemon, & basil

PREPARATION TIME 10 minutes COOKING TIME 15 minutes SERVES 4

12 OUNCES TAGLIATELLE
1 POUND SKINLESS CHICKEN BREASTS, THINLY SLICED
    ACROSS THE GRAIN
VIRGIN OLIVE OIL
1 CUP FROZEN FAVA BEANS, THAWED

JUICE OF 1 LARGE, JUICY LEMON
3 TABLESPOONS CRÈME FRAÎCHE
SALT AND FRESHLY GROUND BLACK PEPPER
LEAVES FROM A SMALL HANDFUL BASIL, SHREDDED
FRESHLY GRATED PARMESAN, TO SERVE

1   Cook and drain the pasta according to the package directions, reserving about ½ cup of the cooking water.
2   Meanwhile, fry the chicken in a little oil in a large skillet until cooked through and golden.
3   Add the fava beans and cook 2 minutes. Stir in the lemon juice and crème fraîche and warm through slowly. Season and toss with the pasta and basil, and enough of the reserved cooking water, if necessary, to moisten. Serve with grated Parmesan.

# vegetable &
# vegetarian dishes

Pasta was originally a staple part of the diet of the less well-off. Many people grew their own vegetables so these made the obvious choice for combining with pasta. In some recipes vegetables are given minimal preparation and quickly sliced or chopped, and cooked briefly to maintain their flavors, texture and nutritive value. On other occasions, they can be cooked slowly to mellow and meld the flavors into a rich-tasting sauce; for example, the slow cooking of the onions in Gemelli with Melting Onion Sauce reduces them to a smooth, sweet sauce. For lovers of lasagne there are popular combinations such as spinach and cheese or, for a lighter dish, a vegetable lasagne where the white sauce is replaced by goat cheese, cream, and eggs.

CHAPTER
**4**

## 257

# torchietti with zucchini, lemon, & pine nuts

PREPARATION TIME 10 minutes COOKING TIME 10 minutes SERVES 4

2 PLUMP GARLIC CLOVES, THINLY SLICED

VIRGIN OLIVE OIL

1¼ POUNDS SMALL ZUCCHINI, PARED LENGTHWISE
   INTO STRIPS (SEE PAGE 212)

GRATED ZEST AND JUICE OF 1 LARGE LEMON

6 TABLESPOONS HEAVY CREAM

SALT AND FRESHLY GROUND BLACK PEPPER

12 OUNCES TORCHIETTI

2 TABLESPOONS FINELY CHOPPED FLAT-LEAF PARSLEY

5 TABLESPOONS PINE NUTS, LIGHTLY TOASTED

FRESHLY GRATED PARMESAN, TO SERVE

1   Warm the garlic in 4 tablespoons oil 5 minutes, but do not let it become too hot; discard the garlic.
2   Fry the zucchini briskly in the garlic-infused oil in batches until golden. Return all the zucchini to
    the pan with the lemon zest and juice and the cream. Bubble 2 to 3 minutes until thickened slightly,
    then season.
3   Meanwhile, cook and drain the pasta according to the package directions. Toss with the zucchini sauce,
    parsley, and pine nuts. Serve sprinkled with Parmesan.

## 258
# trofie with broccoli sauce

PREPARATION TIME 5 minutes COOKING TIME 20 minutes SERVES 3 to 4

1½ POUNDS **BROCCOLI FLOWERETS**
**SALT**
2 **GARLIC CLOVES, FINELY CHOPPED**
**VIRGIN OLIVE OIL**
8 OUNCES **TROFIE***

½ CUP **HEAVY CREAM**
3 TABLESPOONS **LEMON JUICE**
2 TABLESPOONS **FRESHLY GRATED PARMESAN,**
    **PLUS EXTRA TO SERVE**

1   Boil the broccoli in salted water until very tender; drain, reserving ½ cup of the cooking water. Refresh the broccoli under running cold water, then drain and chop very finely.
2   Fry the garlic in a little for 1 minute, then add the broccoli and cook, stirring, about 3 minutes, until dry.
3   Meanwhile, cook and drain the pasta according to the package directions.
4   Stir the cream and lemon juice into the broccoli and simmer 3 to 4 minutes. Add enough of the broccoli water to give the consistency of light cream. Stir in the Parmesan and toss with the pasta. Serve with additional Parmesan.

*   Cavatappi or fusilli lunghi can also be used.

## 259
# eliche with broccoli, bread crumbs, golden raisins, & pine nuts

PREPARATION TIME 10 minutes COOKING TIME 10 minutes SERVES 4

⅓ CUP **GOLDEN RAISINS (OPTIONAL)**
10 OUNCES **ELICHE**
¾ CUP **BROCCOLI CUT INTO FLOWERETS, STEMS VERY**
    **FINELY CHOPPED**
1 TABLESPOON **SUN-DRIED TOMATO PASTE**
1½ CUPS **FRESH BREAD CRUMBS**

½ CUP **VIRGIN OLIVE OIL**
2 **GARLIC CLOVES, FINELY CHOPPED**
3 TABLESPOONS **PINE NUTS**
3 TABLESPOONS **CHOPPED FLAT-LEAF PARSLEY**
**SALT AND FRESHLY GROUND BLACK PEPPER**

1   Soak the golden raisins, if using, in a little boiling water 5 minutes.
2   Cook the pasta according to the package directions, adding the broccoli 4 to 5 minutes before the end. Drain, reserving 1 tablespoon of the cooking water and mixing it with the tomato paste.
3   Fry the bread crumbs in the oil in a skillet until starting to become crisp. Add the garlic and pine nuts and fry, stirring, until the pine nuts begin to color. Stir in the parsley, then toss with the pasta and broccoli, the tomato liquid, drained golden raisins, if using, and seasoning.

## 260
# riccioli with broccoli, parmesan, & pine nuts

PREPARATION TIME 5 minutes COOKING TIME 10 minutes SERVES 4

14 OUNCES **RICCIOLI**
2 CUPS **BROCCOLI FLOWERETS**
4 TABLESPOONS **VIRGIN OLIVE OIL**
2 **GARLIC CLOVES, FINELY CHOPPED**

**JUICE OF 1 LEMON**
**SALT AND FRESHLY GROUND BLACK PEPPER**
2–3 TABLESPOONS **PINE NUTS, LIGHTLY TOASTED**
**FRESHLY GRATED PARMESAN, TO SERVE**

1   Cook the pasta according to the package directions, adding the broccoli the last 4 minutes of the cooking; drain the pasta and broccoli.
2   Meanwhile, combine the oil, garlic, lemon juice, and seasoning. Toss with the pasta, broccoli, and pine nuts. Serve with plenty of Parmesan.

## 261
# orecchiette with peas & feta

PREPARATION TIME 5 minutes COOKING TIME 10 minutes SERVES 4

14 OUNCES ORECCHIETTE*
1 ONION, FINELY CHOPPED
SMALL KNOB OF UNSALTED BUTTER
1¼ CUPS VEGETABLE STOCK, HOT

1 CUP FRESH PEAS
SCANT 1 CUP CRUMBLED FETA
1–2 TABLESPOONS CHOPPED FRESH DILL
FRESHLY GROUND BLACK PEPPER

1  Cook and drain the orecchiette according to the package directions.
2  Meanwhile, fry the onion in the butter until translucent and soft but not colored. Add half the stock and boil until almost evaporated. Pour in the remaining stock, add the peas, and boil until the peas are tender; there should still be some liquid left. Toss with the pasta, feta, dill, and seasoning (salt may not be necessary because of the saltiness of the cheese).

*  Conchiglie can also be used.

## 262
# chifferi with peas & parmesan

PREPARATION TIME 5 minutes COOKING TIME 10 minutes SERVES 4

14 OUNCES CHIFFERI*
1½ CUPS FROZEN PETITS POIS
½ CUP DICED UNSALTED BUTTER

¾ CUP PARMESAN, FRESHLY GRATED
SALT AND FRESHLY GROUND BLACK PEPPER

1  Cook and drain the pasta according to the package directions, adding the peas the final 2 minutes.
2  Toss with the butter and most of the Parmesan. Season, using plenty of black pepper, and serve with the remaining Parmesan.

*  Gnocchi and cavatelli can also be used.

## 263
# cavatappi with minted lettuce & peas

PREPARATION TIME 10 minutes COOKING TIME 10 minutes SERVES 4

1 ONION, FINELY CHOPPED
3 TABLESPOONS UNSALTED BUTTER
6 OUNCES HEARTS OF LETTUCE
⅔ CUP MEDIUM-BODIED DRY WHITE WINE
1½ CUPS FROZEN PETITS POIS

SALT AND FRESHLY GROUND BLACK PEPPER
14 OUNCES CAVATAPPI
2 TABLESPOONS CHOPPED MINT
4 TABLESPOONS CRÈME FRAÎCHE

1  Fry the onion in the butter in a large skillet, preferably nonstick, until softened.
2  Meanwhile, cut off the end of the cores of the hearts of lettuce, but don't remove all the core. Slice each head lengthwise into 6 to 8 wedges; the remaining core will hold the leaves together.
3  Pour the wine into the pan and boil until most of it evaporates, then add the lettuce. Cook, stirring, until wilted and tinged with brown. Stir in the peas to warm through just before the end; season.
4  Meanwhile, cook and drain the pasta according to the package directions, reserving ½ cup of the cooking water. Toss with the lettuce and peas and add the mint. Stir in the reserved cooking water, if necessary, to moisten. Serve each portion topped with a spoonful of crème fraîche.

# pappardelle with roast squash & broiled goat cheese

PREPARATION TIME 10 minutes COOKING TIME 30 minutes SERVES 4

1 SMALL BUTTERNUT SQUASH, PEELED, SEEDED,
  AND CUT INTO 1-INCH CHUNKS
SEVERAL THYME SPRIGS
2 GARLIC CLOVES, CRUSHED
3 TABLESPOONS VIRGIN OLIVE OIL
10 OUNCES PAPPARDELLE*

4 SLICES OF GOAT CHEESE LOG
4 TABLESPOONS FINELY CHOPPED FLAT-LEAF PARSLEY
FINELY GRATED ZEST OF ½ LEMON
SALT AND FRESHLY GROUND BLACK PEPPER
EXTRA-VIRGIN OLIVE OIL AND FRESHLY GRATED
  PARMESAN, TO SERVE

1   Heat the oven to 400°F.
2   Put the squash into a large roasting pan and add the thyme, garlic, and oil. Stir together to coat the squash, then roast in the heated oven 25 to 30 minutes until the squash is tender and tinged with brown; discard the thyme.
3   Meanwhile, cook the pasta according to the package directions, reserving ½ cup of the cooking water.
4   Lay the goat cheese on a piece of lightly greased foil and broil 3 to 4 minutes until light brown and softened.
5   Toss the pasta with the squash and any pan juices, the parsley, lemon zest, and seasoning, adding enough reserved cooking water to moisten. Serve with the oil and Parmesan and top each portion with goat cheese.

*   Cavatappi and eliche can also be used.

# conchiglie with fava beans, nuts, & lemon sauce

PREPARATION TIME 10 minutes COOKING TIME 10 minutes SERVES 4

¾ cup COARSLEY CHOPPED LIGHTLY
  TOASTED HAZELNUTS
4 GARLIC CLOVES, VERY THINLY SLICED
4 TABLESPOONS DICED UNSALTED BUTTER
COARSELY GRATED ZEST AND JUICE OF 1½–2 LEMONS
9 OUNCES CONCHIGLIE

1 cup SHELLED FRESH, OR THAWED FROZEN, BABY
  FAVA BEANS
4 TABLESPOONS SHREDDED BASIL
2 TABLESPOONS CHOPPED FLAT-LEAF PARSLEY
2 TABLESPOONS LIGHT CREAM
SALT AND FRESHLY GROUND BLACK PEPPER
FRESHLY GRATED PARMESAN, TO SERVE (OPTIONAL)

1 Cook the hazelnuts and garlic in the butter 30 to 60 seconds, then add the lemon zest and remove
  from the heat.
2 Cook and drain the conchiglie according to the package directions, adding the beans about 4 minutes
  before the end of the cooking for fresh beans, 2 minutes for frozen ones.
3 Toss the pasta and beans with the butter mixture. Cover for 1 minute, then toss in the herbs,
  lemon juice, cream, and seasoning. Serve with freshly grated Parmesan, if liked.

# orecchiette with broccoli, sun-dried tomatoes, & thyme

PREPARATION TIME 10 minutes COOKING TIME 10 minutes SERVES 4

14 OUNCES ORECCHIETTE
1¼ cups BROCCOLI FLOWERETS
3 GARLIC CLOVES, BRUISED BUT LEFT WHOLE
PINCH OF CHILI FLAKES
1 TABLESPOON FRESH THYME
5 TABLESPOONS VIRGIN OLIVE OIL OR OIL FROM
  THE TOMATOES

10 PIECES OF SUN-DRIED TOMATOES IN OIL, DRAINED
  AND SLICED
4 TABLESPOONS CHOPPED FLAT-LEAF PARSLEY
1 TEASPOON FINELY GRATED LEMON ZEST
3 TABLESPOONS FRESHLY GRATED PARMESAN, PLUS
  EXTRA TO SERVE
FRESHLY GROUND BLACK PEPPER

1 Cook and drain the pasta according to the package directions, adding the broccoli the final
  3 to 4 minutes of the cooking time.
2 Meanwhile, fry the garlic, chili, and thyme in the oil over low heat 5 minutes, so the oil is infused
  with garlic; discard the garlic. Add the sun-dried tomatoes and toss with the pasta, parsley,
  lemon zest, Parmesan, and black pepper. Serve with more Parmesan.

## 267

# trofie with goat cheese & lemon

PREPARATION TIME 5 minutes COOKING TIME 10 minutes SERVES 2

7 OUNCES TROFIE*
5 OUNCES SOFT GOAT CHEESE LOG, THICKLY SLICED
2 GARLIC CLOVES, THINLY SLICED
SMALL KNOB OF UNSALTED BUTTER
2 TABLESPOONS EXTRA-VIRGIN OLIVE OIL

FINELY GRATED ZEST OF 1 LEMON
2 TABLESPOONS LEMON JUICE
2 OUNCES ARUGULA
FRESHLY GROUND BLACK PEPPER

1   Cook and drain the trofie according to the package directions, reserving ½ cup of the cooking water.
2   Meanwhile, place the goat cheese on a lightly greased piece of foil, place under a heated broiler and heat 4 to 5 minutes until pale golden and starting to melt.
3   At the same time, fry the garlic in the butter and oil 30 seconds; add the lemon zest and juice. Toss with the pasta, arugula, black pepper, and a little of the reserved cooking water, if necessary, to moisten. Serve each portion topped with goat cheese.

*   Fusilli and farfalle can also be used.

## 268

# fettuccine with asparagus, peas, & lemon

PREPARATION TIME 5 minutes COOKING TIME 10 minutes SERVES 4

1 POUND SLIM ASPARAGUS, HALVED CROSSWISE
13 OUNCES FETTUCCINE*
1 CUP FRESH PEAS
GRATED ZEST AND JUICE OF 1 LEMON
2 TABLESPOONS OLIVE OIL

4 TABLESPOONS LIGHT CREAM
4 TABLESPOONS FRESHLY GRATED PARMESAN
2–3 TABLESPOONS SHREDDED MINT, TO TASTE
SALT AND FRESHLY GROUND BLACK PEPPER

1   Cook the asparagus on a hot ridged griddle pan until evenly flecked with brown.
2   Meanwhile, cook and drain the pasta according to the package directions, adding the peas the last 3 to 4 minutes, depending on size.
3   At the same time, fry the lemon zest in the oil about 3 minutes. Add the lemon juice and warm through.
4   Toss the fettuccine and peas with the lemon mixture, the cream, basil, asparagus, cheese, mint, and seasoning.

*   Tagliatelle can also be used.

# 269
# lasagnette with mixed mushrooms & herbs

PREPARATION TIME 10 minutes COOKING TIME 15 minutes SERVES 4

1¼ POUNDS ANY COMBINATION OF MIXED
 MUSHROOMS, SUCH AS CEPS, OYSTER, SHIITAKE,
 CREMINI, ENOKI, AND ANY WILD MUSHROOMS
 THAT ARE AVAILABLE, SLICED, HALVED,
 OR QUARTERED AS APPROPRIATE*
3 SHALLOTS, FINELY CHOPPED
VIRGIN OLIVE OIL
3 GARLIC CLOVES, THINLY SLICED

1¼ CUPS MEDIUM-BODIED DRY WHITE WINE
4 TABLESPOONS MIXED CHOPPED FLAT-LEAF PARSLEY
 AND SMALL SAGE LEAVES
SALT AND FRESHLY GROUND BLACK PEPPER
14 OUNCES LASAGNETTE
SHAVED PARMESAN, TO SERVE

1   If using oyster or enoki mushrooms, keep them separate to fry for the shortest time.
2   Fry the shallots and mushrooms in batches in a little oil in a large skillet until lightly colored.
    Add the garlic with the last batch. Remove all the mushrooms from the pan and set aside.
    Stir in the wine and boil until it reduce by about half. Return the mushrooms to the pan,
    add the herbs and seasoning, and warm through slowly.
3   Meanwhile, cook and drain the pasta according to the package directions. Return to
    the pan and lightly toss in the mushroom sauce. Serve with Parmesan shavings.

*   For additional flavor, pour ⅔ cup boiling water over ½ ounce dried wild mushrooms,
    leave to soak 20 minutes before straining off and reserving the liquid.
    Chop the dried mushrooms finely and add them and the liquid with the wine.

VEGETABLE & VEGETARIAN DISHES

161

## 270
# penne with mediterranean vegetables

PREPARATION TIME 10 minutes COOKING TIME 30 minutes SERVES 4

I EGGPLANT, CUT INTO ½-INCH CUBES
VIRGIN OLIVE OIL
8 OUNCES SUMMER SQUASH, SUCH AS PATTY PAN,
   QUARTERED
I RED BELL PEPPER, THINLY SLICED
I RED ONION, THINLY SLICED
4 LARGE WELL-FLAVORED PLUM TOMATOES, CHOPPED
2 GARLIC CLOVES, CHOPPED

I½ TABLESPOONS CHOPPED OREGANO
SALT AND FRESHLY GROUND BLACK PEPPER
14 OUNCES PENNE
FRESHLY GRATED PARMESAN,
   TO SERVE

1   Stir-fry the eggplant in a little oil in a large wok or deep sauté pan until brown; remove with a slotted spoon and drain on paper towels.
2   Then stir-fry the squash until slightly soft. Using a slotted spoon, transfer to paper towels. Repeat with the bell peppers, cooking until limp. Quickly fry the onion until light brown. Return the cooked vegetables to the wok, stir in the tomatoes, garlic, oregano, and seasoning and cook 15 minutes, stirring occasionally, until tender.
3   Meanwhile, cook and drain the pasta according to the package directions.
4   Toss the vegetables with the pasta. Serve with the Parmesan.

## 271
# fusilli lunghi with broiled mediterranean vegetables

PREPARATION TIME 15 minutes COOKING TIME 20 minutes SERVES 4

I FENNEL BULB, CUT LENGTHWISE INTO WEDGES
I SMALL EGGPLANT, SLICED
2 ZUCCHINI, CUT INTO THIN LENGTHWISE STRIPS
   (SEE PAGE 212)
I LARGE, RED BELL PEPPER, CUT INTO STRIPS
5 WELL-FLAVORED PLUM TOMATOES, HALVED
   LENGTHWISE

4 GARLIC CLOVES
3 TABLESPOONS EXTRA-VIRGIN OLIVE OIL
I TABLESPOON THYME LEAVES
I TEASPOON LEMON ZEST
BALSAMIC VINEGAR, FOR SPRINKLING
14 OUNCES FUSILLI LUNGHI
PESTO (SEE PAGE 18), TO SERVE

1   Boil the fennel 2 minutes; drain well.
2   Put all the vegetables and the garlic in an ovenproof bowl. Combine the oil, thyme, and lemon zest, then stir into the vegetables to coat evenly. Cook under a heated broiler 15 to 20 minutes until tender and flecked with brown, stirring as necessary to insure even cooking. Sprinkle with a little balsamic vinegar.
3   Meanwhile, cook and drain the pasta according to package directions. Toss with the vegetables and any juices in the broiler pan, then serve with the pesto.

## 272
# penne rigate with cheeses, celery, & almonds

PREPARATION TIME 10 minutes COOKING TIME 15 minutes SERVES 4

½ CUP **BLANCHED ALMONDS**
**VIRGIN OLIVE OIL**
5 **SMALL CELERY STALKS, THINLY SLICED**
⅔ CUP **LIGHT CREAM**
7 OUNCES **PENNE RIGATE**\*

4 OUNCES **FRESH GOAT CHEESE LOG,**
    **CUT ACROSS INTO 4 SLICES**
½ CUP **CRUMBLED RICOTTA**
⅔ CUP **CRUMBLED GORGONZOLA**
**SALT AND FRESHLY GROUND BLACK PEPPER**
**HANDFUL OF ARUGULA LEAVES, TO SERVE**

1   Lightly brown the almonds in 2 tablespoons oil; scoop out with a slotted spoon and drain on paper towels. Add the celery to the oil and fry until softe but not brown. Pour in the cream and heat slowly to warm through.
2   Meanwhile, cook and drain the pasta according to the package directions.
3   At the same time, place the goat cheese on a sheet of foil under a heated broiler until golden.
4   Toss the pasta with the celery, cream, ricotta, Gorgonzola, almonds, and seasoning. Scatter arugula over each serving, top with a slice of goat cheese, and grind over plenty of black pepper.

\*   Sedani can also be used.

## 273
# taglioni with summer vegetables & fresh herb sauce

PREPARATION TIME 15 minutes, plus standing time COOKING TIME 15 minutes SERVES 4

2 TABLESPOONS **MIXED CHOPPED HERBS, SUCH AS**
    **CHIVES, BASIL, THYME, PARSLEY, AND OREGANO**
**EXTRA-VIRGIN OLIVE OIL**
1½ POUNDS **MIXED VEGETABLES SUCH AS QUARTERED**
    **PATTY PAN SQUASH, SNOW PEAS, BABY FAVA BEANS,**
    **BROCCOLI FLOWERETS, AND CAULIFLOWER**
    **FLOWERETS**

2 **SHALLOTS, FINELY CHOPPED**
14 OUNCES **TAGLIONI**
5 TABLESPOONS **RICOTTA**
**SALT AND FRESHLY GROUND BLACK PEPPER**
**FRESHLY GRATED PARMESAN, TO SERVE**

1   Combine the herbs and 2 tablespoons oil and leave a few hours.
2   Blanch the vegetables (but not the shallots) separately in enough boiling salted water for the pasta, 1 to 3 minutes, according to type, until just tender; drain well. Return the water to a boil.
3   Soften the shallots in 6 tablespoons oil, then add the blanched vegetables and heat through, stirring, but do not brown.
4   Meanwhile, cook the taglioni in the vegetable water according to the package directions; drain, reserving a little of the cooking water. Toss with the vegetables, ricotta, herb sauce, and seasoning. Add enough reserved water, if necessary, to moisten. Serve with plenty of Parmesan.

## 274
# bucatini with roast tomatoes

PREPARATION TIME 10 minutes COOKING TIME 1 hour SERVES 4

6 WELL-FLAVORED PLUM TOMATOES, HALVED
    LENGTHWISE
2 PLUMP GARLIC CLOVES, THINLY SLICED
1 SPRIG OF ROSEMARY, BROKEN INTO PIECES
1 TABLESPOON THYME LEAVES
SALT AND FRESHLY GROUND BLACK PEPPER

5 TABLESPOONS EXTRA-VIRGIN OLIVE OIL
14 OUNCES BUCATINI*
3 TABLESPOONS FRESHLY GRATED PARMESAN,
    PLUS EXTRA TO SERVE
2 TABLESPOONS FRESHLY GRATED PECORINO

1   Heat the oven to 180°F.
2   Place the tomatoes, cut side up, in a single layer on a baking sheet, tucking the garlic and rosemary
    between the pieces. Sprinkle with the thyme and seasoning and trickle a little oil over. Roast in the
    heated oven about 1 hour until the tomatoes shrink slightly and begin to brown; reserve the juices
    in the pan but discard the rosemary. Chop the tomatoes, if liked.
3   Meanwhile, cook and drain the pasta according to the package directions.
4   Toss the pasta with the tomatoes, cooking juices, and cheeses. Serve sprinkled with additional Parmesan.

*   Tagliatelle, spaghetti, pappardelle, or linguine can also be used.

## 275
# cavatappi with spring vegetables & herbs

PREPARATION TIME 5 minutes COOKING TIME 20 minutes SERVES 4

5 OUNCES THIN GREEN BEANS
9 OUNCES SLIM ASPARAGUS
1 GARLIC CLOVE, CRUSHED
5 OUNCES BABY LEEKS, QUARTERED LENGTHWISE
    WITH ROOT ENDS LEFT ATTACHED
1½ CUPS SLICED SMALL ZUCCHINI
VIRGIN OLIVE OIL

12 OUNCES CAVATAPPI*
JUICE OF 1 LARGE LEMON
SMALL HANDFUL CHOPPED MIXED HERBS, SUCH AS
    PARSLEY, THYME, OREGANO, AND TARRAGON
2 TABLESPOONS EXTRA-VIRGIN OLIVE OIL
SALT AND FRESHLY GROUND BLACK PEPPER
FRESHLY GRATED PARMESAN, TO SERVE

1   Cook the beans and asparagus in salted boiling water 3 to 4 minutes until just tender; drain,
    rinse in cold water, and drain again. Cut the asparagus into 1½-inch pieces.
2   Cook the garlic, leeks, and zucchini in a little virgin olive oil in a large skillet until the zucchini
    and leeks are just tender. Stir in the asparagus and beans to warm through.
3   Meanwhile, cook and drain the pasta according to the package directions.
4   Toss the vegetables with the pasta, lemon juice, herbs, a little extra-virgin oil, and seasoning.
    Serve with grated Parmesan.

*   Fusilli can also be used.

## 276
# tagliatelle alla primavera

PREPARATION TIME 10 minutes COOKING TIME 15 minutes SERVES 4

8 OUNCES **SLIM BABY CARROTS**
6 OUNCES **SLIM ASPARAGUS SPEARS**
½ CUP **BROCCOLI FLOWERETS**
4 OUNCES **SUGAR-SNAP PEAS**
2 **ZUCCHINI, DICED**
**SMALL KNOB OF UNSALTED BUTTER**
1 CUP **HEAVY CREAM**

1 BUNCH OF **SCALLIONS, CUT INTO** 1½-INCH **PIECES**
3–4 TABLESPOONS **FRESHLY GRATED PARMESAN**
**SALT AND FRESHLY GROUND BLACK PEPPER**
14 OUNCES **TAGLIATELLE**
2 TABLESPOONS **MIXED THYME, CHOPPED CHIVES,**
   **AND FLAT-LEAF PARSLEY**

1  Cook the carrots, asparagus, and broccoli in boiling salted water 3 to 4 minutes until just tender, adding the sugar-snap peas about 2 minutes before the end of the cooking; drain, refresh under running cold water, and drain thoroughly.
2  Cook the zucchini in the butter until soft but not colored. Stir in the carrots for a couple of minutes.
3  Add the cream and scallions to the zucchini and carrots and bubble, stirring frequently, until slightly reduced by about one-third. Add the asparagus, sugar-snaps, broccoli, Parmesan, and seasoning and warm through.
4  Meanwhile, cook and drain the pasta according to the package directions.
   Toss with the vegetable sauce. Serve sprinkled with the herbs.

## 277
# linguine with new potatoes, beans, & pesto

PREPARATION TIME 5 minutes COOKING TIME 15 minutes SERVES 4

4–5 SMALL NEW POTATOES, UNPEELED
14 OUNCES **LINGUINE**
4 OUNCES **THIN GREEN BEANS**

1 QUANTITY PESTO (SEE PAGE 18), OR TO TASTE
FRESHLY GROUND BLACK PEPPER

1   Boil the potatoes in a pan of water that is large enough for the pasta until tender. Remove the potatoes, drain well, and slice. Bring the water back to a boil.
2   Cook the pasta in the pan according to the package directions, adding the beans 4 to 5 minutes before the end. Add the potato slices the final minute.
3   Drain the pasta, beans, and potatoes, reserving a few spoons of the cooking water. Toss with pesto to taste and black pepper, adding enough of the reserved water to moisten. Serve immediately.

166

## 278
# penne with artichokes, tomatoes, & olives

PREPARATION TIME 5 minutes COOKING TIME 10 minutes SERVES 4

14 OUNCES **PENNE**
1 **RED ONION, THINLY SLICED**
14 **ROASTED ARTICHOKES IN OIL, DRAINED**
  **AND CHOPPED, OIL RESERVED**
2 **GARLIC CLOVES, CHOPPED**
8 **HALVES OF SUN-BLUSH TOMATOES OR PLUMP SUN-**
  **DRIED TOMATOES IN OIL, CHOPPED**

10 **PITTED BLACK OLIVES, CHOPPED**
3 TABLESPOONS **FRESHLY GRATED PECORINO,**
  **PLUS EXTRA TO SERVE**
4 OUNCES **ARUGULA**
**SALT AND FRESHLY GROUND BLACK PEPPER**

1   Cook and drain the pasta according to the package directions.
2   Meanwhile, fry the red onion in 1 tablespoon of the artichoke oil until soft and beginning to brown.
    Add the garlic toward the end of the cooking.
3   Stir in the tomatoes, artichokes, and olives and heat through. Toss with the pasta, cheese,
    arugula, and seasoning. Serve with additional pecorino.

## 279
# fusilli lunghi with spinach & gorgonzola

PREPARATION TIME 5 minutes COOKING TIME 10 minutes SERVES 4

14 OUNCES **FUSILLI LUNGHI**
SCANT 1 CUP **GORGONZOLA, DICED**
5 TABLESPOONS **MILK**
**SMALL KNOB OF UNSALTED BUTTER**

1 POUND **SPINACH**
**FRESHLY GROUND BLACK PEPPER**
**LIGHTLY TOASTED PINE NUTS, TO SERVE**

1   Cook and drain the fusilli lunghi according to the package directions.
2   Meanwhile, gently melt the Gorgonzola in a pan with the milk and butter.
3   Cook the spinach in a dry saucepan 2 to 3 minutes, stirring occasionally, until it wilts; drain well
    in a strainer, pressing out surplus liquid.
4   Toss the spinach, cheese sauce, and plenty of black pepper with the pasta. Serve sprinkled with pine nuts.

## 280
# tagliatelle with green beans & herbs

PREPARATION TIME 10 minutes COOKING TIME 15 minutes SERVES 4

12 OUNCES MIXED SLIM RUNNER BEANS (THINLY
  SLICED LENGTHWISE), THIN GREEN BEANS (HALVED
  ACROSS), AND FRESH PEAS
14 OUNCES TAGLIATELLE
1 GARLIC CLOVE, CRUSHED
OLIVE OIL
5 OUNCES SOFT, MILD GOAT CHEESE, CHOPPED
SMALL BUNCH OF FLAT-LEAF PARSLEY,
  FINELY CHOPPED

LEAVES FROM A SMALL BUNCH OF YOUNG MINT,
  FINELY CHOPPED
⅓ CUP CRÈME FRAÎCHE
SALT AND FRESHLY GROUND BLACK PEPPER
2 TABLESPOONS LIGHTLY TOASTED PINE NUTS
SHAVED PECORINO, TO SERVE

1   Bring the pan of water for the pasta to a boil. Add the beans and peas and cook 3 to 4 minutes
    until almost tender; remove with a slotted spoon. Add the pasta to the pan and cook according
    to the package directions.
2   Meanwhile, fry the garlic in a little oil in a skillet about 2 minutes. Add the goat cheese, herbs,
    and crème fraîche. Warm through and add the beans; season.
3   Drain the pasta and toss with the sauce. Serve scattered with the pine nuts and pecorino.

VEGETABLE & VEGETARIAN DISHES

## 281
# tagliatelle, asparagus, fava bean, & zucchini salad

PREPARATION TIME 10 minutes COOKING TIME 10 minutes SERVES 4

8 OUNCES ASPARAGUS, CUT INTO 1-INCH PIECES
⅓ CUP SHELLED BABY FAVA BEANS
⅔ CUP THICKLY SLICED BABY ZUCCHINI
18 OUNCES FRESH TAGLIATELLE (SEE PAGE 9)
12 SUN-BLUSH TOMATOES
FRESHLY GRATED PARMESAN, TO SERVE

DRESSING
2 TABLESPOONS VIRGIN OLIVE OIL
JUICE OF 1 LARGE LEMON
2 SCALLIONS, FINELY CHOPPED
2 TABLESPOONS COARSELY CHOPPED TARRAGON
SALT AND FRESHLY GROUND BLACK PEPPER

1   Bring a pan of water large enough for cooking the pasta to a boil. Boil the asparagus 2 minutes; remove
    with a slotted spoon. Repeat with the fava beans, cooking them 2 to 3 minutes, and then the zucchini
    slices, cooking them for 1 minute; set aside.
2   Meanwhile, make the dressing by whisking the ingredients together with seasoning.
3   Cook and drain the tagliatelle (see page 13), reserving ½ cup of the cooking water. Toss with the
    vegetables, sun-blush tomatoes, and dressing, and about 4 tablespoons of the reserved cooking water,
    to moisten. Serve with plenty of freshly grated Parmesan.

## 282
# warm pasta, mushrooms, & broiled vegetable salad

PREPARATION TIME 10 minutes COOKING TIME 25 minutes SERVES 4 to 6

I GARLIC CLOVE, SLICED

4 TABLESPOONS OLIVE OIL

I EGGPLANT, CUT LENGTHWISE INTO ½-INCH STRIPS

3¼ CUPS SLICED MIXED OYSTER AND SHIITAKE
   MUSHROOMS

4 OUNCES SUN-DRIED TOMATOES IN OIL

I SMALL RED BELL PEPPER, BROILED,
   PEELED, AND SLICED (SEE PAGE 67)

I SMALL YELLOW BELL PEPPER, BROILED,
   PEELED, AND SLICED (SEE PAGE 67)

I RED CHILI, SEEDED AND THINLY SLICED

8 OUNCES ROAST ARTICHOKES IN OIL,
   DRAINED AND HALVED

⅔ CUP PITTED OIL-CURED BLACK OLIVES

2 TABLESPOONS BALSAMIC VINEGAR

SALT AND FRESHLY GROUND BLACK PEPPER

I POUND RIGATONI

1. Warm the garlic in the oil in a small saucepan over very low heat 15 minutes; do not let it get too hot or the garlic will fry. Scoop out the garlic.
2. Brush the eggplant slices generously with the garlic oil and cook under a heated, very hot broiler about 8 minutes until soft and charred on both sides.
3. Meanwhile, cook the mushrooms with the sun-dried tomatoes and their oil over high heat about 3 minutes, stirring frequently. Transfer to a large bowl and add the peppers, chili, eggplant, artichokes, olives, balsamic vinegar, and seasoning. Cover to keep warm.
4. Cook and drain the pasta according to the package directions. Toss with the vegetable mixture and serve.

## 283
# tonnarelli with roast bell peppers, eggplant, fennel, & olives

PREPARATION TIME 10 minutes COOKING TIME 20 to 25 minutes SERVES 4

2 RED BELL PEPPERS, CUT INTO BITE-SIZE PIECES

I SMALL EGGPLANT, CUT INTO BITE-SIZE PIECES

I SMALL FENNEL BULB, CUT INTO BITE-SIZE PIECES

5 WELL-FLAVORED RIPE PLUM TOMATOES,
   QUARTERED

6 GARLIC CLOVES

PINCH OF CRUSHED CHILI FLAKES

VIRGIN OLIVE OIL

SALT AND FRESHLY GROUND BLACK PEPPER

14 OUNCES TONNARELLI*

⅔ CUP PITTED GREEN OLIVES

½ CUP RICOTTA

SMALL HANDFUL OF BASIL LEAVES, SHREDDED

FRESHLY GRATED PARMESAN, TO SERVE

1. Heat the oven to 400°F.
2. Put the peppers, eggplant, fennel, tomatoes, garlic, and chili flakes in a roasting pan. Trickle some oil over, season, and stir to combine the ingredients. Spread in an even layer. Bake in the heated oven 20 to 25 minutes until soft and lightly charred.
3. Meanwhile, cook and drain the pasta according to the package directions. Toss with 2 tablespoons oil, the cooked vegetables, olives, ricotta, and basil. Serve with freshly grated Parmesan.

\* Penne, ditali, or cavatappi can also be used.

# 284
# strozzapreti with cauliflower, saffron, & tomatoes

PREPARATION TIME 10 minutes plus 10 minutes soaking COOKING TIME 15 minutes SERVES 4

PINCH OF SAFFRON THREADS, CRUSHED

1 SMALL CAULIFLOWER, DIVIDED INTO FLOWERETS

12 ounces STROZZAPRETI

1 SMALL ONION, FINELY CHOPPED

VIRGIN OLIVE OIL

2 GARLIC CLOVES, FINELY CHOPPED

5 WELL-FLAVORED TOMATOES, PEELED, IF LIKED, SEEDED AND CHOPPED

3 tablespoons FRESHLY GRATED PARMESAN, PLUS EXTRA TO SERVE

1  Pour a little boiling water over the saffron and leave to soak about 10 minutes.

2  Meanwhile, cook the cauliflower in boiling salted water until almost tender, then drain. Cook the pasta according to the package directions, then drain.

3  While the cauliflower is cooking, fry the onion in a little oil until soft and transparent, adding the garlic toward the end of the cooking time. Add the tomatoes, drained cauliflower, and saffron water and cook, stirring frequently, 2 to 3 minutes.

4  Stir the pasta and Parmesan into the cauliflower mixture about 30 seconds, then serve with extra Parmesan.

*  Conchiglie, farfalle, or gnocchi can also be used.

## 285
# pasta provençal

PREPARATION TIME 10 minutes COOKING TIME 20 minutes SERVES 4

3 TABLESPOONS **EXTRA-VIRGIN OLIVE OIL**
1½–2 TABLESPOONS **BALSAMIC VINEGAR**
1 SMALL **GARLIC CLOVE, FINELY CHOPPED**
1 TABLESPOON **CHOPPED CAPERS**
2 TABLESPOONS **FRESHLY GRATED PARMESAN**
**SALT AND FRESHLY GROUND BLACK PEPPER**

1 LARGE **RED BELL PEPPER, HALVED**
1 **ZUCCHINI, THINLY SLICED**
3 WELL-FLAVORED **PLUM TOMATOES, QUARTERED**
1 **EGGPLANT, THINLY SLICED**
7 OUNCES **ELICHE\***
2 TABLESPOONS **SHREDDED BASIL**

1 Make a dressing by whisking the oil with the vinegar, garlic, capers, and Parmesan; season.
2 Broil the pepper halves 8 to 12 minutes until charred and blistered. Discard the charred patches and slice the peppers. At the same time, broil the zucchini slices 3 to 4 minutes per side until soft and flecked with brown. When there is space on the broiler, cook the tomatoes about 5 minutes until lightly charred.
3 Meanwhile, cook the eggplant slices on a hot ridged griddle pan 3 to 4 minutes per side until soft and marked with char lines. Cut into strips and toss with the other vegetables.
4 While the vegetables are cooking, cook and drain the pasta according to the package directions. Toss with the vegetables, basil, and dressing.

\* Fusilli and cavatappi can also be used.

## 286
# tagliatelle with red bell peppers & mozzarella

PREPARATION TIME 10 minutes COOKING TIME 15 minutes SERVES 4

9 OUNCES **TAGLIATELLE**
6 MIXED BROILED **RED AND YELLOW BELL PEPPER HALVES IN OIL, DRAINED AND SLICED\***
3 TABLESPOONS **EXTRA-VIRGIN OLIVE OIL**
JUICE OF ½ **LEMON**
LEAVES FROM A SMALL BUNCH OF **FLAT-LEAF PARSLEY, CHOPPED**

**SALT AND FRESHLY GROUND BLACK PEPPER**
SCANT 1 CUP **CUBED BUFFALO MOZZARELLA**
20 PITTED **OIL-CURED BLACK OLIVES, HALVED**
1 TABLESPOON **SALT-PACKED CAPERS, RINSED AND DRIED**

1 Cook and drain the tagliatelle according to the package directions.
2 Meanwhile, place the pepper strips under a hot broiler until sizzling.
3 While the peppers are cooking, whisk the oil with the lemon juice, then add the parsley and the peppers when they are ready; season.
4 Toss the pasta with the cheese, then add the dressing, olives, and capers. Serve straightaway, so the cheese is just melting.

\* If these are not available, use bottled red peppers instead. Rinse them and toss in oil before putting under the broiler.

## 287
# penne with creamy tomato & basil sauce

PREPARATION TIME 5 minutes COOKING TIME 10 minutes SERVES 4

I ONION, FINELY CHOPPED
2 GARLIC CLOVES, CRUSHED
VIRGIN OLIVE OIL
2 CANS (15-oz.) CRUSHED PLUM TOMATOES
½ CUP HEAVY CREAM

SALT AND FRESHLY GROUND BLACK PEPPER
SMALL HANDFUL OF BASIL LEAVES, SHREDDED
14 OUNCES PENNE
FRESHLY GRATED PARMESAN, TO SERVE

1  Fry the onion and garlic in a little oil in a heavy pan until soft. Pour in the tomatoes and simmer slowly, stirring occasionally until thick and darkened to a deeper red. Puree in a blender, return to the pan, and add the cream. Heat though without letting boil; season and add the basil.
2  Meanwhile, cook and drain the pasta according to the package directions.
Toss with the sauce and serve with Parmesan.

## 288
# pappardelle with mushrooms & leeks

PREPARATION TIME 10 minutes COOKING TIME 10 minutes SERVES 4

4¼ CUPS SLICED SHIITAKE MUSHROOMS
5 BABY LEEKS, SLICED
VIRGIN OLIVE OIL
3 GARLIC CLOVES, CRUSHED
SALT AND FRESHLY GROUND BLACK PEPPER
10 OUNCES FRESH PAPPARDELLE

LEAVES FROM A SMALL BUNCH OF FLAT-LEAF
  PARSLEY, FINELY CHOPPED
FINELY GRATED ZEST OF ½ LEMON
4 TABLESPOONS FRESHLY GRATED PARMESAN,
  PLUS EXTRA TO SERVE

1  Fry the shiitake and leeks in oil in a large skillet until golden, adding the garlic toward the end; season.
2  Cook and drain the pasta according to the package directions, reserving ½ cup of the water.
Toss the pasta with the vegetables, parsley, lemon zest, cheese, and about 5 to 6 tablespoons of the reserved water, to moisten. Serve with additional Parmesan.

## 289
# tagliatelle with asparagus & parmesan

PREPARATION TIME 5 minutes COOKING TIME 15 minutes SERVES 4

12 OUNCES **ASPARAGUS, CUT INTO 2-INCH PIECES**
10 OUNCES **TAGLIATELLE**
1 **GARLIC CLOVE, FINELY CHOPPED**
4 TABLESPOONS **UNSALTED BUTTER**

1 TABLESPOON **LEMON JUICE**
**SALT AND FRESHLY GROUND BLACK PEPPER**
**FRESHLY GRATED PARMESAN, TO SERVE**

1   Bring enough water to a boil for cooking the pasta. Add the asparagus, cook 2 minutes, and remove with a slotted spoon. Add the pasta to the water and cook and drain according to the package directions, reserving ½ cup of the cooking water.
2   Meanwhile, fry the asparagus with the garlic in the butter about 3 minutes over medium heat so it does not brown. Add the lemon juice and seasoning. Toss with the pasta, adding a little of the cooking water, if necessary, to moisten. Serve with freshly grated Parmesan.

## 290
# tagliatelle with tomatoes, mozzarella, & herbs

PREPARATION TIME 10 minutes COOKING TIME 10 minutes SERVES 4

1¼ POUNDS **RIPE PLUM TOMATOES, SEEDED AND VERY FINELY CHOPPED**
1½ CUPS **DICED BUFFALO MOZZARELLA**
**LEAVES FROM A BUNCH OF MIXED HERBS, SUCH AS BASIL, PARSLEY, MARJORAM, AND THYME, CHOPPED**

**SALT AND FRESHLY GROUND BLACK PEPPER**
6 TABLESPOONS **EXTRA-VIRGIN OLIVE OIL**
14 OUNCES **TAGLIATELLE**

1   Combine the tomatoes, cheese, herbs, and seasoning.
2   Heat the oil in a small saucepan until it is very hot, then stir into the tomato mixture; set aside.
3   Cook and drain the pasta according to the package directions. Toss thoroughly with the tomato mixture, then cover and leave about 2 minutes so the mozzarella starts to melt.

## 291

# pappardelle with roast mushrooms

PREPARATION TIME 5 minutes COOKING TIME 15 minutes SERVES 4

1½ POUNDS MIXED MUSHROOMS, SUCH AS SHIITAKE
   AND OYSTER, BROKEN INTO HALVES
   OR QUARTERS AS NECESSARY
3½ TABLESPOONS VIRGIN OLIVE OIL
JUICE OF 1 LEMON

SALT AND FRESHLY GROUND BLACK PEPPER
SMALL KNOB OF UNSALTED BUTTER
1 POUND FRESH PAPPARDELLE (SEE PAGE 10)*
2 TABLESPOONS CHOPPED FLAT-LEAF PARSLEY
FRESHLY GRATED PARMESAN, TO SERVE

1   Heat the oven to 350°F.
2   Put the mushrooms in a roasting pan. Trickle the oil and lemon juice over. Add seasoning and stir the mushrooms to coat. Dot with the butter and roast in the heated oven 15 minutes.
3   Meanwhile, cook and drain the pasta (see page 13). Toss with the mushrooms, the cooking juices, and the parsley and serve with freshly grated Parmesan.

*   Dried pappardelle can also be used.

## 292

# casareccia with broccoli & gorgonzola

PREPARATION TIME 5 minutes COOKING TIME 10 minutes SERVES 4

12 OUNCES CASARECCIA*
1¾ CUPS BROCCOLI FLOWERETS
⅔ CUP MEDIUM-BODIED DRY WHITE WINE
1 CUP CHOPPED GORGONZOLA
FRESHLY GROUND BLACK PEPPER

½ CUP WALNUT HALVES, LIGHTLY TOASTED
   AND CHOPPED
FRESHLY GRATED PARMESAN, TO SERVE

1   Cook and drain the pasta according to the package directions, adding the broccoli for the final 3 to 4 minutes of the cooking time.
2   Meanwhile, in a separate pan, boil the wine rapidly until reduced by half. Remove from the heat and stir in the Gorgonzola so it is just beginning to melt. Season with black pepper and toss with the pasta, broccoli, and walnuts; serve with Parmesan.

*   Other pasta shapes such as gnocchi, conchiglie, pipe rigate, or radiatori can also be used.

# 293
# farfalle with peas, mint, & ricotta

PREPARATION TIME 5 minutes COOKING TIME 10 minutes SERVES 4

10 OUNCES **FARFALLE**
3 CUPS **FRESH OR FROZEN PEAS**
HEAPED 1 CUP **RICOTTA**

**SMALL LEAVES FROM A SMALL BUNCH OF MINT**
**SALT AND FRESHLY GROUND BLACK PEPPER**
**PARMESAN SHAVINGS, TO SERVE**

1   Cook and drain the pasta according to the package directions.
2   Meanwhile, cook fresh peas in boiling water 4 to 5 minutes, frozen peas 2 minutes; drain, reserving 2 tablespoons of the cooking water.
3   Puree one-third of the peas with the ricotta, reserved water, and mint leaves. Transfer to a small nonstick saucepan, season, and warm through slowly, stirring frequently.
4   Add the remaining peas to the pasta just before it is ready to warm through. Drain and toss with the sauce. Serve topped with Parmesan shavings.

## 294
# black pepper tagliatelle with three-cheese sauce

PREPARATION TIME 5 minutes COOKING TIME 5 minutes SERVES 4

14 ounces **FRESH BLACK PEPPER TAGLIATELLE (SEE PAGE 10), OR PLAIN FRESH TAGLIATELLE**
½ cup **HEAVY CREAM**
⅓ cup **RICOTTA**
½ cup **FINELY CHOPPED GORGONZOLA**

3 tablespoons **FRESHLY GRATED PARMESAN**
**SALT AND FRESHLY GROUND BLACK PEPPER**
½ cup **WALNUT HALVES, LIGHTLY TOASTED AND CHOPPED**

1  Gently heat the cream, ricotta, Gorgonzola, and Parmesan in a pan, stirring occasionally until the Gorgonzola almost melts. Season; if using plain tagliatelle, use plenty of black pepper.
2  Meanwhile, cook and drain the pasta according to the instructions. Toss with the sauce and walnuts.

## 295
# pasta, leeks, & cheese al forno

PREPARATION TIME 10 minutes COOKING TIME 45 minutes SERVES 4

9 ounces **PASTA, SUCH AS CHIFFERI, FUSILLI, OR MACARONI**
2 **SMALL LEEKS, HALVED LENGTHWISE, THINLY SLICED**
2 **GARLIC CLOVES, FINELY CHOPPED**
**SMALL KNOB OF UNSALTED BUTTER**
3 **EGGS, BEATEN**

scant 1 cup **RICOTTA**
1 cup **MILK**
**SALT AND FRESHLY GROUND BLACK PEPPER**
6 ounces **FONTINA, GRATED**

1  Heat the oven to 375°F.
2  Cook and drain the pasta according to the package directions, giving it 2 minutes less than specified.
3  While the pasta is cooking, fry the leek and garlic in the butter until soft.
4  Meanwhile, stir the eggs into the ricotta, then stir in the milk until smooth; season. Mix with the pasta, cheese, and leek mixture. Pour into a large buttered baking dish. Bake in the heated oven about 35 minutes until just set and golden on top.

## 296
# pappardelle with
# roast cherry tomatoes, basil, & ricotta

PREPARATION TIME 10 minutes COOKING TIME 10 minutes SERVES 4

1½ POUNDS **RIPE, WELL-FLAVORED**
    **CHERRY TOMATOES, HALVED**
2 **PLUMP GARLIC CLOVES,**
    **FINELY CHOPPED**
½ TEASPOON **DRIED OREGANO**

**SALT AND FRESHLY GROUND BLACK PEPPER**
5 TABLESPOONS **VIRGIN OLIVE OIL**
14 OUNCES **PAPPARDELLE**
⅔ CUP **CRUMBLED RICOTTA**
**HANDFUL OF BASIL LEAVES, SHREDDED**

1   Heat the oven to 400°F.
2   Put the tomatoes in a roasting pan. Sprinkle the garlic, oregano, and seasoning over.
    Trickle the oil over and roast in the heated oven 20 to 25 minutes until they begin to collapse.
3   Meanwhile, cook and drain the pasta according to the package directions.
    Toss with the ricotta, tomatoes, and their cooking juices and basil.

## 297
# tagliatelle with fava beans
# & goat cheese

PREPARATION TIME 5 minutes COOKING TIME 10 minutes SERVES 4

14 OUNCES **TAGLIATELLE\***
1 POUND **BABY FAVA BEANS**
3 TABLESPOONS **OLIVE OIL**
10 OUNCES **SOFT, RINDLESS GOAT CHEESE**

**SMALL LEAVES FROM A SMALL BUNCH OF MINT,**
    **CHOPPED**
**SALT AND FRESHLY GROUND BLACK PEPPER**
**FRESHLY GRATED PARMESAN, TO SERVE**

1   Cook and drain the pasta according to the package directions, adding the fava beans about 4 minutes
    before the end of cooking, reserving ½ cup of the cooking water.
2   Meanwhile, stir the oil into the goat cheese, then add the mint and seasoning. Toss with the pasta,
    adding a little of the cooking water, if necessary, to moisten, and serve with freshly grated Parmesan.

\*   Pasta shapes such as conchiglie or gnocchi can also be used.

## 298
# cavatappi with artichokes, mushrooms, & peas

PREPARATION TIME 10 minutes COOKING TIME 10 minutes SERVES 4

10 ounces CAVATAPPI

3 cups SHELLED FRESH PEAS

2¼–3¼ cups QUARTERED CREMINI MUSHROOMS

1 GARLIC CLOVE, CHOPPED

OLIVE OIL

1 BUNCH OF SCALLIONS, COARSELY CHOPPED

6–8 BROILED ARTICHOKES IN OIL, DRAINED AND
  HALVED OR QUARTERED

PINCH OF THYME LEAVES

1 TABLESPOON CHOPPED FLAT-LEAF PARSLEY

SALT AND FRESHLY GROUND BLACK PEPPER

1 TABLESPOON CHOPPED BASIL

FRESHLY GRATED PARMESAN, TO SERVE

1   Cook and drain the pasta according to the package directions.
2   Meanwhile, boil the peas in a smaller pan of water until just tender. Drain, reserving 2 to 3 tablespoons of the cooking water.
3   At the same time, fry the mushrooms and garlic in a little oil, stirring occasionally, 3 to 4 minutes until the mushrooms are tender. Stir in the scallions, artichokes, thyme, parsley, peas, reserved cooking water to moisten, and seasoning. Cover and heat together a couple of minutes. Add the basil and toss with the pasta. Serve with freshly grated Parmesan.

## 299
# linguine, tomatoes, bell peppers, & black olives en papillote

PREPARATION TIME 10 minutes COOKING TIME 20 minutes SERVES 4

2¼ cups PASSATA (BOTTLED STRAINED PUREED
  TOMATOES)

2 GARLIC CLOVES, FINELY CHOPPED

8 ounces LINGUINE

3 PLUM TOMATOES, SEEDED AND SLIVERED

1 SMALL RED BELL PEPPER, THINLY SLICED

20 PITTED OIL-CURED BLACK OLIVES, QUARTERED

LEAVES FROM A SMALL BUNCH OF BASIL, SHREDDED

1 TABLESPOON CHOPPED FLAT-LEAF PARSLEY

SALT AND FRESHLY GROUND BLACK PEPPER

FRESHLY GRATED PARMESAN, TO SERVE

1   Heat the oven to 375°F. Cut 4 pieces of baking parchment measuring 12-inches square and lightly grease.
2   Simmer the passata with the garlic until slightly reduced.
3   Meanwhile, cook the linguine according to the package directions but for 1 minute less than specified, then drain. Toss with the tomato sauce, the slivered tomatoes, red bell pepper, olives, herbs, and seasoning.
4   Place one-quarter in the middle of each of the 4 greased pieces of paper. Fold the paper loosely over the mixture and twist the edges together firmly to seal well. Place in a shallow roasting pan and bake in the heated oven 15 minutes. Serve with freshly grated Parmesan.

## 300
# tortiglioni with eggplant & tomato

PREPARATION TIME 10 minutes plus an optional 30 minutes standing COOKING TIME 35 minutes SERVES 4

2 SMALL EGGPLANTS, COARSELY CHOPPED
SALT AND FRESHLY GROUND BLACK PEPPER
1 ONION, THICKLY SLICED LENGTHWISE
VIRGIN OLIVE OIL
3 GARLIC CLOVES, FINELY CHOPPED
1 CAN (15-oz.) CRUSHED PLUM TOMATOES
4 TABLESPOONS DRAINED AND CHOPPED SUN-DRIED
  TOMATOES IN OIL

⅔ CUP RED OR MEDIUM-BODIED DRY WHITE WINE
⅓ CUP PITTED KALAMATA OLIVES
2 TABLESPOONS OREGANO
12 OUNCES TORTIGLIONI
4 OUNCES FONTINA, GRATED
3 TABLESPOONS FRESHLY GRATED PARMESAN

1   If you wish, so the eggplant absorbs less oil, sprinkle it with salt and leave in a colander placed
    on a plate to drain 30 minutes; rinse well and dry thoroughly.
2   Fry the onion in a little oil in a large skillet and fry until soft. Add the garlic, fry 30 seconds, then add
    the eggplant and cook 3 minutes, stirring frequently. Add the tomatoes, sun-dried tomatoes, and wine.
    Cover and simmer about 15 minutes until the eggplant is tender. Add the olives, oregano, and seasoning.
3   Meanwhile, cook and drain the pasta according to the package directions. Toss with the eggplant sauce.
4   Transfer to a gratin dish, sprinkle the cheeses over and put under a heated broiler until the cheese
    is melted and golden. Alternatively, bake in a heated oven at 400°F 20 minutes.

## 301
# riccioli with broccoli, taleggio, & almonds

PREPARATION TIME 5 minutes COOKING TIME 10 minutes SERVES 4

13 OUNCES RICCIOLI*
1 LEEK, THINLY SLICED
1 GARLIC CLOVE, FINELY CHOPPED
OLIVE OIL
10 OUNCES BROCCOLI FLOWERETS
¾ CUP MEDIUM-BODIED DRY WHITE WINE
2 OUNCES TALEGGIO, GRATED

2–3 TABLESPOONS SLIVERED ALMONDS,
  LIGHTLY TOASTED
SALT AND FRESHLY GROUND BLACK PEPPER
FRESHLY GRATED PARMESAN, TO SERVE

1   Cook and drain the pasta according to the package directions.
2   Meanwhile, fry the leek and garlic in a little oil 2 to 3 minutes until translucent. Add the broccoli and
    cook 1 minute longer before pouring in the wine. Simmer until the broccoli is tender and the wine
    almost evaporated, stirring carefully occasionally; there should be enough wine left to moisten the sauce.
3   Remove the pan from the heat, add the Taleggio and toss with the pasta, almonds, and seasoning.
    Serve with Parmesan.

*   Orecchiette, gnocchi, and conchiglie can also be used.

## 302

# green & white tagliatelle
# with ricotta, tomatoes, & basil

PREPARATION TIME 5 minutes plus 30 minutes standing COOKING TIME 5 minutes SERVES 4

1¼ POUNDS RIPE, WELL-FLAVORED TOMATOES,
  PREFERABLY PLUM, CHOPPED
I GARLIC CLOVE, FINELY CHOPPED
3 TABLESPOONS EXTRA-VIRGIN OLIVE OIL
SALT AND FRESHLY GROUND BLACK PEPPER

13 OUNCES FRESH GREEN AND WHITE TAGLIATELLE
  (PAGLIA E FIENO)
⅔ CUP CRUMBLED RICOTTA
SMALL HANDFUL OF BASIL LEAVES, SHREDDED

I    Combine the tomatoes with the garlic, oil, and seasoning; leave to stand at least 30 minutes.
2    Cook and drain the pasta. Toss with the ricotta, basil, and tomatoes. Serve warm or at room temperature.

## 303

# penne with eggplants, olives, & basil

PREPARATION TIME 10 minutes COOKING TIME 15 minutes SERVES 4

2 EGGPLANTS, ABOUT 1 POUND IN TOTAL, CHOPPED
4 GARLIC CLOVES, THINLY SLICED
5 TABLESPOONS VIRGIN OLIVE OIL
2 TABLESPOONS SUN-DRIED TOMATO PASTE
I TEASPOON DRIED OREGANO

12 PITTED BLACK OLIVES, SLICED
SALT AND FRESHLY GROUND BLACK PEPPER
ABOUT 2 TEASPOONS BALSAMIC VINEGAR
14 OUNCES PENNE
HANDFUL OF BASIL LEAVES, SHREDDED

I    Fry the eggplant and garlic in the oil in a large skillet until brown. Stir in the tomato paste and 4
     tablespoons hot water. Add the oregano and olives and cook slowly until the eggplants are tender, stirring
     occasionally. Add more water if they become too dry. Season and sprinkle with balsamic vinegar to taste.
2    Meanwhile, cook and drain the pasta according to the package directions, reserving ½ cup of the cooking
     water. Toss with the eggplant sauce and basil, adding reserved cooking water if necessary to moisten.

## 304

# strozzapreti with bell peppers & mushrooms

PREPARATION TIME 10 minutes COOKING TIME 15 minutes SERVES 4

4 GARLIC CLOVES, FINELY CHOPPED
I ROSEMARY SPRIG
2 SAGE SPRIGS
5 TABLESPOONS VIRGIN OLIVE OIL
7 CUPS SLICED CREMINI MUSHROOMS
2 RED BELL PEPPERS, SLICED

SALT AND FRESHLY GROUND BLACK PEPPER
14 OUNCES STROZZAPRETI
3 TABLESPOONS FRESHLY GRATED PARMESAN

I    Fry the garlic and herb sprigs in the oil about 2 minutes until the garlic begins to brown. Scoop out with
     a slotted spoon and discard the garlic and herbs.
2    Add the mushrooms to the pan and fry briskly until the moisture evaporates. Add the peppers and cook
     over medium-high heat until tende; season.
3    Meanwhile, cook and drain the pasta according to the package directions. Toss with the vegetables and
     Parmesan and serve.

VEGETABLE & VEGETARIAN DISHES

## 305
# penne rigate with spicy tomato sauce

PREPARATION TIME 5 minutes COOKING TIME 20 minutes SERVES 4

I ONION, THINLY SLICED
5 TABLESPOONS VIRGIN OLIVE OIL
3 GARLIC CLOVES, SLICED
I TEASPOON CRUSHED CHILI FLAKES
2 CANS (15-oz.) CRUSHED PLUM TOMATOES

SALT AND FRESHLY GROUND BLACK PEPPER
14 OUNCES PENNE RIGATE
2 TABLESPOONS SHREDDED BASIL LEAVES
2 TABLESPOONS FRESHLY GRATED PARMESAN

1   Fry the onion in the oil until soft and golden, adding the garlic and chili the last 2 minutes.
    Pour in the tomatoes and simmer about 15 minutes until thick, stirring frequently; season.
2   Meanwhile, cook and drain the pasta according to the package directions.
    Toss with the sauce, basil. and Parmesan.

## 306
# ditali with tomatoes, garlic, & broiled bell peppers

PREPARATION TIME 10 minutes COOKING TIME 25 minutes SERVES 4

2 PLUMP GARLIC CLOVES, FINELY CHOPPED
PINCH OF CHILI FLAKES
VIRGIN OLIVE OIL
1¾ CUPS PEELED, SEEDED, AND CHOPPED WELL-
    FLAVORED TOMATOES

2 PLUMP RED BELL PEPPERS,
    BROILED, PEELED, AND FINELY CHOPPED
14 OUNCES DITALI
FRESHLY GRATED PARMESAN, TO SERVE (OPTIONAL)

1   Fry the garlic and chilies in some olive oil 1 minute. Add the tomatoes and cook about 20 minutes,
    stirring occasionally, until thick. Stir in the peppers and cook gently 5 minutes or so longer;
    do not let the sauce become too thick.
2   Meanwhile, cook and drain the pasta according to the package directions.
    Toss with the sauce and serve with freshly grated Parmesan, if liked.

## 307
# penne with fava beans, parsley, & pecorino

PREPARATION TIME 10 minutes COOKING TIME 10 minutes SERVES 4

14 OUNCES PENNE
2 CUPS FRESH OR FROZEN FAVA BEANS, THAWED
2 GARLIC CLOVES, FINELY CHOPPED
VIRGIN OLIVE OIL

2 TABLESPOONS CHOPPED FLAT-LEAF PARSLEY
4 TABLESPOONS FRESHLY GRATED PECORINO,
    PLUS EXTRA TO SERVE

1   Cook and drain the pasta according to the package directions, adding the fava beans the last
    3 to 4 minutes.
2   Meanwhile, fry the garlic in some olive oil 1 minute. Stir in the pasta and fava beans to
    coat with the oil, then toss with the parsley and pecorino. Serve with extra pecorino.

## 308
# pennette with broccoli, pine nuts, & chilies

PREPARATION TIME 5 minutes COOKING TIME 10 minutes SERVES 4

I HEAPED CUP **BROCCOLI FLOWERETS**
14 OUNCES **PENNETTE**
**PINCH OF CHILI FLAKES**
I **GARLIC CLOVE, FINELY CHOPPED**

4 TABLESPOONS **PINE NUTS**
**OLIVE OIL**
**SALT**
**FRESHLY GRATED PARMESAN, TO SERVE**

1   Bring enough water to a boil for cooking the pasta. Add the broccoli and cook 3 to 4 minutes until just tender; remove with a slotted spoon. Add the pasta to the water, cook and drain according to the package directions, reserving ½ cup of the cooking water.
2   Meanwhile, fry the chili flakes, garlic, and pine nuts in a little oil 2 minutes; do not allow the nuts and garlic to burn. Add the broccoli and heat through, stirring frequently. Season with salt.
3   Toss with the pasta, adding a little of the cooking water, if necessary, to moisten, and serve with freshly grated Parmesan.

## 309
# fusilli with zucchini, tomatoes, & basil

PREPARATION TIME 10 minutes COOKING TIME 10 minutes SERVES 4

12 OUNCES **FUSILLI**
2 **SLIM ZUCCHINI, SLICED INTO DISKS**
**VIRGIN OLIVE OIL**
I **PLUMP GARLIC CLOVE, CRUSHED**
2 **WELL-FLAVORED TOMATOES, SEEDED AND CHOPPED**
I TABLESPOON **CHOPPED FLAT-LEAF PARSLEY**

**JUICE OF ½ LEMON**
**SALT AND FRESHLY GROUND BLACK PEPPER**
⅔ CUP **CHOPPED BUFFALO MOZZARELLA**
1½ TABLESPOONS **SHREDDED BASIL**

1   Cook the pasta according to the package directions and drain lightly.
2   Meanwhile, fry the zucchini in a little oil 3 to 4 minutes until almost tender. Add the garlic and cook 1 to 2 minutes. Stir in the tomatoes, parsley, lemon juice, 2 tablespoons olive oil, and seasoning just to warm through; do not cook.
3   Add the mozzarella and basil and toss with the pasta. Cover and leave 1 to 2 minutes, over a very low heat, if necessary, so the mozzarella begins to melt.

## 310
# agnolotti with broiled vegetable dressing

PREPARATION TIME 10 minutes plus 1 hour standing COOKING TIME 20 minutes SERVES 4

½ RED BELL PEPPER, HALVED
½ YELLOW BELL PEPPER, HALVED
1 ZUCCHINI, HALVED LENGTHWISE
6 GARLIC CLOVES, UNPEELED
SALT AND FRESHLY GROUND BLACK PEPPER
½ CUP MIXED VIRGIN OLIVE OIL AND OIL
  FROM THE TOMATOES

2 TABLESPOONS WHITE WINE VINEGAR
2 SUN-DRIED TOMATOES IN OIL, DRAINED
  (OIL RESERVED) AND FINELY CHOPPED
1 TABLESPOON PINE NUTS, LIGHTLY TOASTED
1 QUANTITY CHEESE AND HERB AGNOLOTTI
  (SEE PAGE 195)*

1   Put the peppers, zucchini, and garlic on a nonstick baking tray. Spray with oil, stirring the vegetables
    so they are evenly coated; sprinkle with seasoning. Broil until lightly charred and becoming tender,
    stirring occasionally.
2   Meanwhile, whisk the oil with the vinegar until emulsified.
3   Peel the garlic and mash the flesh with a pinch of salt. Whisk into the dressing, then add the
    sun-dried tomatoes and pine nuts.
4   Discard charred patches from the other vegetables and chop them finely. Combine the vegetables
    and dressing.
5   Cook the agnolotti, in batches if necessary, in simmering water about 4 minutes; drain. Put into
    a large shallow dish and spoon the roast vegetable dressing over. Leave 1 hour before serving.

*   The dressing can also be served with other stuffed pastas such as tortellini, ravioli, or raviolini.

183

## 311

# farfalle with mushrooms, sun-dried tomatoes, & spinach

PREPARATION TIME 10 minutes COOKING TIME 15 minutes SERVES 4

1 ONION, FINELY CHOPPED
VIRGIN OLIVE OIL
2 GARLIC CLOVES, CHOPPED
3½ CUPS THINLY SLICED CREMINI MUSHROOMS
¾ CUP MEDIUM-BODIED DRY WHITE WINE
6 OUNCES SMALL SPINACH LEAVES

3 OUNCES SUN-DRIED TOMATOES IN OIL,
   DRAINED AND SLICED
SALT AND FRESHLY GROUND BLACK PEPPER
12 OUNCES FARFALLE
CHOPPED FLAT-LEAF PARSLEY, LIGHTLY TOASTED PINE
   NUTS, AND FRESHLY GRATED PARMESAN, TO SERVE

1    Fry the onion in a little olive oil in a large skillet until soft and pale golden. Add the garlic and
     mushrooms and fry briskly 2 minutes. Pour in the wine and bubble to reduce slightly,
     then add the spinach and tomatoes. Cook until the spinach wilts; season.
2    Meanwhile, cook and drain the pasta according to the package directions. Toss with the mushroom
     mixture. Scatter parsley and pine nuts over, toss lightly, and serve with Parmesan.

## 312

# spinach & ricotta ravioli

PREPARATION TIME 45 minutes COOKING TIME 15 minutes SERVES 4

2-EGG QUANTITY OF PASTA DOUGH (SEE PAGE 10)

FILLING
2 GARLIC CLOVES, CRUSHED
1 TABLESPOON UNSALTED BUTTER
7 OUNCES BABY SPINACH LEAVES

⅔ CUP RICOTTA, BEATEN UNTIL SMOOTH
¾ CUP FINELY GRATED PARMESAN,
   PLUS EXTRA TO SERVE
SALT AND FRESHLY GROUND BLACK PEPPER
BROILED TOMATO SAUCE (SEE PAGE 18)

1    Make the pasta dough (see page 9).
2    For the ravioli filling, fry the garlic in the butter 1 minute. Add the spinach and cook, stirring,
     2 to 3 minutes until it wilts. Leave to cool, then mix in the ricotta, Parmesan, and seasoning.
     Fill and shape the ravioli (see page 11).
3    Cook the ravioli in batches in slowly boiling water 4 to 5 minutes per batch.
4    Meanwhile, warm the sauce.
5    Drain the ravioli and serve with the sauce, accompanied by Parmesan.

## 313
# marille with roast vegetables & fontina

PREPARATION TIME 15 minutes COOKING TIME 35 minutes SERVES 4

I EGGPLANT, CUT INTO BITE-SIZE PIECES
4 SMALL ZUCCHINI, CUT INTO BITE-SIZE PIECES
3 MIXED RED AND YELLOW BELL PEPPERS, CUT INTO BITE-SIZE PIECES
6 GARLIC CLOVES
4 TABLESPOONS EXTRA-VIRGIN OLIVE OIL
LEAVES FROM 4–5 THYME SPRIGS

SALT AND FRESHLY GROUND BLACK PEPPER
4 WELL-FLAVORED PLUM TOMATOES, HALVED LENGTHWISE
6 OUNCES MARILLE
5 OUCNES FONTINA, THINLY SLICED
BALSAMIC VINEGAR AND A SMALL HANDFUL OF BASIL LEAVES, SHREDDED, TO SERVE

1  Heat the oven to 425°F.
2  Put the eggplant, zucchini, peppers, and garlic in a large roasting pan. Pour the oil over, sprinkle with thyme and seasoning, and mix together well. Roast in the heated oven about 35 minutes until tender and brown. Add the tomatoes for the final 20 minutes.
3  About 15 minutes before the vegetables are ready, cook and drain the pasta according to the package directions. Toss with the vegetables and fontina, sprinkle with balsamic vinegar and basil, and serve.

## 314
# orecchiette with mushrooms & tomato

PREPARATION TIME 10 minutes plus 15 minutes soaking COOKING TIME 15 minutes SERVES 4

½ OUNCE DRIED MUSHROOMS
14 OUNCES ORECCHIETTE
I SMALL ONION, FINELY CHOPPED
2 GARLIC CLOVES, FINELY CHOPPED
VIRGIN OLIVE OIL
I TABLESPOON FINELY CHOPPED FLAT-LEAF PARSLEY

5 CUPS SLICED CREMINI MUSHROOMS
8 OUNCES CANNED PLUM TOMATOES, DRAINED AND CHOPPED
SALT AND FRESHLY GROUND BLACK PEPPER
FRESHLY GRATED PARMESAN, TO SERVE

1  Soak the mushrooms in just enough boiling water to cover 15 minute; drain, reserving the water. Finely chop the mushrooms.
2  Cook and drain the pasta according to the package directions.
3  Meanwhile, fry the onion and garlic in a little oil in a large skillet until beginning to color. Add the dried mushrooms and reserved water and boil until almost evaporated. Add the parsley and fresh mushrooms and fry briskly, stirring, until their liquid evaporates. Add the tomatoes and heat through briefly; season. Toss with the pasta and serve with plenty of Parmesan.

## 315
# fusilli with leeks, garlic, & parmesan

PREPARATION TIME 10 minutes COOKING TIME 15 minutes SERVES 4

14 OUNCES **FUSILLI**
5 **GARLIC CLOVES, THINLY SLICED**
5 TABLESPOONS **EXTRA-VIRGIN OLIVE OIL**
3 **LEEKS, HALVED LENGTHWISE AND VERY THINLY**
**SLICED ACROSS**

**SALT AND FRESHLY GROUND BLACK PEPPER**
½ CUP **FRESHLY GRATED PARMESAN,**
**PLUS EXTRA TO SERVE**

1   Cook and drain the pasta according to the package directions, reserving ½ cup of the cooking water.
2   Meanwhile, cook the garlic in the oil in a large skillet for about 2 minutes until turning golden.
    Add the leeks and cook, stirring, about 3 minutes until it wilts. Cover and cook about 10 minutes
    until tender, stirring occasionally; season.
3   Toss the pasta with the Parmesan and the leek mixture, adding reserved cooking water,
    if necessary, to moisten. Serve with additional Parmesan.

## 316
# tagliatelle with spinach, lemon, & parmesan

PREPARATION TIME 10 minutes COOKING TIME 10 minutes SERVES 4

12 OUNCES **TAGLIATELLE**
1 POUND 6 OUNCES **BABY SPINACH LEAVES**
6 TABLESPOONS **HEAVY CREAM**

1 CUP **FRESHLY GRATED PARMESAN,**
**PLUS EXTRA, TO SERVE**
**SALT AND FRESHLY GROUND BLACK PEPPER**
**JUICE OF 1 LEMON, OR TO TASTE**

1   Cook and drain the pasta according to the package directions.
2   Meanwhile, cook the spinach in large pan without any water, stirring until it wilts and the liquid
    evaporates. Toss with the pasta, cream, Parmesan, seasoning, and lemon juice, to taste.

## 317
# tagliatelle with peas, asparagus, & saffron sauce

PREPARATION TIME 5 minutes plus 15 minutes soaking COOKING TIME 15 minutes SERVES 4

**PINCH OF SAFFRON THREADS, CRUSHED**
12 OUNCES **SLIM ASPARAGUS SPEARS**
1 CUP **FRESH OR FROZEN PEAS**
14 OUNCES **TAGLIATELLE**

**KNOB OF UNSALTED BUTTER**
1 CUP **HEAVY CREAM**
6 TABLESPOONS **FRESHLY GRATED PARMESAN**
**SALT AND FRESHLY GROUND BLACK PEPPER**

1   Soak the saffron in 3 tablespoons boiling water 15 minutes.
2   Meanwhile, cut the tips off the asparagus and reserve. Cook the stems and peas in a large pan of
    boiling water 2 minutes. Add the asparagus tips and cook 1 minute longer; drain, reserving the
    cooking water.
3   Cook the pasta in the reserved water according to the package directions and drain.
4   While the pasta is cooking, melt the butter, add the asparagus and peas, and stir 1 to 2 minutes before
    adding the saffron liquid and cream. Heat slowly until simmering and then stir in half the cheese
    and seasoning. Toss with the pasta and serve with the remaining Parmesan sprinkled over.

## 318
# tagliatelle with spinach & ricotta

PREPARATION TIME 5 minutes COOKING TIME 10 minutes SERVES 4

14 OUNCES **TAGLIATELLE**
1 POUND **BABY SPINACH LEAVES**
**SALT AND FRESHLY GROUND BLACK PEPPER**

8 OUNCES **CRUMBLED RICOTTA**
½ CUP **FRESHLY GRATED PARMESAN,**
   **PLUS EXTRA TO SERVE**

1   Cook and drain the pasta according to the package directions, reserving ½ cup of the cooking water.
2   Meanwhile, cook the spinach without any water in a large saucepan, stirring occasionally until
    it wilts; season.
3   Toss the pasta with the ricotta and Parmesan and then the spinach. Serve with extra Parmesan.

## 319
# quick pasta with garbanzo beans & spinach

PREPARATION TIME 5 minutes COOKING TIME 10 minutes SERVES 4

2 CANS (15-OZ.) **GARBANZO BEANS, DRAINED AND**
   **RINSED**
1 QUANTITY **WINTER TOMATO SAUCE (SEE PAGE 19)**
18 OUNCES **FRESH PASTA**

8 OUNCES **SPINACH**
**PARMESAN SHAVINGS, AND VIRGIN OLIVE OIL**
   **(OPTIONAL), TO SERVE**

1   Heat the garbanzo beans in the tomato sauce until the sauce is just boiling.
2   Meanwhile, cook the pasta in the boiling water according to the package directions. Drain, reserving about
    4 tablespoons of the cooking water.
3   Toss the spinach with the pasta until it wilts, and then combine with the garbanzo bean mixture and
    reserved water. Serve topped with Parmesan shavings and a trickle of virgin olive oil, if liked.

## 320
# riccioli with bell peppers & cherry tomatoes

PREPARATION TIME 10 minutes COOKING TIME 15 minutes SERVES 4

1 **ONION, CHOPPED**
**VIRGIN OLIVE OIL**
2 **GARLIC CLOVES, CHOPPED**
2 **RED BELL PEPPERS, THINLY SLICED LENGTHWISE**
2 **YELLOW BELL PEPPERS, THINLY SLICED LENGTHWISE**

8 OUNCES **CHERRY TOMATOES, HALVED**
**SALT AND FRESHLY GROUND BLACK PEPPER**
**LEAVES FROM A SMALL BUNCH OF BASIL, SHREDDED**
14 OUNCES **RICCIOLI***
**FRESHLY GRATED PARMESAN, TO SERVE**

1   Fry the onion in a little oil until soft and golden. Add the garlic and fry 1 minute. Stir in the peppers
    and cook, stirring frequently, until they begin to soften. Add the tomatoes and cook about 5 minutes
    longer until they are soft but retain their shape; season and add the basil.
2   Meanwhile, cook and drain the pasta according to the package directions, reserving ½ cup of the
    cooking water.
3   Toss the pasta with the sauce, adding a little of the cooking water, if necessary, to moisten.
    Serve with freshly grated Parmesan.

*   Cavatappi or fusilli can also be used.

## 321
# gnocchi with lentil sauce

PREPARATION TIME 10 minutes COOKING TIME 25 minutes SERVES 4

1¼ cups UMBRIAN (OR PUY) LENTILS
½ ONION, HALVED THROUGH THE ROOT END
1 ROSEMARY SPRIG
1 SAGE SPRIG
14 ounces GNOCCHI*
4 WELL-FLAVORED TOMATOES, SEEDED AND CHOPPED
3 GARLIC CLOVES, CHOPPED

HANDFUL OF FLAT-LEAF PARSLEY, CHOPPED
VIRGIN OLIVE OIL
EXTRA-VIRGIN OLIVE OIL (OPTIONAL) AND FRESHLY
   GRATED PECORINO, TO SERVE

1   Bring the lentils, onion, and herbs to a boil in 3 quarts water, then simmer 15 to 20 minutes until the
    lentils are tender. Return to a boil, add the pasta, stir and cook until al dente, stirring occasionally.
2   Meanwhile, fry the tomatoes, garlic, and parsley in a little oil 3 to 4 minutes until the tomatoes
    are soft but not disintegrating completely.
3   Drain the pasta and lentils, reserving about ½ cup of the cooking water; discard the onion and herbs.
    Toss the pasta and lentils with the tomato mixture. If not serving with the olive oil, add enough of
    the reserved water to moisten. Serve with extra-virgin olive oil trickled into each portion, if liked,
    and pecorino.

*   Chifferi or pipe rigate can also be used.

## 322
# cavatappi with roast eggplants, bell peppers, & basil

PREPARATION TIME 10 minutes COOKING TIME 35 minutes SERVES 4

2 EGGPLANTS, WEIGHING 1–1½ pounds TOTAL
2 PLUMP RED BELL PEPPERS
5 GARLIC CLOVES IN THEIR SKINS
6 tablespoons EXTRA-VIRGIN OLIVE OIL
20 PITTED NIÇOISE OR GAETA OLIVES, CHOPPED
14 ounces CAVATAPPI

SALT AND FRESHLY GROUND BLACK PEPPER
BALSAMIC VINEGAR, TO TASTE
SMALL HANDFUL OF BASIL LEAVES, SHREDDED
FRESHLY GRATED PROVOLONE OR PARMESAN,
   TO SERVE

1   Heat the oven to 400°F.
2   Prick the eggplants in several places and cook in the heated oven 20 to 30 minutes, turning once, until
    soft, wrinkled, and lightly charred. At the same time, cook the peppers in the oven 15 to 20 minutes until
    lightly charred and soft, and the garlic until soft.
3   Peel the peppers and cut into slices. Pop the garlic cloves from their skins into a bowl and mash with the
    oil; transfer to a skillet.
4   When the eggplants are cool enough to handle, peel off the skin, and chop the flesh. Add to the skillet,
    with the red peppers and olives. Season with salt, pepper, and balsamic vinegar and warm slowly.
5   Meanwhile, cook and drain the pasta according to the package directions. Toss with the vegetables and
    basil. Serve with freshly grated provolone or Parmesan.

## 323
# gemelli with melting onion sauce

PREPARATION TIME 10 minutes COOKING TIME 40 minutes SERVES 4

6 CUPS **VERY THINLY SLICED LARGE ONIONS**

3 **GARLIC CLOVES, FINELY SLICED**

1 **BAY LEAF**

**SMALL SPRIG OF ROSEMARY**

3 TABLESPOONS **OLIVE OIL**

**SALT AND FRESHLY GROUND BLACK PEPPER**

½ CUP **MEDIUM-BODIED DRY WHITE WINE**

2–3 TABLESPOONS **CHOPPED FLAT-LEAF PARSLEY**

14 OUNCES **GEMELLI\***

1¼ CUPS **GRATED PECORINO**

1   Put the onions, garlic, bay leaf, and rosemary into a large, heavy skillet with the oil and sprinkle with salt. Cook slowly 10 minutes, then cover the onions closely with a circle of waxed paper and cook over low heat until the onions turn rich golden brown.

2   Stir in the wine and cook briskly, stirring, until the wine evaporates. Discard the bay leaf and rosemary. Add black pepper and the parsley.

3   Meanwhile, cook and drain the pasta according to the package directions. Toss with the onions and most of the pecorino. Serve with the remaining pecorino sprinkled over.

\*   Strozzapreti or penne rigate can also be used.

## 324
# panzarotti

PREPARATION TIME 40 minutes plus 1 hour resting for the dough COOKING TIME 10 to 15 minutes SERVES 4

PASTA DOUGH
2 CUPS **ALL-PURPOSE FLOUR**
2 **EGGS**
2 TABLESPOONS **VIRGIN OLIVE OIL**

½ CUP **FINELY GRATED BUFFALO MOZZARELLA**
½ CUP **RICOTTA**
¼ CUP **FRESHLY GRATED PARMESAN,**
   **PLUS EXTRA TO SERVE**
½ CUP **CHOPPED DOLCELATTE**
**SALT AND FRESHLY GROUND BLACK PEPPER**
**SMALL HANDFUL OF MIXED FLAT-LEAF**
   **PARSLEY AND CHIVES, FINELY CHOPPED**
**OLIVE OIL FOR DEEP FRYING**

1  Make the dough (see page 10), wrap, and leave to rest 30 minutes.
2  Meanwhile, using a fork, mash the 4 cheeses with the seasoning, taking care with the salt but using plenty of black pepper; work in the herbs.
3  Make 2-inch raviolini (see page 12) with the dough and filling. Leave to rest 30 minutes in a cool place but preferably not the refrigerator.
4  Heat a deep pan of oil to 350°F* for frying the panzarotti. Add the panzarotti in batches, frying them 2 to 3 minutes per batch until golden; do not overcrowd the pan. Drain on paper towels and sprinkle with grated Parmesan.

*  If you don't have a suitable thermometer,
   drop a cube of bread into the oil;
   if it turns golden in 1 minute,
   the oil is ready.

## 325
# spinach & lentil lasagne

PREPARATION TIME 10 minutes COOKING TIME 45 minutes SERVES 6

10 OUNCES GREEN LENTILS
1 ONION, FINELY CHOPPED
1 SMALL CARROT, FINELY CHOPPED
2 GARLIC CLOVES, THINLY SLICED
1 POUND SPINACH, CHOPPED
2–3 TABLESPOONS RED PESTO (SEE PAGE 19)

SALT AND FRESHLY GROUND BLACK PEPPER
2 CANS (15-oz.) CRUSHED PLUM TOMATOES
1¼ CUPS PASSATA (BOTTLED STRAINED PUREED
    TOMATOES)
6 OUNCES LASAGNE SHEETS
½ CUP FRESHLY GRATED PECORINO

1   Cook the lentils, onion, carrot, and garlic just covered with water about 20 minutes until tender and
    almost dry; if necessary, strain off surplus liquid. Add the spinach and cook, stirring frequently, until it
    wilts. Stir in the red pesto and seasoning.
2   Meanwhile, simmer the tomatoes and passata about 10 minutes until slightly reduced.
3   While the tomatoes are cooking, cook and drain the lasagne, even if using the no-precook type (see
    page 15) and spread on a clean dish towel to dry.
4   Heat the oven to 400°F.
5   Spread a little of the tomato sauce over the bottom of a greased large, shallow baking dish. Cover with a
    layer of lasagne, then some of the lentil sauce, followed by a layer of tomato. Continue layering, ending
    with spinach sauce. Scatter the cheese over.
6   Bake in the heated oven about 25 minutes until bubbling and golden. Leave to stand 5 minutes
    before serving.

## 326
# spinach & cheese lasagne

PREPARATION TIME 15 minutes COOKING TIME 45 minutes SERVES 4 to 6

12 SHEETS FRESH LASAGNE
2 POUNDS SPINACH
SMALL KNOB OF UNSALTED BUTTER
1 CUP RICOTTA
6 OUNCES GORGONZOLA, CRUMBLED
SALT AND FRESHLY GROUND BLACK PEPPER
4 TABLESPOONS PINE NUTS, LIGHTLY TOASTED
½ CUP FRESHLY GRATED PARMESAN
1¼ CUPS GRATED BUFFALO MOZZARELLA

BÉCHAMEL SAUCE
3½ TABLESPOONS UNSALTED BUTTER
4 TABLESPOONS ALL-PURPOSE FLOUR
3¼ CUPS MILK

1   Cook and drain the lasagne (see page 15) and spread on a dish towel to drain.
2   Meanwhile, make the béchamel sauce (see page 17).
3   Heat the oven to 350°F.
4   While the béchamel is simmering, cook the spinach in a large pan, stirring frequently, until it wilts and is
    soft. Drain, chop coarsely, and then squeeze out as much water as possible. Combine with the butter,
    ricotta, Gorgonzola, and seasoning.
5   Barely cover the bottom of a greased shallow baking dish with béchamel sauce. Cover with 3 of the
    lasagne sheets, then one-quarter of the spinach mixture and scatter one quarter of the pine nuts over.
    Pour a quarter of the remaining béchamel over and sprinkle one-quarter of the Parmesan on top.
    Repeat the layers, adding one-third of the mozzarella with the pine nuts until the ingredients are
    used, ending with mozzarella and Parmesan.
6   Bake in the heated oven 30 to 35 minutes until bubbling and golden. Leave to stand 5 minutes
    before serving.

## 327
# ricotta, parmesan, & squash ravioli

PREPARATION TIME 45 minutes COOKING TIME 1¼ hours SERVES 4

2-EGG QUANTITY PASTA DOUGH (SEE PAGE 10).
4 TABLESPOONS UNSALTED BUTTER
FINELY GRATED ZEST OF 1 LEMON
⅓ CUP PINE NUTS, LIGHTLY TOASTED
PARMESAN, TO SERVE

FILLING
1-POUND PIECE OF BUTTERNUT SQUASH
VIRGIN OLIVE OIL
⅔ CUP RICOTTA, BEATEN UNTIL SMOOTH
¾ CUP FINELY GRATED PARMESAN
SALT AND FRESHLY GROUND BLACK PEPPER

1   Make the pasta dough (see page 10).
2   While the dough is resting, make the filling. Heat the oven to 375°F. Brush the squash flesh with a little
    oil and bake in the heated oven about 1 hour until soft. Cool slightly and then scrape into a bowl.
    Add the ricotta and mash with a potato masher or fork. Mix in the Parmesan and seasoning.
    Fill and shape the ravioli (see page 11).
3   Melt the butter over very low heat, add the lemon zest, and set aside to infuse while cooking the pasta.
4   Cook the ravioli in slowly boiling water, in batches, if necessary, about 4 minutes per batch; drain well.
    Scatter the pine nuts over the ravioli and pour the lemon butter over. Serve with grated Parmesan.

## 328
# pappardelle with roast fennel
# & dolcelatte

PREPARATION TIME 5 minutes COOKING TIME 35 minutes SERVES 4

2 FENNEL BULBS, THINLY SLICED, FEATHERY TOPS
    RESERVED
VIRGIN OLIVE OIL
SALT AND FRESHLY GROUND BLACK PEPPER
1¼ CUPS MEDIUM-BODIED DRY WHITE WINE
12 OUNCES PAPPARDELLE

1½ CUPS CRUMBLED DOLCELATTE
4 TABLESPOONS WALNUTS, LIGHTLY TOASTED
    AND COARSELY CHOPPED

1   Heat the oven to 425°F.
2   Put the fennel slices in a heavy-duty roasting pan, trickle a little oil over, season, and then stir the fennel
    to insure it is evenly coated with oil; spread in a single layer. Roast in the heated oven 25 to 30 minutes
    until lightly charred, stirring occasionally.
3   Remove the fennel from the pan and keep warm. Stir the wine into the pan and boil on the stove top
    until reduced by half.
4   Meanwhile, cook and drain the pasta according to the package directions. Toss with the reduced wine,
    cheese, fennel, and seasoning. Scatter the walnuts and reserved feathery tops over.

# 329
# tonnarelli with radicchio & taleggio

PREPARATION TIME 10 minutes COOKING TIME 25 minutes SERVES 4

1 RED ONION, HALVED LENGTHWISE AND
  THINLY SLICED
VIRGIN OLIVE OIL
1 GARLIC CLOVE, FINELY CHOPPED
4 LARGE HEADS OF RADICCHIO, SHREDDED
½ CUP MEDIUM-BODIED DRY WHITE WINE
5 TABLESPOONS VEGETABLE STOCK OR WATER

4 OUNCES TALEGGIO, CHOPPED
SALT AND FRESHLY GROUND BLACK PEPPER
13 OUNCES TONNARELLI*
FRESHLY GRATED PARMESAN, TO SERVE

1 Fry the red onion in a little oil in a large skillet until soft. Add the garlic and fry 1 minute, then stir in the radicchio and fry, stirring occasionally, until turning brown.
2 Pour in the wine and stock and bring to a boil, then simmer, uncovered, until the liquid evaporates and the radicchio is almost tender; leave some parts with bite. The liquid should almost evaporate. Add the Taleggio and seasoning and warm very slowly until the cheese is just melting.
3 Meanwhile, cook and drain the pasta according to the package directions. Toss with the radicchio sauce. Serve with freshly grated Parmesan.

* Spaghetti can also be used.

# 330
# penne rigate with eggplants & ricotta

PREPARATION TIME 10 minutes COOKING TIME 15 minutes SERVES 4

2 SMALL EGGPLANTS, THICKLY SLICED
EXTRA-VIRGIN OLIVE OIL, PLUS EXTRA FOR BROILING
SALT AND FRESHLY GROUND BLACK PEPPER
1 SMALL ONION, FINELY CHOPPED
3 GARLIC CLOVES, THINLY SLICED
1 RED CHILI, SEEDED AND FINELY CHOPPED

1 CAN (15-OZ.) CRUSHED PLUM TOMATOES
3 TABLESPOONS CHOPPED FLAT-LEAF PARSLEY
12 PITTED BLACK OLIVES, HALVED
14 OUNCES PENNE RIGATE
¼ CUP CRUMBLED RICOTTA
SHREDDED BASIL LEAVES, TO SERVE

1 Spread the eggplant slices in a single layer on a large baking sheet, brush both sides with oil, and sprinkle with seasoning. Cook under a heated hot broiler 3 to 6 minutes per side until brown and soft. When cool enough to handle, cut into strips.
2 Meanwhile, fry the onion in a little oil in a skillet until soft. Add the garlic and chili and fry 1 minute. Stir in the tomatoes and parsley and simmer 10 to 15 minutes until thick. Add the olives and seasoning.
3 Meanwhile, cook and drain the pasta according to the package directions. Toss with half the eggplant strips, half the ricotta, and the tomato sauce. Serve with the remaining eggplant strips on top and scatter the remaining ricotta and the basil over.

## 331
# ziti with red bell peppers & basil

PREPARATION TIME 10 minutes COOKING TIME 20 minutes SERVES 4

3 GARLIC CLOVES, HALVED LENGTHWAYS
3 TABLESPOONS VIRGIN OLIVE OIL
4 LARGE, PLUMP RED PEPPERS,
   QUARTERED LENGTHWISE
SALT AND FRESHLY GROUND BLACK PEPPER

BALSAMIC VINEGAR
14 OUNCES ZITI
SMALL HANDFUL OF BASIL LEAVES, SHREDDED
6 TABLESPOONS FRESHLY GRATED PARMESAN,
   PLUS EXTRA TO SERVE

1   Heat the garlic in the oil over very low heat 10 minutes until the oil infuses; discard the garlic.
2   Meanwhile, slice the pepper quarters lengthwise into ½-inch-wide strips, then cut across the strips, into halves.
3   Cook the peppers in the garlic-infused oil over very high heat until they are tender yet still retain their shape; do not let them become mushy. Season with salt, plenty of freshly ground black pepper, and balsamic vinegar.
4   Meanwhile, cook and drain the pasta according to the package directions.
    Toss with the peppers and the pan juices, the basil, and Parmesan.

*   Penne rigate can also be used.

194

## 332
# artichoke & mushroom lasagne

PREPARATION TIME 15 minutes COOKING TIME 50 minutes SERVES 4 to 6

5 SHALLOTS, FINELY CHOPPED
VIRGIN OLIVE OIL
3 GARLIC CLOVES, FINELY CHOPPED
1 POUND 10 OUNCES MIXED MUSHROOMS SUCH AS
   SHIITAKE, OYSTER, CREMINI, HALVED, QUARTERED,
   OR SLICED ACCORDING TO SIZE
1¾ TABLESPOONS LEMON JUICE
LEAVES FROM A BUNCH OF FLAT-LEAF PARSLEY,
   CHOPPED
SALT AND FRESHLY GROUND BLACK PEPPER

7 OUNCES FRESH LASAGNE VERDE SHEETS
1 CUP RICOTTA
9 OUNCES DRAINED ROAST ARTICHOKES IN OIL, HALVED
½ CUP FRESHLY GRATED PARMESAN

BÉCHAMEL SAUCE
3 TABLESPOONS BUTTER
4½ TABLESPOONS ALL-PURPOSE FLOUR
3 CUPS MILK

1   Fry the shallots in a little oil in a large skillet until soft and becoming golden, adding the garlic the final 3 minutes or so. Add the mushrooms, the lemon juice, and half of the parsley and fry, stirring occasionally, 10 to 15 minutes until soft and brown. Add the remaining parsley and seasoning.
2   Meanwhile, make the béchamel sauce (see page 17). While the sauce is simmering, cook, drain, and rinse the lasagne, even if using the no-precook type (see page 15). Spread on a dish towel to dry.
3   Heat the oven to 400°F.
4   Spread a thin layer of béchamel sauce in the bottom of a greased large shallow baking dish. Cover with a layer of lasagne, then one-quarter of the ricotta, followed by one-quarter of the mushroom mixture and half the artichokes. Sprinkle with some of the Parmesan. Continue layering, ending with a layer of béchamel and a good sprinkling of Parmesan.
5   Bake in the heated oven about 30 minutes until golden and bubbling. Stand 5 minutes before serving.

## 333
# cheese & herb agnolotti

PREPARATION TIME 45 minutes COOKING TIME 15 minutes SERVES 4

2-EGG QUANTITY OF PASTA DOUGH
  (SEE PAGE 10)
I GARLIC CLOVE
OLIVE OIL
1¼ CUPS RICOTTA
¾ CUP FRESHLY GRATED PARMESAN
I EGG YOLK

2 HANDFULS CHOPPED MIXED HERBS, SUCH AS
  BASIL, FLAT-LEAF PARSLEY, THYME, AND OREGANO
FRESHLY GROUND BLACK PEPPER
ABOUT 4 TABLESPOONS UNSALTED BUTTER
¼ CUP FRESHLY GRATED PARMESAN
BROILED CHERRY TOMATOES ON THE VINE,
  TO SERVE (OPTIONAL)

1  While the pasta dough is resting, fry the garlic in a little oil 1 to 2 minutes. Leave to cool, then combine with the ricotta, Parmesan, egg yolk, herbs, and black pepper; salt might not be necessary because of the saltiness of the Parmesan.
2  Make the agnolotti (see page 10) with the pasta dough and herb filling.
3  Cook the agnolotti in batches in gently boiling water 4 to 5 minutes per batch.
4  Meanwhile, melt the butter with the Parmesan, but do not let it become too hot; season with black pepper.
5  Drain the agnolotti and pour the melted butter and Parmesan over.
   Serve accompanied by the broiled tomatoes, if liked.

## 334
# spinach & mushroom lasagne

PREPARATION TIME 10 minutes COOKING TIME 1 hour SERVES 4

2 ONIONS, HALVED AND SLICED
2 BAY LEAVES
I TEASPOON DRIED OREGANO
SALT AND FRESHLY GROUND BLACK PEPPER
VIRGIN OLIVE OIL
3 PLUMP GARLIC CLOVES, CHOPPED
5¾ CUPS SLICED CREMINI MUSHROOMS
I TABLESPOON SUN-DRIED TOMATO PASTE

2 CANS (15-oz.) CRUSHED TOMATOES
6 OUNCES LASAGNE SHEETS
14 OUNCES FRESH SPINACH
I QUANTITY BÉCHAMEL SAUCE (SEE PAGE 17)
6 TABLESPOONS FRESHLY GRATED PARMESAN

1  Cook the onions with the bay leaves, oregano, and seasoning in a little oil in a large skillet, stirring occasionally, until the onions are very soft and light brown, adding the garlic about halfway through.
2  Add the mushrooms and cook, stirring occasionally, until the liquid evaporates. Stir in the tomato paste and tomatoes and bring to a boil, then cook slowly 20 minutes until reduced to a thick sauce.
3  At the same time, cook, drain, and rinse the lasagne, even if using the no-precook type (see page 15). Spread on a dish towel to dry.
4  Meanwhile, cook the spinach in a large covered pan, shaking the pan 2 or 3 times for about 3 minutes until the spinach wilts and is soft. Drain well and squeeze out excess moisture.
5  Heat the oven to 375°F.
6  Spread a thin layer of béchamel sauce over the bottom of a greased shallow baking dish. Cover with a layer of lasagne, followed by the mushroom mixture, then spinach. Repeat the layering until all lasagne and vegetables are used, then end with a layer of béchamel sauce. Sprinkle the Parmesan over.
7  Bake in the heated oven 25 to 30 minutes until bubbling and golden.

## 335
# zucchini & ricotta cannelloni

PREPARATION TIME 15 minutes* COOKING TIME 25 minutes* SERVES 4

APPROXIMATELY 12 LASAGNE VERDE SHEETS
1 ONION, CHOPPED
OLIVE OIL FOR COOKING
4 ZUCCHINI, GRATED
2 GARLIC CLOVES, SQUASHED AND FINELY CHOPPED
ZEST OF 1 LEMON

1 CUP RICOTTA
SALT AND FRESHLY GROUND BLACK PEPPER
1 QUANTITY FRESH TOMATO SAUCE (SEE PAGE 18) OR
   WINTER TOMATO SAUCE (SEE PAGE 19), WARM
½ CUP FRESHLY GRATED PARMESAN

1  Cook and drain the lasagne sheets (see page 15) and spread on a dish towel to dry.
2  Heat the oven to 400°F.
3  Fry the onion in a little oil until soft but not colored. Stir in the zucchini and garlic and continue cooking, stirring frequently, until soft. Remove from the heat and add the lemon zest, half the ricotta, and seasoning.
4  Spread the zucchini mixture down the middle of each lasagne sheet; roll into tubes.
5  Pour half the sauce into a greased large, shallow baking dish. Place the tubes on top, seam-side down. Pour the remaining sauce over, dot with the remaining ricotta, and sprinkle with the Parmesan.
6  Bake in the heated oven 15 minutes until golden.

*  Assumes the sauce is already made.

196

## 336
# squash & mushroom lasagne

PREPARATION TIME 15 minutes COOKING TIME 45 minutes SERVES 4 to 6

2 POUNDS BUTTERNUT SQUASH, HALVED, PEELED,
   SEEDED, AND THINLY SLICED ACROSS
VIRGIN OLIVE OIL
SALT AND FRESHLY GROUND BLACK PEPPER
1½ TABLESPOONS PESTO (SEE PAGE 18)
6 LASAGNE SHEETS
1 POUND 5 OUNCES MIXED MUSHROOMS, SUCH AS
   CREMINI, SHIITAKE, AND OYSTER, SLICED
3 GARLIC CLOVES, FINELY CHOPPED

½ CUP HALF-FAT CRÈME FRAÎCHE
1 POUND 5 OUNCES SPINACH
¼ CUP FRESHLY GRATED PARMESAN
2 OUNCES FONTINA, GRATED

1  Heat the oven to 450°F.
2  Put the squash into a roasting pan, trickle about 2 tablespoons oil over, turn the pieces to coat with oil, season, and bake in the heated oven about 20 minutes until tender and light brown around the edges. Cool slightly and then mix with the pesto. Lower the oven temperature to 375°F.
3  Meanwhile, cook, drain and rinse the lasagne, even if using the no-precook type (see page 15). Spread on a dish towel to dry.
4  While the lasagne sheets are cooking, fry the mushrooms in a little oil until tender and their juices are beginning to flow, adding half the garlic 1 minute before the end. Add 1 tablespoon crème fraîche and simmer 2 minutes; season and set aside.
5  Cook the spinach in a large saucepan, stirring occasionally, until it wilts; drain and squeeze out excess liquid. Stir in the Parmesan, remaining garlic, and 4 tablespoons crème fraîche; season.
6  Reserve a little of each vegetable. Layer the lasagne and remaining vegetables in a greased large dish, starting with spinach and ending with lasagne. Cover with the reserved vegetables and spread the remaining crème fraîche over. Season with pepper and sprinkle the fontina over. Bake 25 minutes until golden.

# 337
# roast vegetable lasagne

PREPARATION TIME 15 minutes plus 1 hour draining COOKING TIME 55 minutes SERVES 6

1 SMALL EGGPLANT, CUT INTO 1-INCH CUBES

2 ZUCCHINI, CUT INTO 1-INCH CUBES

SALT AND FRESHLY GROUND BLACK PEPPER

1 RED BELL PEPPER, CUT INTO 1-INCH SQUARES

1 FENNEL BULB, VERY FINELY CHOPPED

4 PLUMP GARLIC CLOVES, CUT INTO THIN SLIVERS

VIRGIN OLIVE OIL

⅓ CUP PITTED OIL-CURED BLACK OLIVES, HALVED

3 TABLESPOONS COARSELY SHREDDED BASIL

¼ CUP FRESHLY GRATED PARMESAN

APPROXIMATELY 10 SHEETS LASAGNE

1½ OUNCES EACH TALEGGIO AND MOZZARELLA,
   GRATED AND MIXED

## BÉCHAMEL SAUCE

3 TABLESPOONS ALL-PURPOSE FLOUR

2½ TABLESPOONS UNSALTED BUTTER

2½ CUPS MILK

1   Put the eggplant and zucchini in a large colander, sprinkle some salt over and stir to mix,
    then leave to drain about 1 hour; rinse well and dry thoroughly.

2   Heat the oven to 475°F.

3   Put all the vegetables and the garlic in a roasting pan, trickle a little oil over and stir to coat the
    vegetables. Bake on the top shelf of the heated oven 30 minutes until brown at the edges, stirring
    occasionally. Remove from the oven (turn the oven down to 375°F) and mix the olives, basil, and
    seasoning with the cooked vegetables.

4   Meanwhile, cook, drain, and rinse the lasagne, even if using the no-precook type (see page 15).
    Spread on a dish towel to dry.

5   While the lasagne is cooking, make the béchamel sauce (see page 17). Stir 3 tablespoons of the Parmesan
    into the sauce and spread one-quarter over the bottom of a greased large, shallow baking dish.
    Cover with one-third of the vegetables. Scatter one-third of the mozzarella and Taleggio over, followed
    by a single layer of lasagne sheets. Repeat the layering and finish with the remaining cheese sauce.
    Sprinkle the remaining Parmesan over. Bake in the oven 20 to 25 minutes until the top is golden.

## 338
# vegetable lasagne with goat cheese topping

PREPARATION TIME 10 minutes plus 30 minutes standing COOKING TIME 35 minutes SERVES 6

2 EGGPLANTS, CUT INTO ½-INCH CUBES

2 ONIONS, THINLY SLICED

VIRGIN OLIVE OIL

4 GARLIC CLOVES, FINELY CHOPPED

5 PLUM TOMATOES, CUT INTO ½-INCH PIECES

4 TABLESPOONS RED WINE

ABOUT 2 TABLESPOONS SUN-DRIED TOMATO PASTE

1 TABLESPOON DRIED OREGANO

2 RED AND 2 YELLOW BELL PEPPERS

APPROXIMATELY 10 LASAGNE VERDE SHEETS

TOPPING

2 EGGS, BEATEN

⅔ CUP LIGHT CREAM

12 OUNCES SOFT GOAT CHEESE

SALT AND FRESHLY GROUND BLACK PEPPER

3 TABLESPOONS FRESH BREAD CRUMBS

4 TABLESPOONS FRESHLY GRATED PECORINO

1   Sprinkle the eggplant with salt in a colander and leave to drain 30 minutes. Rinse and dry thoroughly.
2   Fry the onions in a little oil until soft and lightly colored. Stir in the garlic and eggplant and cook
    2 to 3 minutes, then add the tomatoes, wine, tomato paste, and oregano. Cover and simmer
    15 to 20 minutes, stirring occasionally to prevent sticking.
3   Meanwhile, broil the peppers, then peel and slice them (see page 67). Cook, drain, and rinse the lasagne,
    even if using the no-precook type (see page 15). Spread on a dish towel to dry.
4   Make the topping by stirring the eggs and cream into the goat cheese until smooth; season.
5   Heat the oven to 375°F.
6   Add the peppers and seasoning to the eggplant mixture and spread about one-third in a greased large,
    shallow baking dish. Cover with a layer of lasagne, trimming to fit the dish as necessary. Repeat the
    layering twice. Pour the topping over to cover evenly. Sprinkle with the bread crumbs and pecorino.
7   Bake in the heated oven about 30 minutes until the top is light brown.
    Leave to stand 5 minutes before serving.

## 339
# tagliatelle with slow-cooked fennel & garlic

PREPARATION TIME 10 minutes COOKING TIME 40 minutes SERVES 4

1 FENNEL BULB, THINLY SLICED,

    FEATHERY TOPS RESERVED

1 ONION, THINLY SLICED

4 GARLIC CLOVES, THINLY SLICED

PINCH OF CHILI FLAKES

4 TABLESPOONS UNSALTED BUTTER

1 TEASPOON SUGAR

SALT AND FRESHLY GROUND BLACK PEPPER

½ CUP MEDIUM-BODIED DRY WHITE WINE

⅔ CUP HEAVY CREAM

14 OUNCES TAGLIATELLE

4 TABLESPOONS FRESHLY GRATED PARMESAN,

    PLUS EXTRA TO SERVE

CHOPPED FENNEL HERB,

    TO SERVE (OPTIONAL)

1   Cook the fennel, onion, garlic, and chili in the butter, sugar, and seasoning in a heavy skillet covered with
    a large disk of waxed paper over low heat, stirring occasionally, 25 to 30 minutes until very soft.
    Stir in 1 to 2 tablespoons hot water if the vegetables become too dry.
2   Stir in the wine, increase the heat, and simmer, uncovered, until it almost evaporates.
    Add the cream and simmer until the sauce thickens, but do not allow it to become too thick.
3   Meanwhile, cook and drain the tagliatelle according to the package directions. Toss with the Parmesan
    and fennel sauce and sprinkle the reserved fennel tops, or chopped fennel herb, over.
    Serve with additional Parmesan.

# 340

# sedani with roast vegetables
# & olives al forno

PREPARATION TIME 15 minutes plus optional 1 hour draining COOKING TIME 50 minutes SERVES 4

2 ZUCCHINI, CUT INTO BITE-SIZE CHUNKS

1 SMALL EGGPLANT, CUT INTO BITE-SIZE CHUNKS

SALT

1 HEAD OF BELGIAN ENDIVE, CUT INTO BITE-SIZE
    PIECES

1 RED ONION, CUT INTO WEDGES

1 RED BELL PEPPER, CUT INTO BITE-SIZE CHUNKS

3 GARLIC CLOVES, CHOPPED

1 SPRIG OF ROSEMARY AND 2 SPRIGS OF THYME

VIRGIN OLIVE OIL

4 RIPE WELL-FLAVORED TOMATOES, QUARTERED

6 OUNCES SEDANI*

⅓ CUP PITTED BLACK OLIVES

1 QUANTITY CHEESE SAUCE (SEE PAGE 17)

3 OUNCES BUFFALO MOZZARELLA, THINLY SLICED

1½ TABLESPOONS FRESHLY GRATED PARMESAN

1   Layer the zucchini and eggplants in a colander, sprinkling salt over each layer. Leave to drain 1 hour;
    rinse well and dry thoroughly**.
2   Heat the oven to 425°F.
3   Put the zucchini and eggplant in a large roasting pan with the endive, onion, pepper, garlic, and
    herbs. Trickle a little oil over, stir together to coat the vegetables, and spread them out. Roast in the top
    of the heated oven about 30 minutes until tender and charred in patches. Add the tomatoes after
    15 minutes; discard the herbs and lower the oven temperature to 400°F.
4   Just before the vegetables are ready, cook the pasta according to the package directions but 1 minute
    less than specified, then drain. Combine with the vegetables, olives, and cheese sauce. Layer in a large,
    shallow baking dish with the mozzarella, finishing with mozzarella. Sprinkle the Parmesan over.
5   Bake about 10 minutes until the top is golden.

*    Penne or rigatoni can also be used.
**   This step can be omitted, if you wish.

# 341

# macaroni, fennel, pine nut,
# & cheese al forno

PREPARATION TIME 15 minutes COOKING TIME 30 minutes SERVES 4

2 CUPS FENNEL, HALVED LENGTHWISE AND THINLY
    SLICED

1 ONION, THINLY SLICED

VIRGIN OLIVE OIL

2 GARLIC CLOVES, CHOPPED

1½ CUPS MACARONI

½ CUP PINE NUTS, LIGHTLY TOASTED

1½ CUPS CRUMBLED RICOTTA

SALT AND FRESHLY GROUND BLACK PEPPER

6 OUNCES BUFFALO MOZZARELLA, THINLY SLICED

1   Heat the oven to 350°F.
2   Boil the fennel 5 minutes until tender; drain well, reserving the cooking water. Coarsely chop
    the fennel.
3   Meanwhile, fry the onion in a little oil until soft. Stir in the garlic and chopped fennel and cook about
    4 minutes until the vegetables are lightly flecked with brown. Remove from the heat and leave to cool.
4   Meanwhile, cook the macaroni in the fennel water plus additional water according to the package
    directions but for 1 minute less than specified; drain well. Spread half in a buttered large, shallow
    baking dish.
5   Add the pine nuts, ricotta, and seasoning to the fennel sauce. Spread half over the macaroni;
    repeat the layers. Lay the mozzarella over the top and bake in the heated oven
    15 to 20 minutes until the mozzarella is golden and melted.

## 342
# fava bean & basil cannelloni

PREPARATION TIME 20 minutes COOKING TIME 40 minutes SERVES 4

12 CANNELLONI TUBES

2 CUPS SHELLED FRESH FAVA BEANS, OR FROZEN BABY
FAVA BEANS

1 CUP RICOTTA

1 GARLIC CLOVE, CRUSHED

2–3 TABLESPOONS FINELY CHOPPED BASIL

FRESHLY GROUND BLACK PEPPER

½ QUANTITY TOMATO AND BASIL SAUCE (SEE
PAGE 18)

½ CUP GRATED MOZZARELLA

2 TABLESPOONS FRESHLY GRATED PARMESAN

## CHEESE SAUCE

3 TABLESPOONS UNSALTED BUTTER

2½ TABLESPOONS ALL-PURPOSE FLOUR

2 CUPS MILK

¼ CUP FRESHLY GRATED PARMESAN

1    Cook and drain the cannelloni tubes (see page 15).
2    Meanwhile, make the simple cheese sauce (see page 17), using the butter, flour, milk, and Parmesan.
3    Heat the oven to 400°F.
4    Boil the fava beans in salted water until tender; drain and rinse in cold water. Put into a food processor
     with the ricotta, garlic, and basil; pulse until mixed to a nubbly texture and season with black pepper.
     Spoon into a large piping bag (or thick plastic food bag with a corner snipped off) and pipe
     into the cannelloni tubes.
5    Spread the tomato sauce over the bottom of a large, shallow baking dish and lay the tubes in the dish.
     Cover completely with the cheese sauce and sprinkle the mozzarella and Parmesan over.
6    Bake in the heated oven 30 to 35 minutes until bubbling and golden.

## 343
# elicoidali with roast vegetables & pesto

PREPARATION TIME 15 minutes COOKING TIME 30 to 40 minutes SERVES 4

2 LEEKS WITH THE ROOT ENDS LEFT ON,
  QUARTERED LENGTHWISE
2 ZUCCHINI, CUT INTO LARGE CHUNKS
2 RED BELL PEPPERS, QUARTERED
1 EGGPLANT, CUT INTO LARGE CHUNKS
1 HEAD OF GARLIC, SEPARATED INTO CLOVES,
  1 FINELY CHOPPED

VIRGIN OLIVE OIL
4 WELL-FLAVORED PLUM TOMATOES, HALVED
12 ounces ELICOIDALI
3 tablespoons PESTO (SEE PAGE 18)
RICOTTA, TO SERVE (OPTIONAL)

1  Heat the oven to 400°F.
2  Put all the vegetables, except the tomatoes, into a large roasting pan with the whole garlic cloves. Trickle some oil over, stir together to coat the vegetables, and spread them out. Roast in the top of the heated oven 30 to 40 minutes until tender and charred in patches. Stir and add the tomatoes after 15 minutes.
3  Just before the vegetables are ready, cook and drain the pasta according to the package directions.
4  When the vegetables are cooked, use scissors to cut the vegetables into small pieces and combine with the chopped garlic.
5  Toss the pasta with the pesto and vegetables Stir in a spoonful or two of the juices remaining in the roasting pan. Serve topped with a spoonful of ricotta, if liked.

## 344
# marille with spinach, eggplants, & bell peppers al forno

PREPARATION TIME 15 minutes COOKING TIME 1¼ hours SERVES 4

1 EGGPLANT, CUT INTO BITE-SIZE PIECES
1¼ cups BUTTERNUT OR ONION SQUASH, CUT INTO
  BITE-SIZE PIECES
1 RED BELL PEPPER AND 1 YELLOW BELL PEPPER,
  CUT INTO BITE-SIZE PIECE
2 GARLIC CLOVES, THINLY SLICED
VIRGIN OLIVE OIL
SALT AND FRESHLY GROUND BLACK PEPPER
4 ounces MARILLE
8 ounces FROZEN SPINACH, THAWED AND SQUEEZED
DRY, OR 1 pound FRESH SPINACH

BÉCHAMEL SAUCE
1½ tablespoons UNSALTED BUTTER
2 tablespoons ALL-PURPOSE FLOUR
SCANT 2 cups MILK
2 tablespoons WHOLEGRAIN MUSTARD
1 cup FRESHLY GRATED PARMESAN
2½ ounces SOFT CHEESE WITH GARLIC AND HERBS

1  Heat the oven to at 425°F.
2  Put the eggplant, squash, peppers, and garlic in a roasting pan, trickle the oil over and sprinkle with seasoning. Stir, then spread in an even layer. Roast in the heated oven 35 to 40 minutes until tender and lightly charred. Lower the oven temperature to 400°F.
3  About 15 minutes before the vegetables are ready, cook and drain the pasta according to the package directions but for 1½ minutes less than specified.
4  Meanwhile, make the sauce (see page 17) and stir in the mustard, half the Parmesan, and the soft cheese.
5  Combine the pasta with the vegetables and cooking juices, the spinach, and sauce. Transfer to a gratin dish, sprinkle the remaining cheese over, and bake 25 to 30 minutes until golden.

# 345
# baked bell peppers & eggplant with three cheeses

PREPARATION TIME 10 minutes* COOKING TIME 40 minutes* SERVES 4

2 RED BELL PEPPERS, CUT INTO ½-INCH PIECES
1 EGGPLANT, CUT INTO ½-INCH PIECES
3 GARLIC CLOVES, CHOPPED
VIRGIN OLIVE OIL
SALT AND FRESHLY GROUND BLACK PEPPER
14 OUNCES RIGATONI

1 QUANTITY WINTER TOMATO SAUCE
   (SEE PAGE 19), WARM
SMALL HANDFUL OF BASIL LEAVES, SHREDDED
1 CUP GRATED BUFFALO MOZZARELLA
½ CUP CRUMBLED RICOTTA
½ CUP FRESHLY GRATED PARMESAN
FRESHLY GRATED PECORINO, TO SERVE

1   Heat the oven to 400°F.
2   Put the vegetables and garlic in a roasting pan. Trickle some olive oil over, season, and stir the vegetables to insure they are evenly coated. Spread in an even layer. Roast in the heated oven 20 to 25 minutes until soft and lightly charred; leave the oven on.
3   Meanwhile, cook and drain the pasta according to the package directions, but giving it 1 minute less cooking time than specified.
4   Toss the pasta with the tomato sauce, the vegetables and cooking juices, and the basil.
    Spread half in a large, shallow baking dish. Cover with the mozzarella, ricotta, and half the Parmesan. Top with the remaining pasta mixture and sprinkle the remaining Parmesan over.
5   Bake in the oven at 400°F about 15 minutes until bubbling and the top is golden.
    Leave to stand 5 minutes before serving.

*   Assumes the sauce is already made.

# 346
# mushroom & eggplant pasticcio

PREPARATION TIME 10 minutes COOKING TIME 1 hour SERVES 6

1 ONION, HALVED AND THINLY SLICED
OLIVE OIL
2½ CUPS THICKLY SLICED CREMINI MUSHROOMS
2 GARLIC CLOVES, CRUSHED
1 LARGE EGGPLANT, CHOPPED
1 ROSEMARY SPRIG AND 3 THYME SPRIGS, TIED
   TOGETHER
2–3 TEASPOONS SUN-DRIED TOMATO PASTE
1 CAN (14-OZ.) CHERRY TOMATOES

SALT AND FRESHLY GROUND BLACK PEPPER
1½ CUPS CAVATAPPI, FUSILLI, OR CURVED MACARONI
1 TABLESPOON RED PESTO (SEE PAGE 19)
2 EGGS, BEATEN
1 CUP RICOTTA
¾ CUP LIGHT CREAM
4 TABLESPOONS FRESHLY GRATED PARMESAN

1   Fry the onion in a little oil in a heavy-bottomed pan until tender and light brown. Add the mushrooms and fry until lightly colored; transfer to a plate and set aside. Stir in the garlic, eggplant, and herbs and cook 2 to 3 minutes until lightly colored.
2   Dissolve the tomato paste in 4 tablespoons water. Return the mushrooms to the pan, stir in the dissolved tomato and the cherry tomatoes and bring to a simmer. Cover and simmer gently, stirring occasionally, about 15 minutes until the eggplant is tender; season and discard the herbs.
3   Heat the oven to 350°F.
4   Cook the pasta according to the package directions but 2 minutes less than specified. Drain and toss with the pesto, then with the eggplant sauce; spread in a large, shallow baking dish.
5   Stir the eggs into the ricotta, then stir in the cream until smooth. Season and pour over the eggplant and mushroom mixture. Scatter the cheese over evenly and bake in the heated oven about 35 minutes until the top is golden and just set.

## 347
# vegetable & smoked mozzarella pasticcio

PREPARATION TIME 15 minutes* COOKING TIME 45 minutes* SERVES 4

I EGGPLANT, CUT INTO ½-INCH PIECES
I RED ONION, SLICED LENGTHWISE
I HEAD OF BELGIAN ENDIVE, CUT INTO ½-INCH PIECES
I LARGE RED BELL PEPPER, CUT INTO STRIPS
2 LARGE GARLIC CLOVES, CRUSHED
PINCH OF CHILI FLAKES
VIRGIN OLIVE OIL

SALT AND FRESHLY GROUND BLACK PEPPER
13 ounces PENNE RIGATE
I QUANTITY BROILED TOMATO SAUCE
  (SEE PAGE 18), WARM
1¼ cups GRATED SMOKED MOZZARELLA
⅔ cup RICOTTA
6 tablespoons FRESHLY GRATED PARMESAN

1   Heat the oven to 425°F.
2   Put the eggplant, onion, chicory, pepper, garlic, and chili into a roasting pan. Trickle a little oil over, add seasoning, and stir the vegetables to coat evenly. Spread out and then bake in the heated oven 25 to 30 minutes until soft and lightly charred; leave the oven on.
3   Meanwhile, cook and drain the pasta according to the package directions. Mix with the vegetables and tomato sauce.
4   Spread half of the vegetable mixture in a greased 8 x 8 x 2-inch baking dish. Cover with three-quarters of the mozzarella, the ricotta, and half of the Parmesan. Top with the remaining vegetable mixture followed by the remaining cheeses.
5   Bake 15 to 20 minutes until bubbling and the top is browned. Leave to stand 5 minutes before serving.

*   Assumes the sauce is already made.

## 348
# mushroom & ricotta cannelloni

PREPARATION TIME 10 minutes* plus 15 minutes soaking and optional 2 hours standing
COOKING TIME 45 minutes* SERVES 4

½ ounce DRIED MUSHROOMS
4¼ cups FINELY CHOPPED CREMINI MUSHROOMS
SMALL KNOB OF UNSALTED BUTTER
I cup RICOTTA
2–3 teaspoons THYME
ABOUT I tablespoon LEMON ZEST
2–3 teaspoons RED PESTO (SEE PAGE 19)

SALT AND FRESHLY GROUND BLACK PEPPER
8 CANNELLONI TUBES
I QUANTITY FRESH TOMATO SAUCE (SEE PAGE 18) OR
  WINTER TOMATO SAUCE (SEE PAGE 19), WARM
½ cup SHAVED PARMESAN

1   Pour ⅓ cup boiling water over the dried mushrooms and leave to soak 15 minutes; drain and finely chop.
2   Fry the fresh and dried mushrooms in the butter in a large, preferably nonstick skillet 10 to 15 minutes until the liquid evaporates and they are beginning to brown. Leave to cool on paper towels.
3   Combine the ricotta with the mushrooms. Stir the thyme, lemon zest, and red pesto to taste into the ricotta; season. If possible, cover and leave 2 hours or overnight.
4   Heat the oven to 400°F.
5   Cook the cannelloni tubes (see page 15), drain, rinse, and drain again. Fill with the mushroom mixture. Place in a greased, shallow baking dish. Pour the sauce over, sprinkle with the Parmesan, and bake in the heated oven about 30 minutes until bubbling and golden.

*   Assumes the tomato sauce is already made.

# 349
# souffléed macaroni cheese

PREPARATION TIME 10 minutes COOKING TIME 30 minutes SERVES 4

2 cups **MACARONI**

1 **LEEK, FINELY CHOPPED**

3½ tablespoons **UNSALTED BUTTER**

4 tablespoons **ALL-PURPOSE FLOUR**

2½ cups **MILK**

1 **BAY LEAF, TORN ACROSS**

¾ cup **RICOTTA**

4 ounces **GRATED FONTINA**

1 cup **FRESHLY GRATED PARMESAN**

4 **EXTRA-LARGE EGGS, SEPARATED**

**SALT AND FRESHLY GROUND BLACK PEPPER**

1　Heat the oven to 375°F.

2　Cook the pasta about 1 minute less then specified, then drain well.

3　Meanwhile, fry the leek in the butter until soft, then stir in the flour 1 minute. Gradually add the milk and bay leaf, stirring constantly. Bring to a boil, stirring, then cook slowly 5 minutes; discard the bay leaf. Off the heat, stir in the ricotta, fontina, half the Parmesan, the egg yolks, and pasta; season.

4　Whisk the egg whites until soft peaks form. Stir a few spoonfuls into the sauce, then carefully fold in the remainder in 3 batches.

5　Transfer the mixture evenly into a large, shallow baking dish, scatter the remaining Parmesan over, and bake in the heated oven 15 to 20 minutes until puffed, golden, and just set in the middle.

## 350
# lentil & tomato cannelloni
# with spinach sauce

PREPARATION TIME 20 minutes COOKING TIME 1 hour SERVES 4

1¾ cups GREEN LENTILS
1 ONION, FINELY CHOPPED
2 CELERY STALKS, FINELY CHOPPED
VIRGIN OLIVE OIL
3 GARLIC CLOVES, FINELY CHOPPED
3 LARGE WELL-FLAVORED TOMATOES, SEEDED
    AND CHOPPED
1 TABLESPOON CHOPPED OREGANO

3 cups FRESH BROWN BREAD CRUMBS
SALT AND FRESHLY GROUND BLACK PEPPER
8 SHEETS FRESH LASAGNE VERDE
6 ounces BABY SPINACH
2 TABLESPOONS ALL-PURPOSE FLOUR
1½ cups MILK
3 TABLESPOONS FRESHLY GRATED PARMESAN

1   Cook the lentils in plenty of boiling water about 30 minutes until tender; drain well.
2   About 5 minutes before the lentils are ready, fry the onion and celery in a little oil in a skillet
    until softened, adding two-thirds of the garlic 2 minutes before the end. Stir in the drained lentils, the
    tomatoes, and oregano and simmer about 10 minutes, stirring occasionally, until thick. Stir in about
    three-quarters of the bread crumbs; season.
3   Meanwhile, cook the lasagne (see page 15) and spread on a dish towel to drain.
4   Heat the oven to 400°F.
5   Fry the remaining garlic in 1 tablespoon oil in a small saucepan 1 minute, then add the spinach
    and cook, stirring, until it wilts. Stir in the flour. Off the heat, slowly pour in the milk, stirring.
    Return to the heat, bring to a boil, stirring, and simmer 2 minutes; season. Spread about
    one-third in the bottom of a shallow baking dish.
6   Divide the lentil mixture between the lasagne sheets and roll them up. Place, seam side down,
    close together on the spinach sauce. Pour the remaining sauce over. Combine the remaining
    bread crumbs with the Parmesan and sprinkle over the sauce.
7   Bake in the heated oven 20 to 25 minutes until the top is crisp and golden.

## 351
# eggplant timballo

PREPARATION TIME 10 minutes* COOKING TIME 35 minutes* SERVES 4

1¾ cups CAVATAPPI, FUSILLI, OR CURVED MACARONI
3 EGGPLANTS, TOTAL WEIGHT ABOUT 1 POUND
    6 OUNCES, CUT INTO ¼ INCH THICK SLICES
VIRGIN OLIVE OIL

1 QUANTITY BROILED TOMATO SAUCE (SEE PAGE 18)
8 OUNCES BUFFALO MOZZARELLA, SLICED
½ CUP GRATED PARMESAN

1   Heat the oven to 375°F.
2   Cook and drain the pasta according to the package directions but 2 minutes less than specified.
3   Meanwhile, brush the eggplant slices with oil and broil until tender and brown. Use most of the slices
    to line an 8½-inch springform cake pan, leaving them to overhang the sides, taking care not to leave any
    gaps; reserve a few slices for the top.
4   Combine the pasta with the tomato sauce.
5   Pack half of the pasta mixture into the pan. Cover with a layer of mozzarella slices and a sprinkling
    of Parmesan. Add the remaining pasta, packing it down well. Cover with the overhanging and reserved
    eggplant slices. Bake in the heated oven 20 to 25 minutes until heated through. Leave to stand
    5 to 10 minutes before carefully turning onto a warm plate, if liked, and removing the pan.

*   Assumes the tomato sauce is already made.

## 352

# elicoidali with eggplants, tomatoes, & green olives al forno

PREPARATION TIME 15 minutes COOKING TIME 40 minutes SERVES 4

1 LARGE ONION, HALVED AND THINLY SLICED
4 OUNCES SUN-DRIED TOMATOES PACKED IN OIL,
   DRAINED WITH 1 TABLESPOON OIL RESERVED
2 GARLIC CLOVES, CRUSHED
1 LARGE EGGPLANT, DICED
1 CAN (15-OZ.) CRUSHED PLUM TOMATOES
8-OUNCE JAR PIMENTO-STUFFED GREEN
   OLIVES, DRAINED
SALT AND FRESHLY GROUND BLACK PEPPER
8 OUNCES ELICOIDALI*

1 CUP DICED BUFFALO MOZZARELLA
2¼ CUPS FRESHLY GRATED PARMESAN
4 OUNCES BABY SPINACH
2 TABLESPOONS PINE NUTS, CHOPPED

WHITE SAUCE
1½ TABLESPOONS BUTTER
2 TABLESPOONS ALL-PURPOSE FLOUR
2¼ CUPS MILK

1   Heat the oven to 375°F.
2   Fry the onion in the oil from the tomatoes until turning golden brown, adding the garlic the last
    2 minutes. Stir in the eggplant and sun-dried tomatoes 1 minute, then add the chopped tomatoes.
3   Cover the pan and simmer 10 to 15 minutes until the eggplants are tender. Stir in the olives, season,
    and pour into a baking dish.
4   While the eggplant is cooking, cook the elicoidali according to the package directions but for 1 minute
    less than specified; drain well.
5   Meanwhile, make the white sauce (see page 17). Stir in the mozzarella and three-quarters of the
    Parmesan, followed by the spinach and pasta. Pile evenly over the eggplant mixture,
    scatter the pine nuts and the remaining Parmesan over.
6   Bake in the heated oven about 30 minutes until bubbling and golden.

*   Penne, rigatoni, or sedani can also be used.

## 353

# spaghettini, tomato, & taleggio al forno

PREPARATION TIME 10 minutes COOKING TIME 35 minutes SERVES 4

8 OUNCES SPAGHETTINI
1 ONION, FINELY CHOPPED
VIRGIN OLIVE OIL
3 GARLIC CLOVES, CHOPPED
SMALL HANDFUL OF FLAT-LEAF PARSLEY
   LEAVES, CHOPPED
1½ TEASPOONS DRIED OREGANO
SMALL HANDFUL OF BASIL LEAVES, SHREDDED

1 EGG, BEATEN
½ CUP RICOTTA
SALT AND FRESHLY GROUND BLACK PEPPER
1 POUND WELL-FLAVORED PLUM TOMATOES, SLICED
3 OUNCES TALEGGIO, SLICED
2 TABLESPOONS FRESHLY GRATED PARMESAN

1   Heat the oven to 375°F. Oil an 8-inch loose-bottomed cake pan.
2   Cook the spaghettini according to the package directions, but for 2 minutes less than specified; drain well.
3   Meanwhile, fry the onion in a little oil until soft. Add the garlic and fry 1 minute. Combine with the
    spaghettini and herbs.
4   Blend the egg into the ricotta and then mix into the pasta; season and put half into the prepared pan.
    Press down lightly and add half the tomato slices and Taleggio. Cover with the remaining pasta, press
    down lightly, and arrange the remaining tomatoes and Taleggio on top. Sprinkle with the Parmesan.
5   Cover the top of the pan with foil and bake in the heated oven 20 minutes. Uncover and bake
    5 minutes or so longer until it is just set and the top is brown.

## 354
# tomato-topped gorgonzola, spinach & leek rigatoni

PREPARATION TIME 10 minutes COOKING TIME 25 minutes SERVES 4 to 6

9 OUNCES RIGATONI*
2¼ CUPS THINLY SLICED LEEKS
OLIVE OIL
1 POUND BABY SPINACH
PINCH OF FRESHLY GRATED NUTMEG
SALT AND FRESHLY GROUND BLACK PEPPER
⅔ CUP CRUMBLED GORGONZOLA
5 WELL-FLAVORED TOMATOES, SLICED

1–2 TABLESPOONS CHOPPED FLAT-LEAF PARSLEY
2 TABLESPOONS FRESHLY GRATED PARMESAN

### WHITE SAUCE
1½ TABLESPOONS BUTTER
2 TABLESPOONS ALL-PURPOSE FLOUR
1¾ CUPS MILK
2 TABLESPOONS WHOLEGRAIN MUSTARD

1  Heat the oven to 375°F.
2  Cook the pasta according to the package directions but giving it 1 minute less than specified; drain well.
3  Meanwhile, fry the leeks in a little oil 3 to 4 minutes. Add the spinach and cook briskly, turning frequently, until it wilts and the liquid evaporates. Add the nutmeg and seasoning to taste and combine with the pasta.
4  Make the sauce (see page 17) and stir in the mustard and seasoning.
5  Cover the bottom of a greased baking dish with a layer of the pasta mixture. Sprinkle half the Gorgonzola over, then add another layer of the pasta mixture followed by half of the sauce. Repeat the layers, ending with a layer of sauce. Arrange the tomatoes slices on top. Scatter the parsley and Parmesan over; season.
6  Bake in the heated oven 20 minutes until the tomatoes are well cooked.

*  Penne, sedani, fusilli, and eliche can also be used.

## 355
# mushrooms, gorgonzola, & tagliatelle al forno

PREPARATION TIME 10 minutes COOKING TIME 25 to 30 minutes SERVES 4

12 OUNCES TAGLIATELLE VERDE
2 SHALLOTS, FINELY CHOPPED
VIRGIN OLIVE OIL
1 GARLIC CLOVE, FINELY CHOPPED
5 CUPS THINLY SLICED CREMINI MUSHROOMS
6 TABLESPOONS LOW-FAT CRÈME FRAÎCHE
½ CUP CRUMBLED GORGONZOLA

2 WELL-FLAVORED TOMATOES, PEELED, SEEDED, AND CHOPPED
1 EGG, BEATEN
SALT AND FRESHLY GROUND BLACK PEPPER
1 CUP GRATED MOZZARELLA

1  Heat the oven to 350°F.
2  Cook and drain the tagliatelle according to the package directions, but for 1 minute less than specified.
3  Meanwhile, fry the shallots in a little oil until soft. Add the mushrooms and garlic and cook, stirring, until the mushrooms are just soft. Stir in the crème fraîche and Gorgonzola and warm through gently, stirring; do not boil.
4  Add the tagliatelle and tomatoes, then remove from the heat and stir in the egg and seasoning, using plenty of black pepper. Pour into a greased shallow baking dish, sprinkle the mozzarella over, and cover with foil.
5  Bake in the heated oven 15 to 20 minutes until the mozzarella melts and is brown.

# 356
# pasta & gorgonzola puff

PREPARATION TIME 10 minutes COOKING TIME 25 to 30 minutes SERVES 4 to 6

4 TABLESPOONS **UNSALTED BUTTER, MELTED**

2 TABLESPOONS **DRY BREAD CRUMBS**

6 OUNCES **SPAGHETTI**

½ CUP **ALL-PURPOSE FLOUR**

2¼ CUPS **MILK**

1 TABLESPOON **DIJON MUSTARD**

1 CUP **CRUMBLED GORGONZOLA**

6 **EGGS, SEPARATED**

**FRESHLY GROUND BLACK PEPPER**

1    Heat the oven to 375°. Brush the inside of a 2¼-quart baking dish thoroughly with some of the butter.
     Sprinkle in the bread crumbs so they adhere evenly.

2    Cook the spaghetti according to the package directions but for 1 minute less than specified; drain well.

3    Make a white sauce (see page 17) with the remaining butter, the flour, and milk. Remove from the heat
     and stir in the mustard, cheese, egg yolks, and cooked pasta. Season using plenty of black pepper.

4    Whisk the egg whites until stiff but not dry. Stir 2 tablespoons into the pasta mixture, then fold
     in the remainder in 3 batches. Transfer to the baking dish and bake in the heated oven
     20 to 25 minutes until puffy and golden and lightly set in the middle.

## 357
# mushroom & squash al forno

PREPARATION TIME 10 minutes COOKING TIME 35 minutes SERVES 3 to 4

1 BUTTERNUT SQUASH, PEELED, SEEDED, AND CUT
  INTO ½-INCH CUBES
4½ CUPS CREMINI MUSHROOMS, HALVED OR
  QUARTERED, DEPENDING ON SIZE
1 SPRIG OF ROSEMARY
3 GARLIC CLOVES, LIGHTLY CRUSHED

VIRGIN OLIVE OIL
SALT AND FRESHLY GROUND BLACK PEPPER
9 OUNCES PENNE
1 CUP HALF-FAT CRÈME FRAÎCHE
5 TABLESPOONS FINELY GRATED PARMESAN
1¼ CUPS FRESH BREAD CRUMBS

1 Heat the oven to 400°F.
2 Put the squash, mushrooms, rosemary, and garlic into a nonstick roasting pan, trickle a little oil over, season, and stir the ingredients together. Spread in an even layer and bake in the heated oven about 30 minutes until soft and slightly charred, stirring a couple of times.
3 Meanwhile, cook and drain the pasta according to the package directions.
4 Toss the pasta with the cooked vegetables (discard the rosemary), then gently stir in the crème fraîche and half the Parmesan; season. Tip into a gratin dish, sprinkle the bread crumbs and remaining Parmesan over, and place under a heated hot broiler until crisp and golden.

## 358
# rotolo

PREPARATION TIME 15 minutes* COOKING TIME 45 minutes* SERVES 4

2-EGG QUANTITY OF PASTA DOUGH (SEE PAGE 10)
1 POUND 10 OUNCES BABY SPINACH
UNSALTED BUTTER
6 OUNCES SOFT GOAT CHEESE,
  RIND REMOVED, CRUMBLED
¼ CUP CRUMBLED RICOTTA

¼ CUP FRESHLY GRATED PARMESAN
FRESHLY GROUND BLACK PEPPER
1 WHOLE EGG AND 1 EGG YOLK, BEATEN
3 TABLESPOONS HEAVY CREAM
RED BELL PEPPER AND TOMATO SAUCE,
  (SEE PAGE 123), TO SERVE

1 Cook the spinach in a large covered pan until it wilts. Drain well and squeeze out as much water as possible; chop finely.
2 Heat a little butter in a skillet and stir in the spinach 2 to 3 minutes, until all the moisture evaporates. Cool slightly, then stir in the goat cheese, ricotta, and two-thirds of the Parmesan. Season with plenty of black pepper. Stir in the egg and egg yolk.
3 Roll out the pasta dough by hand to a rectangle about 12 x 16 inches.** Place on a large piece of cheesecloth.
4 Using a spatula, spread over the filling to within ½ inch of the edges. Roll up like a jelly roll, dampen the ends, and pinch them together. Wrap the roll tightly in the cheesecloth and tie the ends with string.
5 Place in a fish kettle or large flameproof dish of boiling water, half cover with a lid, and simmer 20 to 25 minutes, turning carefully twice; lift out carefully and leave to cool before unwrapping.
6 Heat the oven to 400°F.
7 Using a large, sharp knife cut the roll into ½-inch slices and arrange in a buttered gratin dish. Melt a small knob of butter in the cream, pour over the slices, and sprinkle with the remaining Parmesan. Bake in the heated oven about 15 minutes until golden. Serve with the tomato sauce.

\* Times for making pasta dough or red bell pepper and tomato sauce not included.
\*\* If using a pasta machine, roll 3 strips about 16 inches long, lay them side by side, overlapping slightly. Moisten the overlap with water to stick the edges together.

## 359
# broccoli & pasta bake

PREPARATION TIME 10 minutes COOKING TIME 25 minutes SERVES 4

8 ounces PENNE RIGATE
I LARGE HEAD OF BROCCOLI, DIVIDED
  INTO FLOWERETS
1¼ cups FRESHLY GRATED PARMESAN
4 tablespoons PINE NUTS, LIGHTLY TOASTED

SIMPLE WHITE SAUCE
1½ tablespoons UNSALTED BUTTER
2 tablespoons ALL-PURPOSE FLOUR
2¼ cups MILK
I tablespoon WHOLEGRAIN MUSTARD

1 Heat the oven to 400°F.
2 Cook the pasta according to the package directions, adding the broccoli the last 4 minutes.
  Drain the pasta and broccoli thoroughly. Tip in an even layer in a gratin dish.
3 Meanwhile, make a white sauce with the butter, flour, and milk (see page 17). Remove from the heat
  and stir in the mustard and half the cheese. Pour over the broccoli and pasta.
  Scatter the pine nuts and remaining cheese over.
4 Bake in the heated oven about 15 minutes until golden.

## 360
# pappardelle with fresh artichokes

PREPARATION TIME 15 minutes COOKING TIME 15 minutes SERVES 4

6 ARTICHOKES
½ LEMON
2 GARLIC CLOVES, FINELY CHOPPED
I DRIED CHILI, SEEDED AND FINELY CHOPPED

4 tablespoons EXTRA-VIRGIN OLIVE OIL
2 tablespoons BOILING WATER
18 ounces PAPPARDELLE
FRESHLY GRATED PARMESAN, TO SERVE (OPTIONAL)

1 Remove the outer leaves from the artichokes and cut off the tough tips from the remaining leaves.
  Cut the artichokes into quarters. Rub the cut surfaces with the lemon. Remove the hairy "choke"
  and thinly slice each segment.
2 Fry garlic and chili in the oil 2 minutes. Add the artichoke slices and cook slowly, stirring, about
  3 minutes before adding the boiling water. Cover and simmer 10 minutes.
3 Meanwhile, cook the pasta according to the package directions. Drain, reserving about ½ cup of
  the cooking water. Toss the pappardelle with the artichoke mixture. If the pasta seems too dry,
  add sufficient of the reserved pasta cooking water. Serve with freshly grated Parmesan, if liked.

# 361
# spinach & cheese pasticcio

PREPARATION TIME 10 minutes COOKING TIME 1 hour 10 minutes SERVES 4

4 ounces **TAGLIATELLE**

18 ounces **SPINACH**

1¼ cups **MILK**

10 ounces **SOFT GOAT CHEESE, CHOPPED***

⅓ cup **RICOTTA***

ABOUT ½ cup **FRESHLY GRATED PARMESAN**
  **(OPTIONAL)*****

3 EGGS, BEATEN

SALT AND FRESHLY GROUND BLACK PEPPER

RED PEPPER AND TOMATO SAUCE (SEE PAGE 123)
  OR ½ QUANTITY BROILED TOMATO SAUCE
  (SEE PAGE 18), TO SERVE (OPTIONAL)`

1   Heat the oven to 350°F.
2   Cook the tagliatelle 2 minutes less then specified; drain well.
3   Meanwhile, cook the spinach without any additional water in a large pan, stirring frequently, until it wilts and is soft. Drain, then squeeze out excess moisture. Combine with the milk, cheeses, eggs, and seasoning. Mix with the drained pasta and pour into a greased, large baking dish.
4   Bake in the heated oven about 1 hour until light brown and just set in the middle.
5   To turn out the pasticcio, invert onto a warm plate and give a slight shake. Serve with the sauce, if liked.

\*    The proportions can be varied, to taste.
\**   The addition of Parmesan will depend on the amount of goat cheese used and the mildness of its flavor.

## 362

# farfalle, artichoke, mushroom, & egg salad

PREPARATION TIME 10 minutes plus 2 hours standing COOKING TIME 10 minutes SERVES 4

14 OUNCES **FARFALLE**
8 OUNCES **MIXED MUSHROOMS SUCH AS SHIITAKE,**
  **OYSTER, CHANTERELLE, AND ENOKI**
2 **SHALLOTS, FINELY CHOPPED**
2 **GARLIC CLOVES, FINELY CHOPPED**
9 OUNCES **ROAST ARTICHOKES IN OIL, DRAINED**
  **(RESERVE THE OIL) AND HALVED**

1 TABLESPOON **BALSAMIC VINEGAR**
**SALT AND FRESHLY GROUND BLACK PEPPER**
2 **EGGS, BOILED TO TASTE, PEELED, AND CHOPPED**
**LEAVES FROM A BUNCH OF FLAT-LEAF PARSLEY,**
  **FINELY CHOPPED**

1   Cook and drain the pasta according to the package directions.
2   Meanwhile, break the mushrooms into pieces if large. Fry the mushrooms and shallots in a little of the artichoke oil in a large skillet over brisk heat, until light brown, adding the garlic 2 minutes before the end.
3   Toss the mushrooms with the pasta, artichokes, balsamic vinegar, and seasoning. Cover and leave in a cool place (preferably not the refrigerator) at least 2 hours.
4   Just before serving, toss the egg with the parsley and seasoning. Scatter over the pasta salad to serve.

## 363

# tagliatelle with zucchini ribbons

PREPARATION TIME 15 minutes plus 30 minutes standing COOKING TIME 10 minutes SERVES 4

12 OUNCES **SMALL ZUCCHINI**
**SALT AND FRESHLY GROUND BLACK PEPPER**
2 CUPS **DRY WHITE BREAD CRUMBS**
½ CUP **FRESHLY GRATED PARMESAN**
2 **EGGS, BEATEN**

14 OUNCES **TAGLIATELLE**
**OIL FOR DEEP FRYING**
**KNOB OF UNSALTED BUTTER, MELTED**
**SMALL HANDFUL OF BASIL LEAVES, SHREDDED**

1   Cut the zucchini into fine ribbons lengthwise using a mandoline, food processor, or vegetable peeler with firm pressure. Layer with salt in a colander and leave 30 minutes; rinse well and dry thoroughly.
2   In a shallow bowl, combine the bread crumbs with black pepper and half the cheese. Pour the eggs into another shallow bowl. Dip the zucchini ribbons individually first into the egg, allowing the excess to drain off, then into the bread crumb mixture to coat well and evenly.
3   Cook and drain the pasta according to the package directions.
4   Meanwhile, deep-fry the zucchini ribbons in batches in hot oil 1 to 2 minutes until crisp and golden; drain on paper towels. Toss the pasta with the butter, basil, and remaining cheese and transfer to a warm large, shallow serving dish. Pile the zucchini strips on top.

## 364

# cavatappi with zucchini, tomatoes, & capers

PREPARATION TIME 10 minutes plus 30 minutes standing COOKING TIME 10 minutes SERVES 4

14 OUNCES ZUCCHINI, CUT INTO SHORT STRIPS
SALT
4 LARGE WELL-FLAVORED PLUM TOMATOES, CHOPPED
2 GARLIC CLOVES, FINELY CHOPPED
3 TABLESPOONS CAPERS

2 TABLESPOONS CHOPPED OREGANO
2 TABLESPOONS WHITE WINE VINEGAR
EXTRA-VIRGIN OLIVE OIL
12 OUNCES CAVATAPPI*

1   Put the zucchini in a colander, sprinkle salt over, and leave 30 minutes. Rinse well, squeeze, and pat dry with paper towels.
2   Meanwhile, combine the tomatoes, garlic, capers, half the oregano, the vinegar, and 3 tablespoons olive oil; set aside 15 minutes.
3   Cook and drain the pasta according to the package directions.
4   Meanwhile, quickly fry the zucchini in a little oil until light brown. Add the tomato mixture to the pan to warm through. Toss with the cavatappi and remaining oregano.

*   Fusilli lunghi, fusilli, or farfalle can also be used.

## 365

# tagliatelle with zucchini, ricotta, & basil

PREPARATION TIME 10 minutes COOKING TIME 10 minutes SERVES 4

1 GARLIC CLOVE, THINLY SLICED
4 TABLESPOONS VIRGIN OLIVE OIL
11 OUNCES TAGLIATELLE
1 POUND SMALL, FIRM BABY ZUCCHINI, VERY THINLY SLICED
JUICE AND GRATED ZEST OF 1 LARGE LEMON

¼ CUP FRESHLY GRATED PARMESAN, PLUS EXTRA TO SERVE
1 CUP RICOTTA
SMALL HANDFUL OF BASIL LEAVES, SHREDDED
2 TABLESPOONS PINE NUTS, LIGHTLY TOASTED
SALT AND FRESHLY GROUND BLACK PEPPER

1   Warm the garlic in the oil 5 minutes; do not let it become too hot. Discard the garlic.
2   Meanwhile, cook and drain the pasta according to the package directions.
3   While the pasta is cooking, fry the zucchini in batches in the garlic oil until soft and flecked with brown. Return all the zucchini to the pan. Add the lemon juice to warm through.
4   Toss the zucchini with the pasta, Parmesan, ricotta, lemon zest, basil, pine nuts, and seasoning. Serve with extra Parmesan.

# Index

**ANCHOVIES**: black olive pasta with
broccoli, capers, & anchovies 70
bucatini with melting onion
& anchovy sauce 75
farfalle with bell peppers,
anchovies, & capers 62
fusilli with sun-blush tomatoes,
anchovies, & olives 38
linguine with anchovies, chili, & olives 31
orecchiette with cauliflower,
anchovies, & tomatoes 66
penne with cauliflower,
anchovies, & garlic 89
puffed spinach & anchovy bake 93
spaghetti alla puttanesca 64
spaghetti with anchovies, lemon,
chilies & thyme pangritata 39
spaghetti with capers, olives, & anchovies 41
spaghetti with cherry tomatoes,
anchovies, & basil 65
spaghetti with garlic, anchovies, & parsley 30
spaghetti with summer puttanesca sauce 40
**ARTICHOKES**: artichoke
& mushroom lasagne 194
cavatappi with artichokes,
mushrooms, & peas 178
elicoidali with artichokes, bell peppers,
zucchini, & prosciutto 135
farfalle, artichoke, mushroom,
& egg salad 212
fusilli with artichokes, tomatoes, & olives 32
lumache with pancetta & artichokes 137
pappardelle with fresh artichokes 210
penne with artichoke, tomatoes, & olives 167
tagliarini with artichokes & gremolata 29
**ARUGULA**: cavatappi with arugula,
tomatoes, & olives 31
farfalle with arugula, walnuts, & dolcelatte 47
fusilli, arugula, & tomato frittata 35
gnocchi, arugula, tomato,
& black olive salad 46
orecchiette with tomatoes, arugula,
& pine nuts 47
spaghetti with goat cheese,
arugula, & walnuts 48
tagliatelle with arugula pesto 47
tagliatelle with arugula,
pine nuts, & thyme 55
**ASPARAGUS**: agnolotti with
asparagus & prosciutto 129
fettuccine with asparagus, peas, & lemon 160
fusilli with asparagus & prosciutto 141
riccioli with shrimp & asparagus 80
tagliatelle, asparagus, fava bean,
& zucchini salad 168
tagliatelle with asparagus & Parmesan 173
tagliatelle with peas, asparagus,
& saffron sauce 186
**AVOCADO**: cavatappi with tomatoes,
avocado, & basil 52

**BEANS**: fava bean & basil cannelloni 200
conchiglie with fava beans,
nut, & lemon sauce 159
gnocchi with borlotti beans & pancetta 150
linguine with new potatoes,
beans, & pesto 166
macaroni, beef, & beans 134
penne with fava beans,
parsley, & pecorino 181
tagliatelle with fava beans
& goat cheese 177
tagliatelle with green beans & herbs 168
**BÉCHAMEL** sauce 17, 79
**BEEF**: baked rigatoni alla Bolognese 146
cannelloni with beef,
roast shallots, & garlic 145

lasagne 139, 143
macaroni, beef, & beans 134
ragù 16
tagliatelle alla Bolognese 113, 120
Bolognese sauce 113, 120, 143
**BRESAOLA**: tagliatelle with bresaola,
peas, & leeks 125
**BROCCOLI**: black olive pasta with
broccoli, capers, & anchovies 70
broccoli & pasta bake 210
cannelloni with sausages & broccoli 143
casareccia with broccoli & Gorgonzola 174
conchiglie with broccoli,
walnuts, & pancetta 129
eliche with broccoli, bread crumbs,
golden raisins, & pine nuts 155
orecchiette with broccoli,
sun-dried tomatoes, & thyme 159
pennette with broccoli, pine nuts,
& chili 182
riccioli with broccoli, Parmesan,
& pine nuts 156
riccioli with broccoli, Taleggio, & almonds 179
trofie with broccoli sauce 155

**CARBONARA** sauce 40
**CAULIFLOWER**: orecchiette with
cauliflower, anchovies, & tomatoes 66
orecchiette with cauliflower,
chorizo, & black olives 116
penne with cauliflower, anchovies, & garlic 89
strozzapreti with cauliflower,
pancetta, & parsley 139
strozzapreti with cauliflower,
saffron, & tomatoes 170
**CELERY**: penne rigate with cheeses,
celery, & almonds 163
**CHEESE**: black pepper tagliatelle
with three-cheese sauce 176
cheese & herb agnolotti 129, 183, 195
conchiglie with Gorgonzola & walnuts 57
linguine with Gorgonzola & watercress 32
panzarotti 190
pasta, basil, & goat cheese frittata 30
pasta & Gorgonzola puff 208
pasta with roast garlic, thyme,
& crumbled goat cheese 54
penne rigate with cheeses,
celery, & almonds 163
souffléed macaroni cheese 204
spaghetti with goat cheese,
arugula, & walnuts 48
trofie with goat cheese & lemon 160
**CHICKEN**: campanelli with chicken,
prosciutto, & basil 130
chicken & prosciutto cannelloni
on spinach & mushrooms 144
chicken & spinach pasticcio 127
chicken & walnut cannelloni 127
chicken soup with tortellini 23
chicken-stuffed pasta shells 123
conchiglie with chicken,
cherry tomato, & herb sauce 126
fusilli, chicken, & fennel salad 44
fusilli lunghi chicken with avocado
& green pesto sauce 138
garganelle with chicken
& watercress sauce 124
gnocchi with chicken ragù 135
lasagne 122
lumache with chicken,
eggplant, & oregano 132
Mediterranean chicken &
pasta al forno 117
penne with chicken, leeks,
& Gorgonzola 121
pennette with chicken livers & marsala 147

spiced chicken tortellini 23, 120
tagliatelle with chicken, zucchini,
& red bell peppers 133
tagliatelle with chicken, lemon, & basil 151
tagliatelle with chicken & sage 113
**CLAMS**: linguine with red clam sauce 86
linguine with white clam sauce 64
tonnarelli with shrimp, clams, & arugula 87
**COD**: cod, shrimp, & leek lasagne 78
smoked fish raviolini 76
spaghetti with cod & pangritata 72
**CRAB**: cavatappi with crab & basil 45
crab & dill cannelloni 74
crab & shrimp ravioli 100
crab in conchiglie with red pesto sauce 95
riccioli with crab, avocado,
& fresh tomatoes 90
tagliarini with crab & fennel 94
taglioni with crab sauce 102

**EGG** pasta 9–12
**EGGPLANTS**: eggplant timballo 205
baked bell peppers & eggplant
with three cheeses 202
cavatappi with roast eggplants,
bell peppers, & basil 188
elicoidali with eggplants, tomatoes,
& green olives al forno 206
lumache with chicken,
eggplant, & oregano 132
mushroom & eggplant pasticcio 202
penne with eggplants, olives, & basil 180
penne rigate with eggplants & ricotta 193
sausage & eggplant lasagne 149
tortiglioni with eggplant & tomato 179
**EGGS**: farfalle, artichoke,
mushroom, & egg salad 212

**FENNEL**: bucatini with sardines,
lemon, & fennel 68
fusilli, chicken, & fennel salad 44
macaroni, fennel, pine nut,
& cheese al forno 199
pappardelle with roast fennel
& dolcelatte 192
tagliatelle with slow-cooked
fennel & garlic 198
**FRITTATA** 30, 35, 107

**GARBANZO** beans: quick pasta with
garbanzo beans & spinach 187
**GNOCCHI** 12, 43, 58, 59

**HADDOCK**: haddock, spinach,
& pasta al forno 84
smoked fish & mushroom cannelloni 79
smoked fish pie 77
smoked fish raviolini 76
**HAM**: agnolotti with asparagus
& prosciutto 129
fusilli lunghi with asparagus & prosciutto 141
tagliatelle with prosciutto, peas, & lemon 117
taglioni with prosciutto, peas, & parsley 125
**HERB** pasta 10, 195

**LAMB**: bigoli with lamb,
tomatoes, & olives 121
braised lamb shanks with pasta 145
lamb ragù 107, 108
pappardelle with lamb & rosemary 131
**LEEKS**: fusilli with leeks,
garlic, & Parmesan 186
lasagne 78, 122
pappardelle with mushrooms & leeks 172
pasta, leeks, & cheese al forno 176
penne with chicken, leeks, & Gorgonzola 121
tagliatelle with bresaola, peas, & leeks 125

214

tomato-topped Gorgonzola, spinach, & leek rigatoni 207
**LEMON** sauce 56
**LENTILS**: chifferi with lentils & pancetta 142
gnocchi with lentil sauce 188
lentil & tomato cannelloni with spinach sauce 205
spinach & lentil lasagne 191
**LETTUCE**: cavatappi with minted lettuce & peas 157
**LOBSTER**: fidelini with lobster, basil, & wilted tomatoes 82
green fettuccine & lobster with vodka-cream sauce 92

**MEATBALLS** 106, 119, 148
**MINESTRONE** 27
**MUSHROOMS**: cavatappi with shrimp, mushrooms, & tomatoes 81
farfalle, artichoke, mushroom, & egg salad 212
farfalle with mushrooms, sun-dried tomatoes, & spinach 184
fettuccine with mushrooms, pancetta, & wine 110
lasagne 94, 195, 196
lasagnette with mixed mushrooms & herbs 161
mushroom & ricotta cannelloni 203
mushroom & salami al forno 151
mushroom & squash al forno 209
mushrooms, Gorgonzola, & tagliatelle al forno 207
orecchiette with mushrooms & tomato 185
pappardelle with mushrooms & leeks 172
pappardelle with roast mushrooms 174
smoked fish & mushroom cannelloni 79
strozzapreti with bell peppers & mushrooms 180
**MUSSELS**: cavatelli with mussels, tomatoes, & chilies 103
linguine with mussels & zucchini 81
orecchiette with smoked mussels, spinach & cashews 91
smoked mussel & pimento pasta salad 80
tagliatelle with mussels & pesto 82
taglioni with mussels, wilted greens, & lardons 71

**NUTS:** cavatappi with spinach, raisins, & pine nuts 53
chicken & walnut cannelloni 127
conchiglie with fava beans, nuts, & lemon sauce 159
conchiglie with broccoli, walnuts, & pancetta 129
conchiglie with Gorgonzola & walnuts 57
eliche with broccoli, bread crumbs, golden raisins, & pine nuts 155
farfalle with arugula, walnuts, & dolcelatte 47
fettuccine with scallops, buttered pine nuts, & shredded lettuce
fidelini with walnut sauce 33
green & white tagliatelle with pine nuts, & Parmesan 49
macaroni, fennel, pine nut, & cheese al forno 199
orecchiette with smoked mussels, spinach, & cashews 91
orecchiette with tomatoes, arugula, & pine nuts 47
penne rigate with cheeses, celery, & almonds 163
pennette with broccoli, pine nuts, & chilies 182
pennette with tomato & almond sauce 54

riccioli with broccoli, Parmesan, & pine nuts 156
riccioli with broccoli, Taleggio, & almonds 179
spaghetti with goat cheese, arugula, & walnuts 48
spaghetti with parsley & pine nuts 46
spaghetti with tomatoes, olives, & walnuts 51
tagliatelle with arugula, pine nuts, & thyme 55
torchiette with zucchini, lemon, & pine nuts 154
trenette with pine nuts & herbs 52
trenette with quick spinach & walnut sauce 57

**ONIONS**: bucatini with melting onion & anchovy sauce 75
gemelli with melting onion sauce 189

**PANCETTA**: bucatini with pancetta, tomatoes, olives, & herbs 136
bucatini with pancetta, tomatoes, & chilies 147
bucatini with sausage & pancetta 125
cavatappi with pancetta, bell peppers, & tomatoes 122
chifferi with lentils & pancetta 142
conchiglie with broccoli, walnuts, & pancetta 129
conchiglie with pancetta, peas, & ricotta 136
fettuccine with mushrooms, pancetta, & wine 110
gnocchi with borlotti beans & pancetta 150
lumache with pancetta & artichokes 137
orecchiette with peas, pancetta, & sage 140
pancetta-stuffed tomatoes 37
spaghetti with tuna, pancetta, & tomatoes 66
strozzapreti with cauliflower, pancetta, & parsley 139
tagliatelle with pancetta, arugula, & Gorgonzola 147
taglioni with mussels, wilted greens, & lardons 71
taglioni with seared scallops, pancetta, & tomatoes 95
**PANZAROTTI** 190
**PASTA**: buying 7, 8
cooking 14–15
homemade 8–13
stuffed 11, 13, 15, 63, 76, 100, 120, 134, 183, 184, 190, 195, 209
**PEAS**: cavatappi with artichokes, mushrooms & peas 178
cavatappi with minted lettuce & peas 157
chifferi with peas & Parmesan 157
farfalle with peas, mint, & ricotta 175
fettuccine with asparagus, peas, & lemon 160
fettuccine with peas, prosciutto, & sage 131
orecchiette with peas, pancetta, & sage 140
orecchiette with peas & feta 157
pasta e piselli (pasta & peas) 50
riccioli with peas & saffron 52
tagliatelle with bresaola, peas, & leek 125
tagliatelle with prosciutto, peas, & lemon 117
tagliatelle with peas, prosciutto, & basil 131
taglioni with prosciutto, peas, & parsley 125
**PEPPERS**, bell: ditali with tomatoes, garlic, & broiled bell peppers 181
farfalle with hot-smoked salmon & red bell peppers 64
fidelini-stuffed bell peppers 42
fusilli lunghi with fresh tuna & roast bell peppers 67
potato gnocchi with red bell pepper & red pesto sauce 43

red bell pepper & tomato sauce 123, 209
riccioli with bell peppers & cherry tomatoes 187
spaghetti with broiled bell peppers & garlic 48
spaghetti with simple red bell pepper sauce 41
strozzapreti with bell peppers & mushrooms 180
tagliatelle & jumbo shrimp with red bell pepper sauce 98
tagliatelle with red bell peppers & mozzarella 171
warm pasta with mixed bell peppers & tomatoes 50
ziti with red bell peppers & basil 194
**PESTO** 10, 18, 19, 33, 38, 47
**PORK**: cavatappi with pork ragù 114
pasta with pork, spinach, & lemon 126
pork & spinach cannelloni 144
tonnarelli with pork & mushrooms 112
**POTATOES**: linguine with new potatoes, beans, & pesto 166
potato gnocchi with red pepper & pesto sauce 43
spinach & potato gnocchi with fontina 59
**PROSCIUTTO**: bucatini with prosciutto, radicchio, capers, & lemon 111
cannelloni with spinach & prosciutto filling 148
eliche with prosciutto, bell peppers, & peas 140
elicoidali with artichokes, bell peppers, zucchini, & prosciutto 135
fettuccine with peas, prosciutto, & sage 131
lumache with prosciutto, arugula, & capers 128
penne with mushrooms & frazzled prosciutto 138
penne rigate with spinach, prosciutto, & crumbled goat cheese 140
tagliatelle with peas, prosciutto, & basil 131
tonnarelli with radicchio, rosemary, & prosciutto 137
tortellini with spinach, ricotta, & prosciutto 150
**PUTTANESCA** sauce 40, 64

**RADICCHIO**: bucatini with prosciutto, radicchio, capers, & lemon 111
tonnarelli with radicchio, rosemary, & prosciutto 137
tonnarelli with radicchio & Taleggio 193
**RAGÙ**: beef ragù 16, 111, 113
chicken ragù 135
lamb ragù 107, 108
pork ragù 114
Sardinian ragù 107
**ROTOLO** 209

**SAFFRON** pasta 10
**SALADS**: farfalle, artichoke, mushroom, & egg salad 212
fusilli, chicken, & fennel salad 44
gnocchi, arugula, tomato, & black olive salad 46
Mediterranean seafood & pasta salad 84
Mediterranean vegetable & pasta salad 43
olive & triple tomato salad 59
roast vegetable, seafood, & pasta salad 92
smoked mussel & pimento pasta salad 80
tagliatelle, asparagus, fava bean, & zucchini salad 168
warm fresh tuna salad niçoise 72
warm fusilli & seafood salad 69
warm pasta, mushroom, & broiled vegetable salad 169

INDEX

**SALMON**: farfalle with hot-smoked salmon
& red bell peppers 64
fettuccine with smoked salmon,
dill, & ricotta 89
green & white tagliatelle with smoked
salmon, spinach, & lemon 73
salmon ravioli 63
salmon shells with pesto
& tomato sauce 75
spaghetti with salmon eggs & chives 57
**SARDINES**: bucatini with sardines,
lemon, & fennel 68
spaghetti with slivered sardines
& tomatoes 70
**SAUSAGES**: bucatini with sausage
& pancetta 125
cannelloni with sausages & broccoli 143
elicoidali, sausages, &
bell pepper al forno 115
mushroom & salami al forno 151
orecchiette with cauliflower,
chorizo, & black olives 116
penne with chorizo, arugula, & tomatoes 112
penne with sausages & mushrooms 114
penne rigate with sausages al forno 119
sausage & eggplant lasagne 149
sedani with tomatoes,
sausages, & mushrooms 108
strapiozi with sausages,
mixed bell peppers, & tomatoes 128
strozzapreti with sausages,
onions, & bell peppers 115
vermicelli, chorizo, & mozzarella torta 118
**SCALLOPS**: black spaghettini with
scallops, white wine, & parsley 83
fettucine with scallops, buttered
pine nuts, & shredded lettuce
scallop & shrimp lasagne 79
tagliatelle with scallops,
bell peppers, & basil 97
taglioni with seared scallops,
pancetta, & tomatoes 95
**SEAFOOD**: conchiglie with
seafood sauce 97
linguine with seafood, saffron, & tomatoes 98
Mediterranean seafood & pasta salad 84
quick linguine with seafood 65
roast vegetable, seafood, & pasta salad 92
seafood cannelloni 76
seafood linguine en papillote 88
seafood spaghetti with saffron 93
seafood tossed with spaghetti,
lemon, & arugula 86
shellfish spaghetti with
sun-blush tomatoes 99
warm fusilli & seafood salad 69
**SHRIMP**: bucatini with squid, shrimp,
lemon, parsley, & garlic 102
cavatappi with shrimp,
mushrooms, & tomatoes 81
conchiglie with shrimp sauce 100
crab & shrimp ravioli 100
fettuccine with jumbo shrimp,
tomatoes, & basil 96
fusilli lunghi with shrimp,
fennel, & tomatoes 94
lasagne 78, 79
pasta, shrimp & pesto 41
shrimp & pasta al forno 91
quick tagliatelle with shrimp & red pesto 87
riccioli with shrimp & asparagus 80
spaghetti with shrimp,
tomatoes, & capers 69
tagliatelle & jumbo shrimp with
red bell pepper sauce 98
taglioni with shrimp & spinach 82
tonnarelli with shrimp, clams, & arugula 87

**SNAPPER**: linguine with roast snapper
& cherry tomatoes 71
**SOUPS** 22–28
**SPINACH**: cannelloni with spinach
& prosciutto filling 148
cavatappi with spinach, raisins,
& pine nuts 53
chicken & prosciutto cannelloni
on spinach & mushrooms 144
chicken & spinach pasticcio 127
fusilli with spinach,
sun-dried tomatoes, & olives 36
fusilli lunghi with spinach & Gorgonzola 167
tomato-topped Gorgonzola,
spinach, & leek rigatoni 207
lentil & tomato cannelloni
with spinach sauce 205
lasagne 191, 195
pasta with pork, spinach, & lemon 126
penne rigate with spinach, prosciutto,
& crumbled goat cheese 140
pork & spinach cannelloni 144
puffed spinach & anchovy bake 93
quick pasta with
garbanzo beans & spinach 187
rotolo 209
spinach & cheese pasticcio 211
spinach & potato gnocchi with fontina 59
spinach & ricotta gnocchi 51
spinach & ricotta ravioli 184
tagliatelle with spinach,
lemon, & Parmesan 186
tagliatelle with spinach & ricotta 187
tortellini with spinach,
ricotta, & prosciutto 150
trenette with quick spinach
& walnut sauce 57
warm pasta salad with spinach,
tomatoes, & olives 34
**SQUASH**: mushroom & squash al forno 209
pappardelle with roast squash
& broiled goat cheese 158
ravioli with squash & prosciutto 134
ricotta, Parmesan, & squash ravioli 192
squash & mushroom lasagne 196
**SQUID**: bucatini with squid, shrimp,
lemon, parsley, & garlic 102
linguine with squid, basil, & chili 101
spaghetti with squid, tomatoes, & herbs 100
**STEAK**: pappardelle with
steak & mushrooms 109
tagliatelle with steak & onions 110
**SWORDFISH**: spaghetti with swordfish,
lemon, capers, & arugula 101

**TAPENADE** 33
**TOMATOES**: bucatini with
roast tomatoes 164
cavatappi with arugula,
tomatoes, & olives 31
cavatelli with fresh tomatoes,
herbs, & mozzarella 39
eliche with tomatoes, olives, & basil 48
fettuccine with fresh tomatoes & basil 45
fusilli, arugula, & tomato frittata 35
gnocchi, arugula, tomato,
& black olive salad 46
green & white tagliatelle with ricotta,
tomatoes, & basil 180
linguine, tomatoes, bell peppers,
& black olives en papillote 178
olive & triple tomato salad 59
orecchiette with tomatoes,
arugula, & pine nuts 47
pancetta-stuffed tomatoes 37
pappardelle with roast
cherry tomatoes, basil, & ricotta 177

penne with creamy tomato
& basil sauce 172
penne with spicy tomato sauce 181
sauces 14, 15, 18, 19
tagliatelle with Sicilian tomato pesto 38
tagliatelle with tomatoes,
mozzarella, & herbs 173
tonnarelli with tomato
& red pesto sauce 42
trenette with wilted tomatoes 35
warm pasta salad with spinach,
tomatoes, & olives 34
warm pasta with mixed
bell peppers & tomatoes 50
**TORTA** 118
**TUNA**: fusilli lunghi with fresh tuna
& roast bell peppers 67
fusilli with tuna, olives, & garlic 62
penne with tuna in tomato
& olive sauce 69
pipe with tuna, lemon, & basil 74
rotelle with tuna & arugula 89
spaghetti with tuna,
pancetta, & tomatoes 66
strozzapreti with fresh tuna,
chili, tomatoes, & olives 65
tuna & broccoli bake 103
warm fresh tuna salad niçoise 72
**TURKEY**: fusilli with turkey,
mortadella, & mozzarella 132
tagliatelle with turkey,
marsala, & mushrooms 142
turkey meatballs al forno 148

**VEGETABLES**: agnolotti with
broiled vegetable dressing 183
cavatappi with spring vegetables
& herbs 164
elicoidali with roast vegetables & pesto 201
fusilli lunghi with broiled
Mediterranean vegetables 162
lasagne 197, 198
marille with roast vegetables & fontina 185
marille with spinach, eggplants,
& bell peppers al forno 201
Mediterranean vegetable & pasta salad 43
pasta provençal 171
penne with Mediterranean vegetables 162
sedani with roast vegetables
& olives al forno 199
tagliatelle, asparagus,
fava bean, & zucchini salad 168
tagliatelle alla primavera 165
taglioni with summer vegetables
& fresh herb sauce 163
tonnarelli with roast bell peppers,
eggplants, fennel, & olives 169
vegetable & smoked
mozzarella pasticcio 203
warm pasta, mushrooms, & broiled
vegetable salad 169

**WATERCRESS**: garganelle
with chicken & watercress sauce 124
linguine with Gorgonzola & watercress 32
linguine with watercress & capers 45
**WHITE SAUCE** 17

**ZUCCHINIS**: cavatappi with
zucchini, tomatoes, & capers 213
zucchini & ricotta cannelloni 196
fusilli with zucchini, tomatoes, & basil 182
linguine with mussels & zucchini 81
tagliatelle with zucchini ribbons 212
tagliatelle with zucchini, ricotta, & basil 213
torchiette with zucchini,
lemon, & pine nuts 154